THE COMPLETE BOOK OF

Flyfishing

Stoeger Publishing Company

THE COMPLETE BOOK OF

Flyfishing

THE COMPLETE BOOK OF FLYFISHING has been originated, produced and designed by AB Nordbok, Gothenburg, Sweden.

Editorial chief: Göran Cederberg
Editorial assistant: Annika Nilsson
Designer: Mats Persson
Consultant: David Evans
Translator: Jon van Leuwen
Cover design: Munir Lotia

World copyright © 1990 / 1998
AB Nordbok, Box 7095,
402 32 Gothenburg, Sweden

Published 1998 in the United States of America by
Stoeger Publishing
5 Mansard Court
Wayne, NJ 07470

ISBN 0-88317-208-9
UPC 0-37084-06189-4
Printed and bound in Portugal 1998

Photography
Johnny Albertsson: pages 4-5, 19, 54-55, 79, 80-81, 88, 96, 102-103, 137, 142-143, 163, 168-169, 170, 194-195, 200.
Erwin Bauer: pages 56, 58-59, 62, 71, 74, 226-227.
Bill Browning: pages 68-69.
Göran Cederberg: pages 186, 216-217.
Göran Clareus: page 171.
Mikael Engström: pages 102, 132-133, 172, 191.
Mikael Frödin: pages 178, 202-203, 204.
Peter Grahn: pages 180-181, 183.
Jens Ploug Hansen: pages 90-91, 92-93, 120-121, 123, 165, 167, 230.
Roland Holmberg: pages 220-221.
Christian Hvidt: pages 31, 33, 39, 40-41, 43, 49, 53.
Heinz Jagusch: pages 37, 44, 48, 126-127, 140-141, 152-153.
Curt Johansson: page 223.
Jan Johansson: page 10.
Gunnar Johnson: pages 21, 45, 48 (inset), 64.
Lefty Kreh: pages 206-207, 209, 210-211, 213, 214.
Åke Lindau: pages 92, 106-107.
Benny Lindgren: pages 176.
Christer Mattson: pages 174-175.
Leif Milling: pages 6, 8, 10-11, 50, 100-101, 104, 117, 128-129.
Arthur Oglesby: page 232.
Björn Thomsen: page 13.
Steen Ulnitz: pages 61, 66, 124, 166.
Roland Vogel: pages 146-147, 156-157.

The Editor

GÖRAN CEDERBERG is an enthusiastic, experienced flyfisherman and contributes regularly to Scandinavian sportfishing publications. He was the editor of Nordbok's "Complete Book of Sportfishing", and has been the project leader of the present volume on flyfishing – responsible for editing, the choice and arrangement of illustrations, and adaptation to the international public. Göran Cederberg has written Chapters 1 and 3.

The Authors

STEEN ULNITZ is a fishing journalist whose specialty is flyfishing. He contributes to a number of European fishing magazines and has written several books on fish biology, flyfishing and flytying. His experience with flyfishing covers almost all corners of the world. Steen Ulnitz has written Chapters 2, 5 and 8.

ARTHUR OGLESBY is without doubt one of the "grand old men" of English salmon flyfishing. He is a well-known casting instructor, with the Spey as his home water, and has written both books and a large number of magazine articles. In addition, he is a staff member of "Field and Stream". Arthur Oglesby has written Chapter 6.

BENGT ÖSTE has contributed for many years to Scandinavian sportfishing publications and was previously editor of the journal "Flugfiske i Norden" (Flyfishing in Scandinavia). His books, TV programs and articles have been a main force in the development of flyfishing in still waters, notably in Sweden. Bengt Öste has written Chapter 4.

LEFTY KREH is one of the world's authorities on saltwater flyfishing and an able commentator on the scene in North America. He has written several books and a wide range of articles on coastal and sea fishing with flies, for tarpon and bonefish as well as other big sea game. Lefty Kreh has written Chapter 7.

The Illustrators

GUNNAR JOHNSON has created most of the illustrations in this book. He is well-known as an artist when it comes to fish, animals and nature – and as an illustrator of books and magazines both in Scandinavia and elsewhere. Also editor of "Flugfiske i Norden" (Flyfishing in Scandinavia), he has written several books about flyfishing.

TOMMY GUSTAVSSON is a graphic designer, illustrator and nature-painter. Being a devoted flyfisherman as well, he has contributed beautiful water-colours to this book. For many years he has published articles and illustrations in the sportfishing press, mainly in Scandinavia, and he has illustrated several other books.

Contents

For the confirmed flyfisherman, the great adventure beckons from all waterways. Every ripple becomes an attraction, and each shadow on the bottom is a challenge. With a devotion which seems obsessive to outsiders, we can devote days and weeks, indeed months and years, to our attempts at catching fish with our ingeniously tied decoys. Yet only in happy, and often all too brief, moments do these monumental efforts yield the desired returns.

The long time which generations of more or less successful flyfishermen have spent on different fishing waters around the world – in studying insects, observing the behaviour patterns and eating habits of fish, choosing flies, and casting at real or imagined quarry, as well as contemplating the always fascinating diversity and unpredictability of nature – has naturally resulted in an amazing store of knowledge about the conditions and requirements of flyfishing.

To give a coherent picture of where modern flyfishing stands today is a difficult task, though not a hopeless one. No other type of fishing has so many common denominators and so few national peculiarities as flyfishing.

The flyfisherman's prey, consisting primarily of salmonoids, are generally the same everywhere, as are our equipment and the types of water in which we choose to try our flies. To be sure, insect fauna, and therefore their elegant – if also inadequate – imitations, vary from region to region. Yet the fact remains that the principles for tying, selecting and presenting a seductive imitation to an often highly fastidious fish are, on the whole, quite similar.

Göran Cederberg

HENRY WILKES & Co
Studley
REDDITCH
ENGLAND
REGISTERED
TRADE MARK
QUALITY
902

Mustad fder

farve Jr. 330
March Brow

The evolution of modern flyfishing

*Flyfishing is
undeniably more a way of life than
a mere hobby or an everyday sport. Being a
flyfisherman frequently means a special
attitude towards the nuances
of nature on and under the water surface.
Qualities such as watchfulness, good
observational ability, patience, imagination,
and reaction speed are often ascribed to a
clever flyfisherman. To this can
be added an almost scientific accuracy in
studying what the fish eats, as well as
where, when and how it
consumes its food.*

*I*t should be emphasized, to begin with, that flyfishing is an extraordinarily effective method of fishing – on many occasions superior to any other technique – and that successful fishing with more or less close imitations of the fish's natural prey is essentially the result of experience.

Flyfishing is by tradition associated mainly with fresh waters, in particular flowing waters. Trout and salmon are the classic quarry, perhaps due to their strength and willingness to bite. But during recent years other species have also become interesting, such as grayling, char, pike, perch and bass. Besides, many of us have discovered the terrific excitement of using a fly rod to challenge saltwater species which are undoubtedly magnificent opponents, despite their lack of an adipose fin.

In fact a dramatic evolution of flyfishing has occurred during the twentieth century alone. From the English chalk streams, where only small and exact imitations of insects could be used, to flyfishing with large, hairy saltwater flies for tarpon and other great fighting fish on the flats in North America, is a very long step. An important link in the sport's development has also been the early spread of English flyfishing to colonial lands, such as Australia, New Zealand and parts of Africa. Flyfishing in the United States was originally also based in large part on the English flyfishing tradition, as are many classic fly patterns which are now well known: March Brown, Greenwell's Glory, Butcher, Red Tag, Teal and Red, and Zulu are a few random examples.

The history of flyfishing is, of course, relatively brief. This is eloquently illustrated by the fact that several of the flyfishermen who have had great, even decisive significance for the sport have lived into the middle of our century. It is also noteworthy that rapid changes have often been due to

provincial ideas which won new enthusiasts, who in turn have refined and passed on innovations from the viewpoint of their own special conditions.

It is admittedly impossible to present a true picture of flyfishing history without granting a leading role to England and its many forward-looking flyfishermen. After all, the cradle of the sport once stood in that country. Still, we may thus be underemphasizing developments which have occurred elsewhere in the world and which have played a momentous part in the growth of modern flyfishing over the last half-century. Developments not least in the United States and Scandinavia have been extremely rapid. In addition, new ideas are spread like the wind today through the mass media and tend to sow revolutionary findings.

Which, then, are the principal ingredients in the mixture of achievements which we shall use to weave our delightful tale? The development of flyfishing in literature, and the authors who have been and still are active? The evolution of equipment from natural materials to the high-technology products of the space age? The

Greenwell's Glory, one of the classic English wet flies which are still popular among many flyfishermen.

progress of the art of flytying and the advent of new, more practical materials? Or is it simply the case that the history of flyfishing can be told on the basis of careful observations which attentive flyfishermen have made in order to learn more about the behaviour of fish and their food on diverse waters?

Well, the truth is probably that in such a historical drama, neither discoveries due to exact observations while fishing, nor the seemingly inexorable march of progress toward the high-tech society, should be excluded. It must also be kept in mind that a number of leading personalities continue to have a great influence on the development of the flyfishing which we call modern.

The beginnings of flyfishing

Archaeologists believe that the fishing hook was discovered sometime around 30,000 years ago in southern Europe. The hooks, which were eventually provided with barbs, were first manufactured of bone and probably also of different wooden materials. But just when man first found that feather-covered hooks could be very effective fishing equipment is shrouded in the mists of time.

The first literary description of flyfishing comes from about the year AD 200. In his book *On the Nature of Animals*, the author Claudius Aelianus described how people fished with a fly in the river Astraeus in Macedonia. The prey is presumed to have been trout, since it had a "spotted exterior". To judge from this description, the Macedonians fished with hooks which had been covered with red wool and wax-coated cock feathers. These feather creations presumably were more reminiscent of today's jigs than of flies, but we have no reason to doubt their fishing ability.

Although these true pioneers of flyfishing probably fished mainly for their daily food, that naturally does not mean that the Macedonians found no pleasure in fishing with a rod, top-knotted line and flies.

It was not until the end of the fifteenth century – to be exact, the year 1496 – that we find the first certain proof that people fished with flies for the sake of the sport. In her *Book of St. Albains*, Dame Juliana Berner described fishing methods of the time in an article entitled "A Treatyse of Fysshynge Wyth an Angle". This shows that feather-clad hooks were also used as prey.

Dane Juliana Berner is believed to have been the abbess of a Benedictine nunnery in Sopwell. Her article, written in 1425 and subsequently hand-copied by monks until it was printed seventy years later, is absolutely decisive for the early development not only of flyfishing but of sportfishing in general. Here too is described, in detail and for the first time, how fishing for trout and salmon was conducted with artificial flies. She had discovered, among other things, a seasonal regularity in the insects which she observed on her fishing waters. Her conclusion was that the fish's choice of diet depended largely on the supply of swarming insects. With her observations of insect life as a starting point, she developed twelve different fly patterns – one for each month – which are so well described that a flytier today can tie them without much trouble.

Dame Juliana's "Treatyse" had a considerable impact on sportfishermen's attitude to their sport for a long time afterward. The "proper" fisherman had to be an idealist, a philosopher and a nature-worshiper, and had to master the sport down to the smallest details. The perfection of the sport, flyfishing, meant for example that the fisherman should build his own rods, twine his lines and tie his flies. He should on the whole possess the qualities of the true sportsman. The greatest pleasure was indubitably provided by the fish which was hardest to overcome.

In this connection it should obviously be pointed out that the entire *Book of St. Albains* was devoted to the greatest arts of the age, such as heraldry and hunting, and that it was written for nobles and gentlemen. Thus to the great arts was now added fishing with a rod, line and hook for the sake of pleasure and as a source of recreation. At the same time Dame Juliana devoted her work to all virtuous, well-meaning and freeborn individuals – in other words, not only the upper class. With that, the basis for a long tradition was laid.

Fishing equipment in those days was described as consisting of relatively simple tied flies, long rods of ash, hazel and willow, and lines braided with horsehair. The rods, which are assumed to have been about 15 feet (4.5 metres) long, were made of two parts joined by iron or tin links. We may imagine that it could be problematic to play large fish with this primitive gear.

The next milestone in the development of sportfishing was *The Compleat Angler*, which appeared in 1653 and was written by Isaak Walton, then aged 60. In 1676 it was expanded with a section on flyfishing by Charles Cotton. By now the book has seen almost 400 editions and been translated into many languages. With time it has become one of the real classics in fishing literature.

Charles Cotton's flyfishing section has been widely regarded as very significant for the progress and orientation of flyfishing until the beginning of the nineteenth century. He can therefore be called something like the founding father of modern flyfishing.

Through the book's dialogue between Mr Piscator and Mr Venator, we get a good view of how fishing with a rod and hook was done at the time. The tradition from Dame Juliana Berner is clear: fishing was done for enjoyment and was in large part a means for the romantic adventurer to experience nature. We follow the writer to remote brooks and rivers where he is forced to use all his knowledge in order to vanquish the elusive fish, accompanied by the babbling of waters and the song of birds.

Izaak Walton was no devoted flyfisherman, but he undoubtedly became one of the great founding fathers of sportfishing. In the inset picture below, we see his fishing basket, now kept at the Flyfisher's Club in London.

The Compleat Angler may also be called the first true handbook of sportfishing. In lyric phrases it describes not only the eating habits of fish and their resting places, but also how to go about luring them onto the hook with all manner of baits, as well as how to serve up the catch.

Fishing equipment during the seventeenth century was simple and not very different from that employed in Berner's time. The rods were often made of jointed wood, long and – by our standards – colossally clumsy. The lines were made of twined horsehair and, since no reels were available, they were top-knotted.

The breakthrough of split-cane rods

Progress in improving fishing equipment was quite slow. In the mid-1660s, however, hooks began to be made more durable by hardening them. Plagues and fires forced needlemakers, among others, to move out of London. Redditch soon become a center of hookmaking, and the old handicraft of smithing was transformed into a large-scale operation. Industrialization also brought with it improvements in the quality of hooks: they became thinner and lighter, though still thick and unwieldy compared with those of today.

Even if both Berner and Walton/Cotton showed great interest in the insects taken by fish, it was first in 1747 that the initial book on flytying first appeared, *The Art of Angling* by Richard Bowlker. This is widely regarded as the first handbook on the subject and something of a trendmaker. He not only presented a list of his own flies, indicating some knowledge of entomology, but gave direct instructions for special types of fishing, such as upstream fishing.

The rods which were used during the eighteenth century were primarily for the purpose of taking up the fish's strike. On the whole, flyfishing in those days bore little resemblance to that of today. The line and fly were not cast, but swung out to the presumed holding spot of the fish. Only at the end of the century did small primitive reels began to be manufactured, with room for storing a small amount of line. At about the same time, it had been discovered that the lines could be tapered by twining in more horsehairs at the middle than at the end.

By the outset of the nineteenth century, the rod's length had been considerably shortened from 16-18 to 11-12 feet (around 5 to 3.5 metres). There were frequent experiments with different kinds of rod materials such as greenheart, hickory and bamboo. In the mid-1840s, an American violin-maker managed to construct the first split-cane rod by gluing bamboo ribs together. This was a real breakthrough, as a perfect rod material had now been found along with a superior method of construction in order to build really strong, practical rods.

Split-cane rods, compared with earlier types, were light and pliable. In addition, they cast significantly better than their predecessors. However, they were still heavy and hard to handle as casting tools. Despite their overall advantage, it was to be some years before their production could be effectivized to make mass manufacture profitable. Two not entirely unknown names figure in this connection: the Americans Charles Orvis and Hiram Leonard. After about another decade, an Englishman named Hardy began his production of quality rods in the British Isles.

It was not only the development of the fly rod which started things moving in the mid-nineteenth century. Lines were also greatly improved. Thanks to the introduction of oiled silk lines, the casting length could be as much as tripled. More or less simultaneously, the horsehair was replaced by silk gut. Today's modern flyfishing had thus begun to take shape.

Flyfishing as a whole underwent extensive changes during the nineteenth century. The development of equipment, the interest in entomology, the creation of new fly patterns and techniques are all indications of this. A further factor, to be sure, was that flyfishing began to be popular in the true sense of the word. But with the popularization of flyfishing, the distance widened between it and other kinds of sportfishing. It became snobbish, ceremonial, and regarded as a fine art. There were echoes from the days of Berner: such a noble sport should be conducted and perfected by gentlemen.

Flyfishermen during the nineteenth century were evidently very conservative. Flyfishing was, and remained, a way of fishing surrounded by a certain mysticism – an attitude which has indeed persisted far into our own century.

Entomology and flytying, though, became ever more interesting, and the fly was what most captured the attention of flyfishermen. A number of books on this very subject appeared during the nineteenth century, some of the best known being *Fly Fisher's Legacy* by Scotcher (ca. 1810), *Fly Fisher's Guide* (1816), *Fly Fisher's Entomology* by Alfred Ronald (1836), and *Floating Flies and How to Dress Them* by Frederic M. Halford (1886).

Flyfishing tended ever more to become a science. Alfred Ronald was the first author to point out the relevance of insect breeding. His book of 1836 was, in fact, the first entomological description of insects in nature and their imaginary equivalents. Ronald's book inevitably increased the interest in insect studies. It suddenly became a matter of great concern to tie exact insect imitations by carefully observing all sorts of flying creatures at the water and recreating these faithfully for the fish.

During the second half of the nineteenth century, a lively debate blossomed about how the fly should be laid out. Upstream casting, downstream casting, and casting more or less across the stream were important questions. It was W. C. Stewart who made himself the champion of the upstream cast in his book *Practical Angling* (1857) which presented the technique and its advantages: by approaching the fish from the rear it is easier to imitate the insects' natural route downstream, and playing can occur without disturbing the fish upstream (that is, in as yet unfished water). Stewart was also of the opinion that it was more important to show the insect's size, form and appearance than to tie exact imitations.

Early attempts were made to tie flies that imitated the natural food of fish. Shown here are some flies from the late seventeenth century, together with their real prototypes.

The reign of the dry fly

Around 1860, dry-fly fishing began to take off in southern England. This new technique gathered ever more enthusiasts, and it did not take many decades before dry flies became ubiquitous, not least in English chalk streams. In the wake of this innovation, there followed a total devaluation of all that wet flies and wet-fly fishing stood for. It was regarded as unsporting and virtually immoral to fish with any kind of wet fly.

It had long been noticed that fish gladly took a wet fly just when it had landed on the water surface or had broken through. The new technique started by trying to get wet flies to fish dry. The fly was dried by means of a number of air casts, then landed on the water and floated until it eventually got soaked and sank under its own weight. Although dry-fly fishing is generally thought to have been "discovered" in England during the mid-nineteenth century, there is proof that the technique was used in Spain already during the seventeenth century, according to the *Manuscrito de Astorga* (1624).

In any case, the basis of today's dry-fly fishing was developed in the south English chalk streams, for example at Itchen where there were plenty of hungry – although sometimes quite selective – trout and loads of insects. As the fish "learned" to see the difference between real and imitation prey, the wet flies which were dried out by air casting fished less well. The "true and proper" dry fly therefore came as a fresh start, not only because it was a new fashion in itself, but because it fished more effectively.

As for who was actually the first to introduce the dry fly is, as with so much else, a controversial question. Some maintain that it was Pullman in his *Vade Mecum of Fly Fishing for Trout* (1851), while others claim that it was a professional flytier, James Ogden, who made the innovation. At all events, it was an article in *The Field* during 1857 written by Francis Francis which spread the principles of dry-fly fishing beyond a rather small circle of fishermen.

What then of Frederic M. Halford, widely considered the indisputable father of dry-fly fishing? The fact is that he, according to reliable sources, did not attempt dry-fly fishing until 1868 – that is, several years after the "discovery" of dry flies. Yet what Halford did do was to perfect the technique with floating dun hooks.

The last decades of the nineteenth century brought a strong upsurge in flyfishing, not least due to Halford and the group of outwardly passionate flyfishermen who sur-

(Above) The fly reel certainly created new opportunities and made the old fishing with a top-knotted line obsolete. These beautiful old reels are made of brass.

(Below) Interest in dry-fly fishing surged at the end of the nineteenth century. Here we see six of Halford's original flies, which he himself tied.

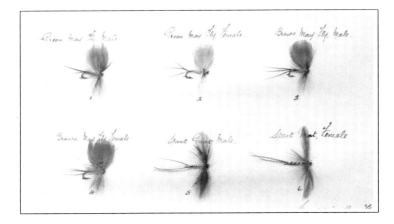

in a systematic way all the phases of dry-fly fishing. This is a virtually comprehensive work on fishing with dry flies in the English chalk streams. On certain waters, such as slow-flowing streams with selective trout, it is still of great value.

We can say without exaggeration that Halford released an avalanche: interest in dry-fly fishing grew at a raging pace. It became modern to collect insects and make naturally faithful copies with Halford's theories of imitation and his flytying technique as a basis. However, the other side of the coin became a fanatical attitude that only dry-fly fishing was the correct way to seek contact with the fish. True believers would never have picked up a wet fly with a pair of pincers.

For this tragic development, Halford bears great responsibility, since in his later days he became quite intolerant of divergent opinions. The "father of dry-fly fishing" was unimpressed by wet flies and nymphs. Rather he tried to combat them as if they were a dangerous nuisance in the fly box. Fishing with dry flies for standing fish was the only proper method for him, while downstream fishing with a wet fly was not only ineffective but also a destructive and immoral form of flyfishing.

The challenging nymph

Along with the strong expansion and popularization of fly-fishing, equipment was improved as well. Rods became easier to handle and the lines smoother to cast. Not least the Americans contributed much to these developments. When this fishing tackle came to England around 1900, nymph fishing slowly began to arise.

A central figure in nymph fishing was George Edward Mackenzie Skues, the technique's inventor and chief theoretician. Born in 1858, he died in 1949, a full 91 years old – and it may be surmised that his success at fishing was one reason for his long life.

Like dry-fly fishing, nymph fishing was developed in the English chalk streams. This is because such streams are fine to experiment in, with their clear water, abundant insect life, and selective fish which have become familiar with hooks due to the active flyfishing.

Skues fished mainly at Itchen and is said to have been a clever dry-fly fisherman, although not a narrow-minded or fanatical one, in contrast to Halford. Despite, or perhaps because of, the predominance of dry-fly fishing in the chalk streams of the late 1800s, Skues began to experiment. He

rounded him. Enormous pains were taken to develop both equipment and techniques. The oiled silk lines were improved, body materials were tested which did not draw water, and new techniques were sought for tying more durable flies. Halford became a dry-fly fisherman by profession. At the age of 45 he retired in order to devote all his time to the sport. This unbelievable commitment, of cour-se, yielded returns. Together with his fishing friends he developed a standard in regard to rods, lines and flies which maintained its relevance long into our century.

His passionate activity also resulted in a couple of books which are regarded today as established works for flyfisher-men. His first and best-known, *Floating Flies and How to Dress Them* (1886), presented, after years of intensive insect studies in the chalk stream district of Hampshire, nearly 100 duns and spinners. Three years later came his *Dry Fly Fishing in Theory and Practice* (1889): here Halford described asked himself: why fish with dry flies when the quarry take food in or just under the water surface?

The idea of fishing with a wet fly when the quarry did not take insects on the water surface was, at the time, heretical to many flyfishermen in conservative England. But this did not prevent Skues from pursuing his research: he developed methods and patterns on the theory that fish were occasionally more interested in the hatching insects than in the already hatched ones. Thus soft-hackled, unweighted flies became the alternative to dry flies.

In 1910 came Skues' first book, *Minor Tactics of the Chalk Stream*. It meant a revolution for the chalk streams, in view of the overwhelming adherence to dry-fly fishing. His concepts were widely regarded as logical, well thought out, and in some respects obvious. Yet the most doctrinaire dry-fly fishermen choked on their whiskey at the mere mention of Skues.

It should be noted that these attitudes existed only in the chalk stream area. People in northern England for centuries had fished upstream with wet flies, this being sometimes necessary to make the fish take at all – and Skues received a ready audience there. What has been magnified by some histories of flyfishing into a life-and-death battle between the two methods was, in other words, actually limited to a small though significant district. Indeed many sportfishermen, particularly outside England, regarded the debate as a storm in a teacup. Still, the events in England were important due to the country's leading role, during much of our century, in the theoretical and practical development of flyfishing, as well as in generating new ideas and in publishing much of the best literature on the subject.

Skues' nymph fishing was refined further, in the face of long opposition from England's numerous old-fashioned flyfishermen. Frank Sawyer and Major Oliver Kite, also acute observers of nymph behaviour in the water, were main proponents of the method in the mid-1900s. Skues had concentrated on fish that took hatching nymphs near the water surface, calling for a vigil – whereas Sawyer and Kite focused on fishing with imitations of swimming and drifting nymphs in deeper water. The weighted Pheasant Tail is the fly most closely associated with Sawyer's name. Kite, one of Sawyer's own disciples, was soon fascinated by nymph fishing and wrote *Nymph Fishing in Practice* (1963), which is still considered the most complete treatment of the Netheravon school of fishing.

The embroiled controversy about dry versus wet flies must have accelerated the development of nymph fishing in England. Things went more slowly elsewhere in the world. Classic wet flies were long the obvious alternative when the fish did not rise, creating no great need for nymphs. In Scandinavia, for example, nymph fishing did not see a breakthrough until the 1960s, and it was primarily done with Frank Sawyer's method. The faster development of nymph fishing in England was, indeed, the only positive effect of the dogmatic attitude among dry-fly fishermen towards all sorts of wet-fly fishing.

Salmon fishing stimulates progress

By and large, salmon fishing runs parallel to the emergence of flyfishing as a whole. But salmon fishermen have probably been the driving force in regard to reels, obviously because the rushing of salmon demanded an ability to store a reasonable quantity of loose line as easily windable as possible.

Even though Isaak Walton described some sort of prototype fly reel for salmon fishing already during the seventeenth century, it was not until well into the eighteenth that the development of equipment began to get under way. Yet the rods were still heavy and clumsy, while the few existing reels were very simply constructed and were quite small in comparison to the rods. The rotating spool lacked a brake and actually had only one function – to store the line on.

Salmon flies are commonly associated with the large, colourful, feathered creations which seem more attractive to the flyfisherman than to the salmon. A typical example is Jock Scott, which reputedly first saw the light of day in 1845 on a boat between England and Norway, and which in its original form probably contained 42 different parts. Its opposite is the American hairwing fly – tied simply, often with only a few ingredients, but no less effective for that.

It is believed that salmon flies until the mid-eighteenth century consisted primarily of the same fly patterns as those for trout, except that they were tied on larger and stronger hooks. But during the nineteenth century, interest in salmon fishing grew explosively, bringing with it a powerful development in flies and equipment. Rods became more flexible, and more purposeful reels began to be used. With the need of greater casting lengths and possibilities of playing the fish, reels were made which not only served as a

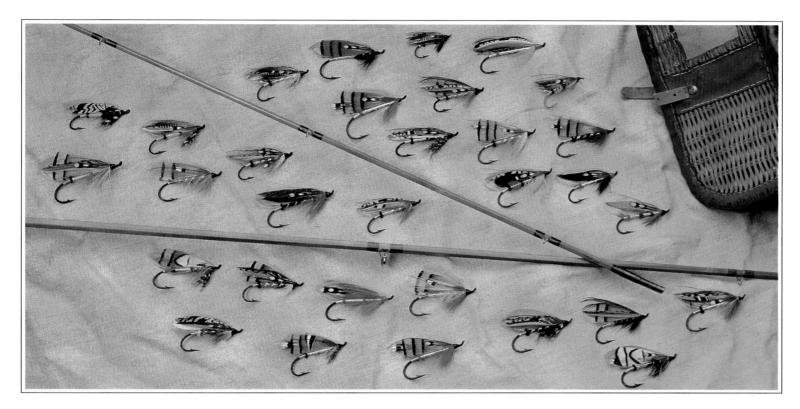

Fully dressed classic salmon flies.

line-winder between fishing tours, but also fulfilled their function during the fishing itself. They still had overdimensioned spools and were simply built, but the salmon fisherman no longer needed to leave all the loose line on the ground while casting and playing.

Yet it was not until the end of the nineteenth century that fly reels were more or less fully developed. Soon afterward, the equipment firm of Hardy began to produce "The Perfect", which became one of the world's most desirable fly reels.

Many now well-known classic salmon-fly patterns can be traced back to that time. Just like Jock Scott, the first classic salmon flies were colourful and elaborately dressed. The connection between overdimensioned salmon flies and the Victorian era in English history is not hard to see. Ladies' interest in showy clothes and feathered hats made the importation of exotic feathers a profitable business. Salmon-fishing gentlemen did their part to expand the area of use. Patterns such as Thunder and Lightning, Black Dose,

Silver Doctor, Black Doctor, and other fully dressed salmon flies derive from the same period, when overdimensioning was in fashion.

Some literary milestones of that period are George M. Kelson's *The Salmon Fly: How to Dress it and How to Use It* (1895) and Pryce-Tannatt's *How to Dress Salmon Flies* (1914). But the pendulum soon swung back, and fishermen began to undress the "Victorian" salmon flies, in particular making the wings much simpler. Ernest Crossfield was the man who led this new orientation. He appreciated simplicity and practicality in flies – the qualities which he thought were responsible for their fishing ability. Flies like Jimmie, Silver Blue and Blue Charm are good representatives of this school.

It was not only in England that new winds were blowing. In the USA around the turn of the century, fishermen began to experiment with new patterns and flytying materials. Hairs from bear, fox, mink, beaver, hare, squirrel and other animals became the "new" stuff of salmon fly wings. Today

Scandinavian flyfishing

George M Kelson.

the American hairwing type is more common than traditional featherwing flies on salmon rivers all over the world. American influence in fly material has even pushed out deeply rooted English traditions. Nowadays even classic British flies in simplified variants are tied with hairwings. Also artificial materials such as fluorescent ones have recently become ever more common in salmon flies.

The change which has occurred in salmon fly materials is profound and the trend is quite clear. Hairwing materials have come to stay among flytiers. The reason is plainly that it is easier to tie hairwing flies and they fish at least as well as the classic salmon flies.

Today, flyfishing in Scandinavia is mainly inspired by the Americans, even though England lies geographically closer and the first impulses came from there. Although we have proof that the Lapps in the Swedish mountains fished with streamer-like flies already in the mid-eighteenth century, it was undoubtedly Englishmen who initiated the sport here during the nineteenth century.

Scandinavia, primarily Sweden and Norway, received many visits by a long series of adept British flyfishermen. Undisturbed salmon rivers and virgin trout streams were the two main sources of their interest. Thus one of the first Swedish flyfishing handbooks, *Om Flugfiskeriet* (1844), was written by an Englishman, Robert Dalton Hutchinson.

In general, the English flyfishing guests played a prominent role in the development of Scandinavian flyfishing. The seemingly inexhaustible fishing resources made Norway and Sweden especially attractive travel goals for the adventurous Britons, and it was naturally the fantastic salmon fishing which drew them most.

One of the pioneers was the great fisherman and bear-hunter Arthur Llewellyn Lloyd. Among his better-known books is *Field Sports in the North of Europe* (1830), which can be characterized as a bold travel journal more than a handbook. Still, it came to inspire Britons for generations afterward. It became the highest fashion to sail over the North Sea to the Scandinavian peninsula in order to challenge big trout, grayling and salmon.

The English began to travel to Norway in the 1820s, bringing with them a knowledge of salmon fishing with flies to, for example, the Norwegian rivers Nidelva, Namsen and Gaula. Hutchinson, already mentioned, travelled around Norway in the 1830s, and came out with the first Norwegian flyfishing book, *Fluefiskeriets Anvendelse i Norge* (1839).

The English "salmon lords", or visiting fishermen, were almost always lords, barons, landowners, officers or very high-ranking civil servants. They dominated Norwegian salmon fishing and flyfishing throughout the nineteenth century and well into the twentieth. This period is usually termed "the Englishmen's era" and is marked not only by a great development of salmon fishing in Norway, but also by a widespread collision between English upper-class habits and the west Norwegian farming culture.

Incredible quantities of salmon were caught in rivers during the entire period. If fishing luck was good, the catch was best counted in wagonloads – daily catches of up to 50

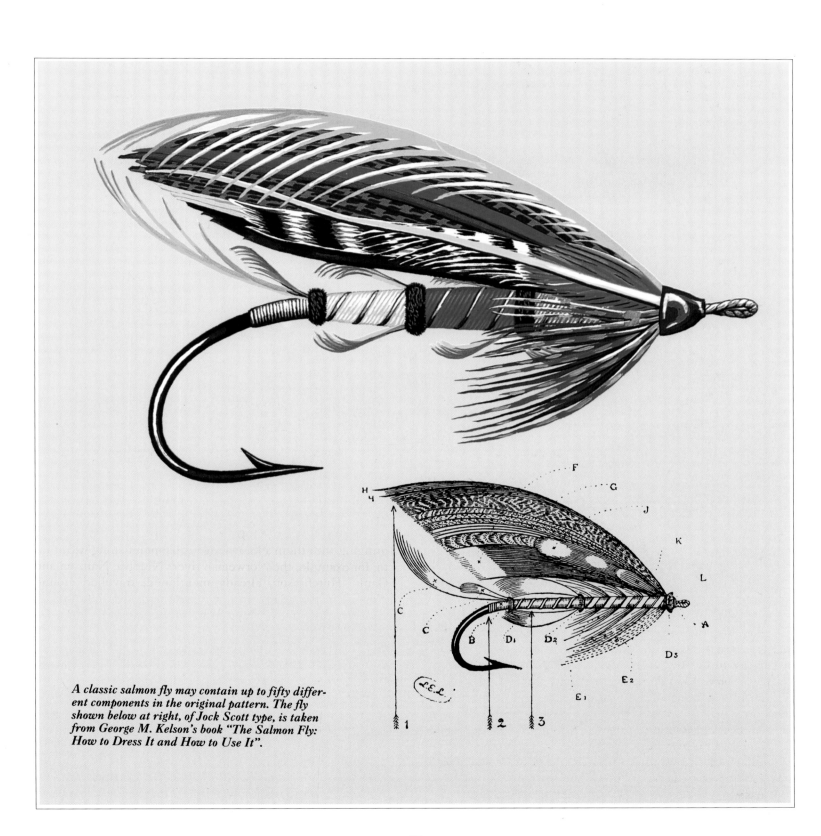

A classic salmon fly may contain up to fifty different components in the original pattern. The fly shown below at right, of Jock Scott type, is taken from George M. Kelson's book "The Salmon Fly: How to Dress It and How to Use It".

An afternoon's catch of about ten big salmon was, once upon a time, nothing unusual on the Norwegian salmon rivers.

salmon occurred – rather than in the number of fish. A clever rower and guide, however, was often a prerequisite for normal fishing. These gillies came mostly from the fishing district in question, and knew exactly how the river ought to be fished. In return, they learned how effective flyfishing should be conducted. Not seldom, they acquired rods, reels, lines and flies from their guests. Many Norwegians also learned how to tie flies and, with time, became clever flyfishermen.

Thus Norwegians first gained the knowhow of salmon fishing from Englishmen. This period laid the basis for the widespread sportfishing after World War II in Norwegian rivers, which are probably the world's best waters for salmon in terms of both number and size. Salmon of 12-15 kg are nothing unusual there.

Flyfishing in the United States

The English colonists who reached the North American continent during the eighteenth and nineteenth centuries naturally brought with them a knowledge of, and interest in, flyfishing to their new land. The sport had taken root by the end of the eighteenth century, and it is even thought that special shops then existed for flyfishing materials and equipment.

Serious fishing with a fly began in the United States around 1850. At this time the Wild West was still living up to its name. It was therefore mainly in the eastern parts of the country that people diverted themselves by fishing with made the first split-cane rods. After about 25 years, they began to be mass-produced and the rods were improved in features like casting ability and weight – so much that the English began to import them around the turn of the century. English rods at the time were long, heavy and stiff; thus gradually the English took over the American type of rod, which many have seen as a prerequisite for the development of nymph fishing.

The American equivalent of the chalk streams in Hampshire became the Catskill rivers in the state of New York. Rivers such as the Neversink and the Beaverkill are today classic waters in the history of American flyfishing.

In Europe and England, the brown trout was the target for the hardily casting flyfisherman. This species, however, did not originally exist in the USA. There, people fished instead for brook trout in the eastern states, and for steelhead or cutthroat in the west.

With the growing popularity of fishing, the supply of brook trout in particular decreased drastically. During the 1880s, trout consequently began to be imported from Europe. The first fish were taken from Germany and the species is thus called the "German trout".

As brown trout, and later rainbow trout, were implanted in rivers, the waters became harder to fish. The traditional downstream wet-fly fishing proved ineffective. These trout were simply not as easy to fool as the brook trout, and flyfishermen were slowly but surely forced to reconsider.

One of those who perhaps came to mean most for the development of American flyfishing was Theodore Gordon. He was something of a loner who, in 1905, settled on the Neversink in order to be able to tie flies and do his fishing in peace and quiet. His literary production was primarily a number of articles in the journals *Forest and Stream* (USA) and *Fishing Gazette* (England). He also corresponded fluently with Halford and Skues. Through this lofty correspondence with two of the great men of flyfishing, he acquired a fine insight into the development of English flyfishing.

At the end of the nineteenth century, Gordon obtained some 50 dry flies from Halford. However, these were tied according to English conditions and were therefore poor imitations of the insects which existed in Gordon's home waters. As a flytier, though, Gordon began to tie his own dry flies with Halford's technique, but modelled on local insects. He created many original patterns, the best known being Gordon Quill, and he also developed the so-called "bumble-puppies" in the Neversink. These flies were the predecessors of the bucktail patterns, subsequently so much used.

Salmon fishing from a boat on a Norwegian salmon river in the mid-nineteenth century (illustrated by Lloyd's "Scandinavian Adventures", Volume 1, in 1853).

a rod, line and hook. In the more civilized Eastern states, people also began to realize that flyfishing was an unusually rewarding form of sportfishing.

In 1887 the book *Fly-Fishing and Fly-Making* by John H. Keene came out. Its main interest is that it shows that people in the USA had come farther in the development of flyfishing than we have tended to believe. The book not only describes how to tie dry flies, for example, but also displays a degree of innovative thinking which was long thought to have been reserved for greater luminaries such as Theodore Gordon.

Despite the country's late entry into flyfishing history in relation to England, the refinement of rods, spools, reels and lines was steadily driven forth. As mentioned previously, it was an American violin-maker who, in the mid-1840s,

Gordon laid the foundations for the Catskill School, which came to have a huge impact on American flytying. The fanaticism which marked English dry-fly fishing never reached the USA and there were thus larger possibilities of experimenting. The results were significantly more sparingly dressed flies than the typical dry flies from the Halford epoch in England.

Another American who has acquired a leading place in the history of flyfishing is George LaBranche. In 1914 his first book came out: *The Dry Fly and Fast Waters*. He is regarded for this and other reasons as the man who made American dry-fly fishing really popular. In the book was presented a technique for effective dry-fly fishing even in relatively rapid waterways. It differed in various respects from Halford's theories, which were primarily suited to the English chalk streams.

LaBranche's fishing technique was distinctive in many ways from the Catskill school, one essential difference being the size and bushy appearance of the flies, which made them float high and remain easily visible to the fish. LaBranche also belongs to those who developed the technique of fishing salmon with dry flies.

In general a different style of flyfishing and flytying arose in the USA as compared with England. An example is the special type of wet flies called bucktails and streamers. They grew up in America during the 1920s and are refinements of the classic wet fly. Observant flyfishermen had discovered that wet flies with silver or gold bodies could be identified as fry by the fish. Gradually there arose a whole lot of different patterns of bucktails (hairwing flies) and of streamers (featherwing flies) which, in one way or another, imitated fish fry in different species and stages.

In addition to those authors already named, Edward R. Hewitt had a great influence on this progress. He was a contemporary of LaBranche, and was one of the great flyfishing authors between the two World Wars. Today he is perhaps best known for his division of flyfishing development into three phases: (1) as many fish as possible, (2) as big fish as possible, (3) as difficult fish as possible to catch. Hewitt also advanced the view that the presentation of the fly was extremely important: the main thing according to him was not to have as great a range of flies as possible, but to have a smaller number and be able to present them correctly.

In the same way as Gordon, through correspondence with Halford, became something of a pioneer in American dry-fly fishing, Hewitt continually corresponded with Skues and thereby gained impetus for trying nymph fishing in the USA. But it was, of course, essential to adjust the English nymphs to suit American conditions. Much of this work took place in the Neversink River itself.

Yet another pioneer in American flyfishing was James (Big Jim) Leisenring, who also corresponded with Skues. In the middle of the war, he published *The Art of Tying the Wet Fly* (1941). Although in many ways it had a more up-to-date attitude towards wet-fly and nymph fishing than did earlier authors, Big Jim's book received no wide recognition until much later. The flymph (something in between a dry fly and a nymph), which tries to copy the insect in the transition between nymph and flying insect (actual hatching), was among other things a result of Leisenring's intensive observations on the water.

The Catskill rivers continued long into the twentieth century to be a principal centre for the development of flyfishing. Besides the Catskill school's typical lightly dressed flies, the American imitation doctrine also got its nourishment from that area. Lewis Rhead, Preston Jennings, Art Flick and several other devoted flyfishermen collected insects in the Catskills for a long time, resulting in two standard works on trout flies and the natural prototypes which they imitate: *American Trout Stream Insects* by Lewis Rhead (1916), Preston Jennings' *A Book of Trout Flies* (1935) and *Streamside Guide to Naturals and Their Imitations* by Art Flick (1947).

The basis of the American imitation school was now laid, and the outcome was an improvement of the traditional patterns and a reduction in the number of necessary imitations to about ten patterns.

Lake flyfishing presents new possibilities

During the twentieth century, Americans have increasingly dominated the development of flyfishing in running waters. As English fishing in such waters has declined due to factors like pollution, however, there have been attempts to expand flyfishing into other types of waters. Lake flyfishing for trout, and for the rainbow trout implanted from the USA, has thus acquired great significance. Actually, lake flyfishing has a long tradition in Great Britain, primarily from the Scottish and Irish lochs – but naturally the fish in inland lakes, ponds and reservoirs have quite different behaviour patterns and eating habits than those in running waters. It was only in the mid-twentieth century that flyfishermen began consciously to study these differences.

In 1952 the first book on lake flyfishing came out: *Still Water Fishing* by Tom Ivens. The English continued to refine this special type of fishing. Their exact observations on the water gave rise to new patterns and improved methods, so that a fresh generation of flyfishermen founded yet one more English tradition. C. F. Walker, Geoffrey Bucknall and John Goddard are now well-known authors and good proponents of this sport. Among the flies which have become popular for lake fishing are imitations of midges and snails.

Flyfishing is a passion for many people – and for some, a real addiction – which often lasts a lifetime and can seldom be completely cured...

The fish, the insects, and the fly

A skilful flyfisherman is
something of a universal genius. He
knows about fish and their biology, studies
insect life in and around fishing
waters, has sound
insight into the chemistry and physics
of water, and pays close attention to the
weather, wind and water level. Although
well-informed and conscious
of the environment, he
never stops learning. There are
always new things to discover and fresh
experiences to gather. This is what makes
flyfishing a lifelong passion for many –
and for some of us, almost
a religion.

Today we are flyfishing for innumerable species in a wide variety of places. The sport has developed so far that it ranges from stream- to still-water fishing, from fresh to salt water, and from the Arctic to the tropics. But the dominant quarry around the world are salmonoids, which were the original inspiration of modern flyfishing. In the following pages we shall therefore concentrate chiefly on salmon, trout and grayling.

Our prey

All fish are cold-blooded, which means that their metabolism – and consequently their activeness – depend directly on the water temperature. Very few flyfishermen, however, realize how much this relationship influences the fish, or what it implies for the choice of equipment, flies, and fishing methods.

Every species has a range of temperatures in which it can survive. If their surroundings become too hot or too cold, the fish simply die. By the same token, there is a certain temperature at which they feel best: then they are extremely active, hunt eagerly and grow rapidly. On the warmer or cooler side of this optimum temperature, their energy and appetite decrease, so a flyfisherman cannot get them to bite as easily, and the striking periods are not as long or remarkable.

Temperature affects the fish's behaviour and vigour in further ways. Salmon are typical as regards their love of cold water and their need of oxygen. Since cold water usually holds more oxygen than warm water, rising temperature lowers the water's oxygen content. Thus, salmonoids can reach a point where their increasing activity is suffocated by a deficiency of oxygen.

In such situations the fish are forced to seek waters that are cooler, richer in oxygen, or both. Those in streams soon find their way to rough rapids, which enable more oxygen to dissolve – and those in still waters sink to deeper levels with low temperature. A good flyfisherman is aware of this phenomenon and pursues the prey accordingly, without wasting time at places poor in fish!

Most fish also follow a certain daily rhythm in their activity, due to both the water temperature and the light conditions. Early in the year, when the waters are cold and the

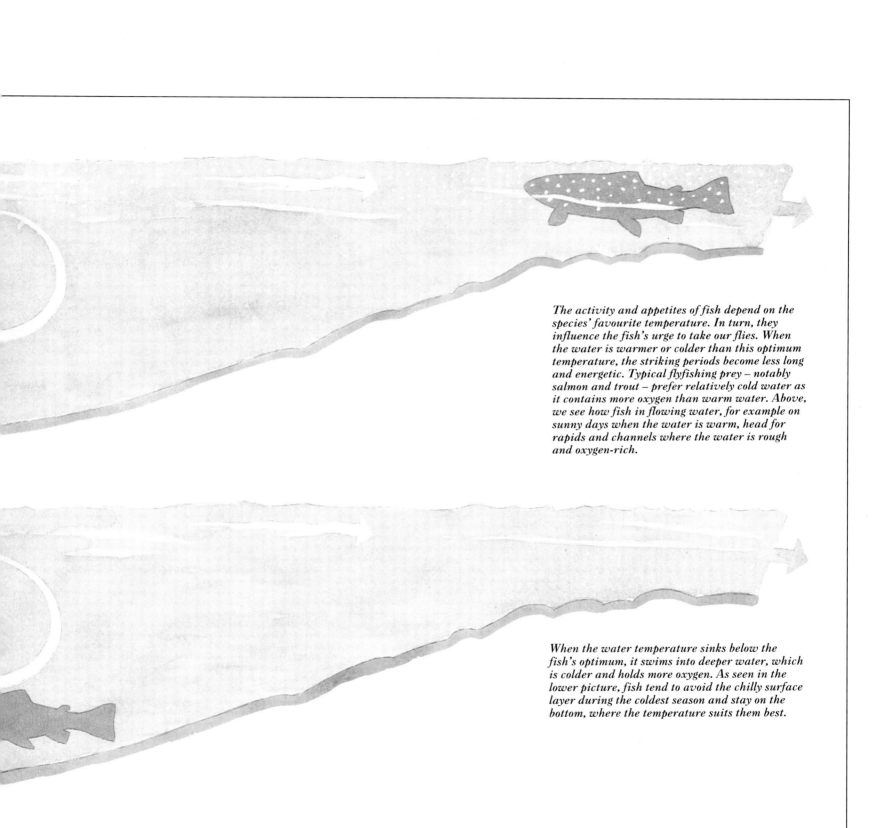

The activity and appetites of fish depend on the species' favourite temperature. In turn, they influence the fish's urge to take our flies. When the water is warmer or colder than this optimum temperature, the striking periods become less long and energetic. Typical flyfishing prey – notably salmon and trout – prefer relatively cold water as it contains more oxygen than warm water. Above, we see how fish in flowing water, for example on sunny days when the water is warm, head for rapids and channels where the water is rough and oxygen-rich.

When the water temperature sinks below the fish's optimum, it swims into deeper water, which is colder and holds more oxygen. As seen in the lower picture, fish tend to avoid the chilly surface layer during the coldest season and stay on the bottom, where the temperature suits them best.

During the warm season, with strong sunlight and high temperatures, fish are often very shy in the daytime. They prefer to hide in deep, shadowy and even overgrown places that offer good protection.

fish sluggish, midday is normally the best time to catch them, as the sun shines most brightly and the water is warmest. Even fractions of a degree's rise in temperature can start the prey swarming. By the same token, in summer the ideal hours are early morning and late evening, when the temperature becomes more favourable. Sunshine combined with low, clear, warm water makes the fish shy and reserved; they are often active only in the cool darkness of night. Feeling secure, they can then leave their hideouts to hunt in the shallows near land. Many of the animals they feed upon obey a similar daily rhythm.

In sum, how active fish are, and how willing they are to bite, is determined by several factors which are well worth knowing. Moreover, a number of biological circumstances shape the behaviour of fish in relation to the fishing hook. What is it that drives a fish to devour our flies?

Hunger and aggression are, generally speaking, the main motives for a strike. But another reason may be the plain curiosity of a fish when it sees something new – the fly. Simply because it has no hands, the only way in which it can investigate more closely is to take the fly with its mouth. Before going into details about such behaviour, though, we must distinguish between salmonoid fish that are hunting for food and those which are travelling to their spawning grounds or defending their territory.

Hunger

All salmonoids are territorial, from the moment when they leave the protective gravel of the river bed until the day they die. Ever since the fry stage, and during their last – perhaps only – spawning period, they will have fought over shelters in streaming water. Some species, however, are more territorial than others. Among the most aggressive is the brown trout *(Salmo trutta)*. If introduced to a waterway which is already populated by rainbow trout *(Salmo gairdneri)* or brook trout *(Salvelinus fontinalis)*, it will outcompete them and become the dominant species. At the other end of the spectrum we find grayling *(Thymallus thymallus)*, which gladly swim in small schools and belong to the least aggressive salmonoids.

Competition between salmonoids is hard in general, when it comes to the limited numbers of resting places and the equally restricted amounts of food in fresh waters. A waterway's permanent residents, such as brown trout, fight each other for the best holding or resting places and feeding sites – in other words, those spots which offer protection from the current as well as good and stable access to food. Usually the resting place is a deep calm one, and certainly brook trout prefer a shadowy abode with a roof over their heads. But the feeding site, not far away, is more open and

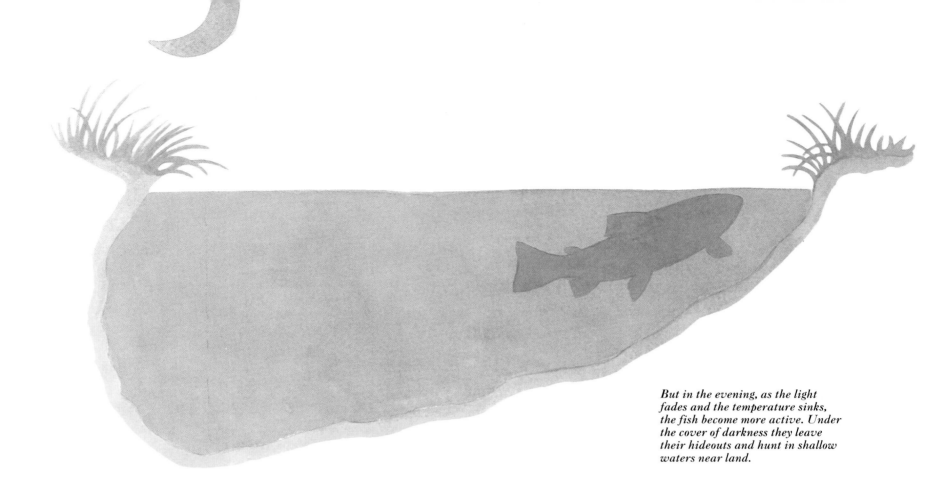

exposed, so the fish risk their safety in the resting place when they have to go out and eat. Many salmonoids, notably members of *Salmo trutta*, are therefore active at night and stay hidden by day. Yet all salmonoids are extremely active at dusk, which makes it a good time for fishing. At that hour, everything in nature wakes up!

As the amount of food in a waterway is limited, several salmonoids have developed subspecies which migrate into lakes or seas for a crack at their far richer food supply. Large lakes and the open ocean offer a virtually infinite diet for salmonoids, and enable them to grow many times faster there than in the tributaries.

Salmonoids are true freshwater fish in that they require fresh water in order to breed and survive as species. A number of their species can tolerate the very saltiest sea water, but not immediately. First the fish must go through a process known as smolting: the little salmon or trout changes in appearance from a round, dark one to a slim, silvery "smolt". This shiny exterior provides excellent camouflage in free waters, at the same time as the fish acquires an ability to tolerate salt water. Whereas it stays near the dark bottom in a waterway, it has to hunt small fish near the surface when in the sea.

Size, not age, is what determines the point at which a young salmon, trout, steelhead or seagoing char becomes mature for smolting. For example, an Atlantic salmon may do so already as a one-year-old in a warm, nutritious Spanish river. By contrast, the Atlantic salmon in Greenland have only a couple of short summer months to grow in, and may take up to five years before reaching a sufficient size of 10-15 cm (4-6 in).

The ability to tolerate sea water depends on its temperature, not just on the fish's size. If too cold, it lowers the fish's metabolism so much that there is no surplus energy to regulate the internal salt balance. Likewise, the migration of smolt from fresh to salty water begins during the springtime, when the water temperature is high enough. On the other hand, we may observe a migration of, for example, trout into relatively fresh – or less salty – waters during the cold winter months. Hard winters can force them all the way up into tributaries or make them overwinter in brackish coves. Here they can naturally be fished with a fly rod, but the fishing has to be done slowly and deeply in such cold water.

In the sea, fish devote themselves wholeheartedly to eating. There is plenty of food and consequently, with their open surroundings and shiny hunting coats, fish no longer need to be territorial. Instead, their decisive trait is a so-called striking reflex. When the fish sees something edible, such as a smaller fish or crustacean, its striking reflex is activated automatically. The hungrier it is, the more easily this reflex operates. Conversely, a fish full of food is difficult to attract with a fishing fly: it simply stands digesting its meal, apparently uninterested in anything else. Nor will it swim after the fly, which therefore has to be served right in front of its nose, and perhaps more than once before the fish will strike. Hungry, hunting fish are eager to swim quite a distance for a fly, and are generally easy to deal with, having few scruples about the fly's nature or presentation.

We often encounter fish which follow the fly all the way up to the rod end without striking. They may have recently satisfied their appetite for everything except curiosity. Or else the fly may not be quite right in its size, form, colour or movements. A fish that follows a fly out of sheer interest, however, collects impressions. If it collects enough of them, its striking reflex is triggered – as if you were pressing a button. After all, fish are simple creatures with elementary behaviour. Rather than thinking about objects, they react to external influences. And similarly, if they do not collect enough impressions, they turn round and abandon the enterprise. Then you have to try a different fly or technique until you find the right one.

Aggression

The above remarks apply to fish that are eating, by actively hunting at sea or in lakes and streams. But the situation is different with fish that are defending their territories, whether they be stationary species (such as brown trout) or are migrating in order to breed (such as salmon or sea trout).

Fish in the sea frequently undertake long migrations in search of food. One of the best-known examples is the European Atlantic salmon *(Salmo salar)*, which roams up to the Davis Strait between Canada and Greenland for a meal from its rich supplies. At some time, though, the fish become sexually mature – perhaps as young males after only one summer at sea, or after as many as four summers – and then they turn homeward.

On the way back to their childhood rivers, guided exactly by their sense of smell, they gradually lose their appetites. By the same token, their striking reflex diminishes. Fish which have been migrating for a long time will have entirely stopped eating when they reach home. They have begun to live on the fat reserves which they built up during months at sea. As their body fat is used up, they also lose

the red colour of flesh which is the hallmark of salmon. This is because the red colour comes from pigments in crustaceans that are eaten. Fish that need not travel so far to reach home will, to some extent, retain their fine red flesh as well as the striking reflex which is so important to us fly-fishermen.

Most migratory fish – whether salmon, sea trout, steelhead or seagoing char – still possess a degree of striking reflex when they have just swum up from the sea. These fish are, as a result, usually easiest to catch if other conditions are right, particularly the water level and temperature. But the striking reflex diminishes with every day spent in fresh water, and eventually it disappears. Moreover, during this transitional period, great hormonal changes occur inside the fish. Its production of sexual substances is in full swing, taking a further toll of its fat reserves, so that the fish becomes quite worthless as a food animal at the end of the season. Its value is far higher if it is allowed to spawn!

Along with these hormonal changes, the fish reverts in a way to its childhood nature. It repeats the habits and behaviour patterns which characterized its youth before going to sea. Thus it begins again to defend territory, a trait that becomes ever more marked as the fish approaches spawning.

Corresponding changes are seen in the fish's appearance. The reflective hunting garb which it wore at sea is gradually transformed into a darker, more colourful breeding costume. Its skin turns thick and the silver hue vanishes. Loose scales, typical of the shiny fish while at sea, now become attached and absorbed into the skin. Its outer coating of mucus is also strengthened.

Whereas the fish in the sea thought only of eating, in the rivers they think only of reproducing. Increasingly aggressive, and looking ever more scary, they ultimately boast the bright colours of breeding, and the males can display impressively long jaws with powerful hooks.

Although the old striking reflex has faded into memory, the fish can still be caught. However, it now bites only due to aggressiveness or plain irritability. Flies that come too close are immediately chased out of its territory, either with a swat of its tail or with a direct bite. The shiny summer fish was happy to rise up to the surface for a tiny black fly, but the well-dressed breeding fish has to be tempted with big flies in brilliant colours.

In conclusion, we must consider two different kinds of fish – the glistening mariner and the gaudy marrier. They belong to the same species, yet each has its own personality.

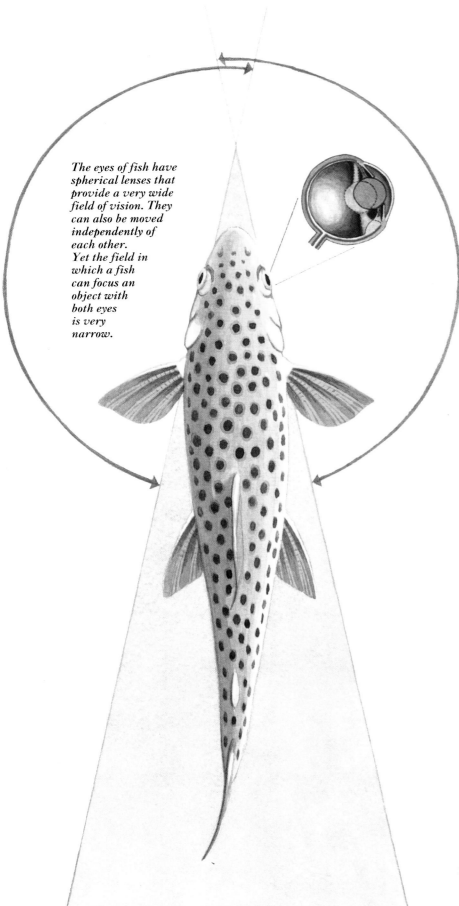

The eyes of fish have spherical lenses that provide a very wide field of vision. They can also be moved independently of each other. Yet the field in which a fish can focus an object with both eyes is very narrow.

How fish view the fly and fisherman

For us flyfishermen, the fish seem to enjoy an obscure existence under the water surface. They have a better chance of watching us than we have of glimpsing them. Nevertheless, we can penetrate their cover with a little science.

Air and water do not have the same density. Water is much more dense than air, and this fact not only enables us to see farther on land than underwater, but also causes light to refract when passing between air and water. How much, then, can a fish see?

To begin with, the common idea that fish are nearsighted is not entirely true. A fish hardly needs to see very far, since the water itself sets limits – so a fish's eye is mostly focused at short distances. But its eyes, unlike those of us mammals, has a spheroidal lens which gives it an enormous field of vision. In addition, its eyes project and can move independently of each other. On this basis alone, we should not be surprised that fish are easy to frighten!

Fish were also long thought to be colour-blind, yet they can see colours very well. Just like humans, they have special colour-sensitive cells in their eyes. Still, everything looks grey in the dark to them as well, because colour vision requires a minimum amount of light, and too little light leaves only black and white impressions. This is why black flies are best for night fishing, since these create the clearest silhouette against the dimly lit sky. A fly's colour can be effective only in daylight.

In front and overhead, the fish has a fairly narrow field of vision where it can focus objects with both eyes at once. There alone, it is able to judge distances – an ability which is crucial for its willingness to rise and take an insect at the surface. Obviously, an absolute requirement for the dry-fly fisherman is to present his fly inside this field.

Above the fish is its "window" to the outer world, a circular field in which it can see through the surface and, if it wishes, up onto the land. Beyond the window's edges, the water surface resembles a vast mirror to the fish, simply reflecting light from underwater. The window is sharply outlined in calm weather, but becomes less transparent when the surface is disturbed by wind and waves.

A fish can "see round the corner" of its window's edges, due to the refraction of light at the surface between air and water. Thus, a fisherman who stands on land and may think

27

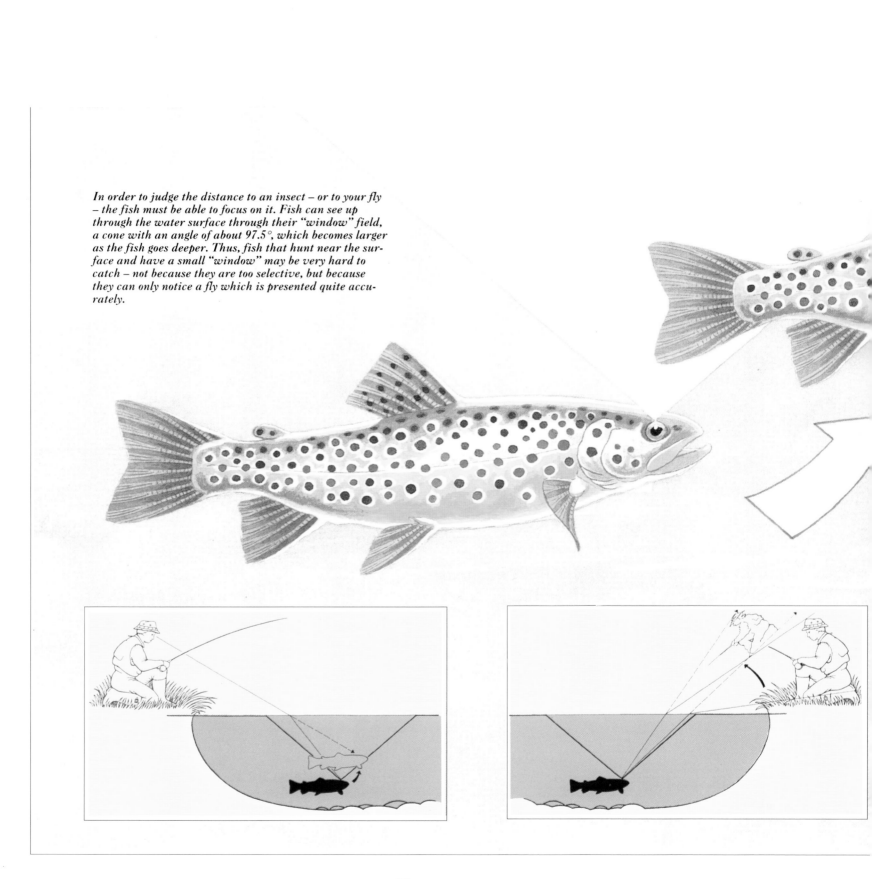

In order to judge the distance to an insect – or to your fly – the fish must be able to focus on it. Fish can see up through the water surface through their "window" field, a cone with an angle of about 97.5°, which becomes larger as the fish goes deeper. Thus, fish that hunt near the surface and have a small "window" may be very hard to catch – not because they are too selective, but because they can only notice a fly which is presented quite accurately.

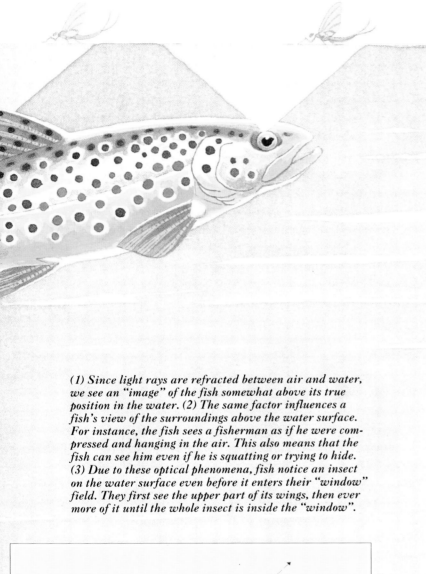

(1) Since light rays are refracted between air and water, we see an "image" of the fish somewhat above its true position in the water. (2) The same factor influences a fish's view of the surroundings above the water surface. For instance, the fish sees a fisherman as if he were compressed and hanging in the air. This also means that the fish can see him even if he is squatting or trying to hide. (3) Due to these optical phenomena, fish notice an insect on the water surface even before it enters their "window" field. They first see the upper part of its wings, then ever more of it until the whole insect is inside the "window".

himself hidden by shore vegetation is often visible to his quarry. The same phenomenon makes it easier for us to notice a fish hidden in deep water. However, refraction also shows the fish to be shallower and farther away than it really is. This illusion must be taken into account, especially by nymph fishermen when presenting a weighted nymph.

The fish's picture of the world above the surface through its window is compressed, and ever more so as it looks toward the edges. So a fisherman sitting on land will seem abnormally low and broad to a fish, as though viewed in a "funny" mirror. For the same reason, when an insect approaches on the water surface, the first thing that a fish sees is the insect's "footprint" where it has made an impression on the surface. If it is a mayfly, the next to be seen are its high wings, which are actually the first to enter the window field. Only when the insect is entirely inside the window does the fish see it clearly.

On the other hand, if an insect comes drifting or swimming under the water surface, and if the surface is smooth in calm weather, a fish will see two insects instead of one — that is, both the insect and its reflection from the surface. Yet the reflection disappears when the insect enters the underwater part of the fish's window field.

A fish carries its window with it everywhere, into the depths and up to the shallows, swimming and resting alike. The window merely becomes larger when the fish sinks, and smaller as it rises toward the surface. This explains, for instance, why fish that are specialized to eat very small insects can be hard to catch. They lurk just beneath the surface and have an extremely narrow field of vision. So a fly must be cast with great precision if they are to see it at all. Their attention is directed only toward this window and, if the fly does not pass through it, they can hardly react. Often we think that a fish is highly selective, whereas in reality we are simply poor casters!

A general rule is that fish should be approached from behind, supposedly in order to make use of their "blind angle". But the supposition is wrong. The location of a fish's eyes, already mentioned, would easily enable it to see a fisherman who tries to sneak up on it from behind. What makes the fish vulnerable is that its attention is directed forward — up the stream which brings food to it. Naturally this can be exploited by approaching from the rear direction that it watches least.

Food and environment

The food supply largely determines where fish are to be found. It is therefore essential to know the kinds, appearance and behaviour of the animals on which the fish feed. A flyfisherman must be able to recognize these different insects, crustaceans and other prey, if he or she is to have any hope of success. Such awareness makes it possible to decide upon the right fly and to be in the right place at the right time.

Flyfishing is an intimate interplay between the sportsman, his quarry, and the fish's food. The fish hunts for food and is hunted in turn by the fisherman. The fisherman, who enters into the fish's ecosystem, should know not only about its biology and the food it eats, but also about the entire watery environment – streams, lakes or the sea in which he is fishing. And the feeding habits of fish are a good clue to the environment. Which animals or insects occur, and which are caught by the fish, reveal much about the water's quality and its special properties for fishing, one reason being that certain creatures tolerate more pollution or acidification of the water than do others.

Even if a number of particular environments contain the same kind of fish, they may differ radically. Trout, for instance, can be found in fresh or salt water, running or still water, nutritious or depleted water. The ability of trout to adapt themselves is impressive, and goes far beyond what their feeding habits alone indicate.

The food supplies in such environments may vary in great detail. Several of the kinds of animals eaten by trout are the same everywhere, yet their subgroups or species depend on the surroundings. Most insects and crustaceans are adapted to life in either running or still water, but not in both. If mayflies dominate in streams, midges are often the main insects in lakes and ponds. No insects at all exist in the sea, where small fish and crustaceans are predominant. Thus, our choice of fly and fishing technique must be varied accordingly.

The majority of insects and crustaceans on a fish's menu are consumers of plants and of algae which grow atop the sediment. They graze on algae or gobble up the dead, partly decomposed, plant material known as detritus. Evidently the fish's prey are themselves dependent on having enough food and an abundant supply of microscopic algae.

These conditions, however, apply only to relatively clean and clear water, which can transmit light most easily. The light is what activates the process of photosynthesis, creating algae at a basic stage in the food chain. With the energy of sunlight and the building materials of water, carbon dioxide and salts, the algae can produce their organic components. While carbon becomes part of the algae, oxygen is released into the water. As a result, plants in the water do more than provide nourishment for insects and crustaceans. They also generate much of the oxygen needed by both a fish and the animals it eats.

If the water quality is ruined by run-off from a source such as nutrient-rich sewage, which uses up the water's oxygen when decomposing, the fish in the water will naturally disappear fast. A similar but indirect effect can occur in a larger lake or enclosed sea bay. Nutritious run-off water will overfertilize the environment, causing "eutrophication", and the free-swimming planktonic algae will experience a population explosion due to the abundance of nutrient salts. When the water becomes murky with algae, no light can reach the bottom where other algae and plants are rooted, so these die out for lack of energy. This leads to a decline in production of the insects and crustaceans eaten by fish – which are the very foundation of our flyfishing!

Although water environments are harmed by an excess of nutrient salts, the world has numerous excellent fishing waters that are rich in nutrients and provide fish with a huge range of diverse prey. Good examples are the classic chalk streams, which come from sources in land with plenty of limestone and calcium. Their water dissolves the salts from the earth and becomes alkaline – with a high pH value – forming the best possible conditions for animal and plant life.

Quite the opposite are waterways that receive run-off from rain and melting snow in the countryside. Such water is virtually sterile, containing almost no dissolved salts, and its low pH value tends to make streams unproductive. The consequent poverty of food limits the growth of fish and keeps them hungry. Whereas the water level and temperature in a chalk stream are more or less constant all year round, the variations are great in a "freestone stream" of the nutrient-poor kind. It takes in masses of ice-cold water during the spring when most snow is melting; afterwards its level sinks, and its temperature rises with the warmth of summer. Sudden rain on nearby land will cause the water

Dense swarms of insects usually attract fish to the surface. They may rise enthusiastically, but often become very selective and hard to catch.

level to rise again, and perhaps even to flood over – as is indicated by the term "spate river".

Waterways and lakes with a low pH value are, moreover, extremely sensitive to acidification and its effects. Acid rain lowers the pH value rapidly to a critical point, where only a few plants and animals can survive. The animals eaten by fish are the first to perish in such bitter surroundings.

The insects
Mayflies
(Ephemeroptera)

Mayflies have always had a special significance for modern flyfishing. A main reason is that the cradle of dry-fly fishing lay in the English chalk streams, where mayflies were overwhelmingly predominant. Anyone could see that the trout took mayflies up at the surface. Until then, fishing had been done only with sinking flies, but the development of fishing equipment and the production of dry-fly oil made it possible to get densely hackled flies to float. With that, modern flyfishing became a reality. Thus the mayfly has played an important role in the progress of flyfishing.

A mayfly undergoes three stages in its life cycle, and all are of interest to the flyfisherman and flytier. First, the nymph stage is spent in the water, and makes up most of the mayfly's life. As a nymph it feeds on algae and rotting vegetation, moulting its skin several times while it grows. Its colour is dark before moulting, and lighter again afterwards.

There are various forms of mayfly nymphs, but they can be divided into four chief groups, each with its own appearance and way of life. These are the burrowing, the creeping, the crawling, and – last but not least – the swimming kind. Almost all are characterized by three tail antennae.

Among the burrowing nymphs are the large "drake" *(Ephemera danica)* and the "dark mackerel" *(Ephemera vulgata)*. The former lives in running water, the latter in lakes and ponds. Both stay buried most of the time, but must come up to moult their skins, and may then become a fine meal for fish. The drake is declining in many places, as it demands a lot from the environment.

The creeping mayfly nymphs include common species such as the "may duns" *(Heptagenia)*. Creeping nymphs have

a flat body which facilitates their grip on slippery stones in fast waters. Many of them are by nature demanding in regard to the water quality, and therefore have widely died out.

Better able to survive are the crawling nymphs, which show less sensitivity to the water quality. They vaguely resemble the creeping nymphs in body form, but are not quite as flat, since they prefer slower waterways. Living on bottoms or water plants, the well-camouflaged nymphs pursue a rather inconspicuous career. Their camouflage may consist of algae or clay particles stuck to the body. The most widespread crawling species include the Blue Winged Olive Dun *(Ephemerella ignita)* and the small but prominent "white midges" *(Caenis)*.

Swimming nymphs are the commonest of all mayflies. Slim and active insects, they can move very fast in water. When swimming, they draw their legs in toward the body, becoming streamlined in shape. We find these fast swimmers in both flowing and still waters. The classic "olives" *(Baetis)* dominate in running water, while lakes and ponds favour their relatives which, aptly enough, are called "pond olives" *(Cloeon, Procloeon)*. The species living in waterways have fixed gills, but those in lakes have movable gills – and need them, since there is no current in a lake to move fresh water over the gills. In contrast to the burrowing nymphs at places with sand or soft bottoms, and the creeping nymphs on stony bottoms in streams, the swimming nymphs stay close to water plants. Here they swim about and become easy prey for trout. Hence they are among the most important water insects for us flyfishermen.

Mayflies are peculiar in many ways. For one thing, they exhibit what is called incomplete metamorphosis, lacking a pupal stage. Nymphs, the insect larvae, instead gradually resemble the adult insects ever more closely. In other words, they never undergo any rapid change to define a pupal stage.

After a year as nymphs, most mayflies are ready to hatch, turning into adult winged insects. Some species, however, produce two generations annually, while others – such as the drake – produce only one generation every second year. Consequently, drakes need two years to reach their impressive size. After numerous moultings, the wings are fully developed and the nymphs find their way up to the surface. Some species crawl up onto stones or plants; others ascend passively or swim busily upward. During their journey to the surface, they face a considerable risk of ending as food for fish.

Mayflies have always been quite important for flyfishing. Their many species look much alike. Winged mayflies are characterized by upright wings and three tail antennae. Shown here are a typical mayfly nymph (at left) and an adult winged mayfly (above and at far right).

Once on the surface, the skin cracks between the wings, and what emerges from the water is a winged mayfly in the "dun" stage. This hatching takes a longer time during the early and late months of the year than during summer, because the temperature determines the rate of hatching.

A dun mayfly has dull colours with opaque wings and relatively short tail antennae. It is a fairly clumsy flier and can have trouble in lifting from the water. If the water is cold, it sits for a long time on the surface before taking off. On warmer water, its wings speedily harden and it can fly away almost immediately. It then heads inland to find a hiding-place.

There the dun moults again and turns into the third, last stage of the mayfly, a "spinner". The time between these two moultings can vary from several days in cold and windy weather, to a few hours or even minutes in warm weather. A spinner has clear colours, transparent wings, long tail antennae and excellent flying ability. But it cannot consume any nourishment, so it does not live long.

Towards afternoon, and especially in the evening, may-flies form swarms if the weather is suitable. The males swarm thickly above the trees and bushes where the females are hiding. Soon the females fly up, and mating occurs while they are airborne. Then the males immediately die, but the females follow the current upstream and lay their eggs on a suitable stretch of water.

The eggs can be laid in different ways. Large drakes sit on the surface and lay several batches of eggs, which the fish are not slow to observe! Others lay their eggs in a single clump. Some *Baetis* species, quite common in flowing waters, crawl down on stones or plants beneath the surface to lay eggs. Afterwards, the females too die: they drift downstream as "spent spinners", offering the fish an easy and concentrated meal. Such an occurrence of dead or dying females is termed a "spinner fall". Thus, the females are far more significant as food than the males, which seldom end up in the water.

The descent of *Baetis* species into water for egg-laying is very important to flyfishermen. In some cases there is no spinner fall of spent females on the water. Instead, after laying eggs, the females rise to the surface, where the fish can see them clearly and eat them with no difficulty. However, they are almost invisible to us, unless we know exactly what to look for. One must bend right down to the surface in order to see them thronging just beneath it.

Places full of mayflies are rich feeding areas for trout and grayling. The fish take them deep down near the water

Mayflies undergo an incomplete metamorphosis – as do stoneflies. This means they have no pupal stage. The nymph keeps growing and increasingly resembles the adult insect. After about a year, it rises to the water surface, its skin cracks between the wings, and the winged insect hatches. In this dun stage, the wings are dull and opaque, and the tail antennae relatively short. Soon the dun flies away inland to moult its skin again, thus becoming a spinner. In this final stage, the insects swarm and the females lay eggs, then die as spent spinners.

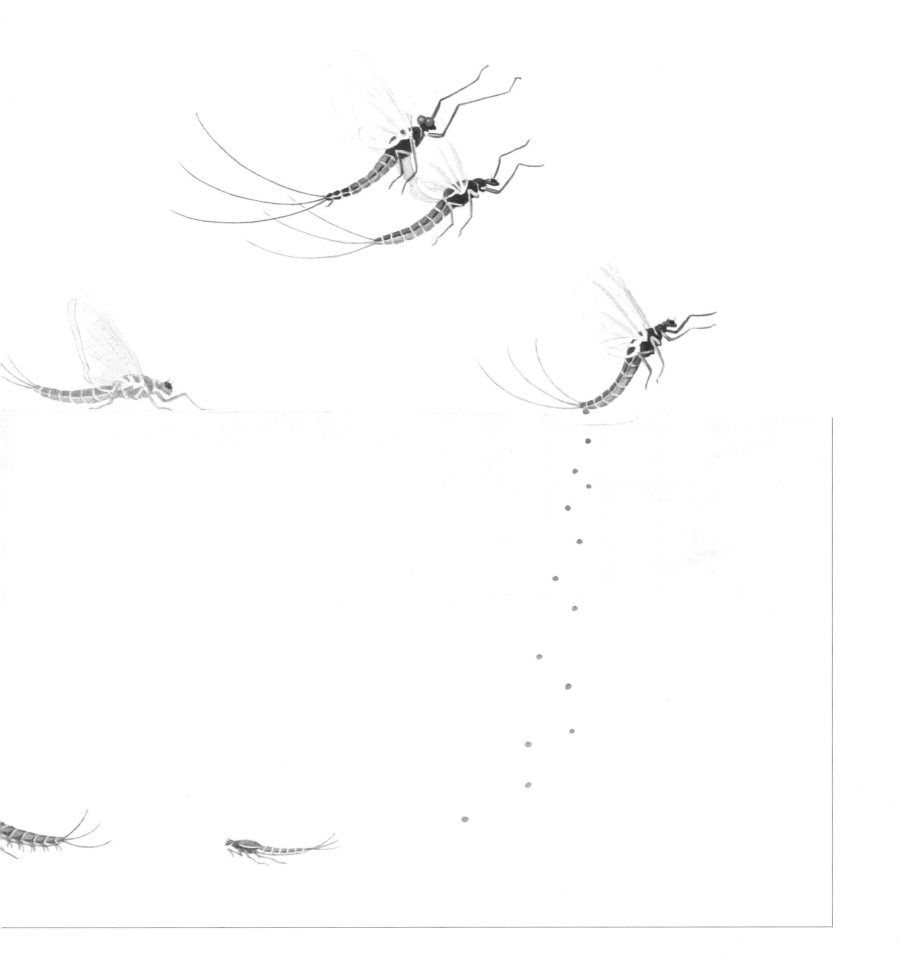

plants, or when they climb toward the surface to hatch, or when hanging dead at the surface while hatching; or again, when the bold fliers with their big wings are blown down in hard wind, or when they have laid their eggs and fall lifeless into the stream.

Caddis flies (Trichoptera)

The mayfly has been in the limelight ever since we invented the dry fly. But things are different with the caddis fly, which has long been neglected. Its status has nonetheless grown greatly in recent years, partly since caddis flies tolerate more pollution than do mayflies. Relatively robust, they get along better with the poor water qualities of the late twentieth century, although many species still require excellent water quality.

All caddis flies, unlike the mayflies, undergo a complete metamorphosis: their larvae pass through a pupal stage before becoming winged adults. The caddis fly is interesting to flyfishermen in both its larval and pupal stages as well as when an adult.

Caddis flies are divided into three main groups: the free-living, the net-spinning, and the case-building. Best known among the free-living larvae are the *Rhyacophila* species. These large greenish predators stay on the stony bottoms of clean waters, and are therefore becoming scarce in many places. The larvae live freely all the time, and only when about to pupate do they build a little flat house on a stone.

More common are the net-spinners, a frequent example being the larvae of *Hydropsyche* species. They are easily recognized by three conspicuous back-plates just behind the head and on the light rear body. This is a specialized creature which spins small hunting-nets between stones. The net opens upstream, and the larva sits on the bottom waiting for the catch – namely algae and bacteria which come along with the current. At some sites, *Hydropsyche* larvae are plentiful and provide much of the food for fish. Such conditions often occur at the outlets of lakes whose water contains a lot of planktonic algae that the larvae can catch and eat.

The last and most perplexing group are case-builders. They include the big *Phryganea* species, which are very hard to mistake in view of their sheer size. Most of us are familiar with the larvae, which are seldom abundant in rapid waters and prefer calm places in waterways or lakes. The larvae are elaborately camouflaged with cut-out plant parts or mosaics of small pebbles. They are usually not seen until they move. Each of the numerous species builds a characteristic kind of "house". The *Phryganea* erect spiral abodes with bit-off vegetation, whereas larvae of the family *Leptoceridae* construct slightly curved cones with glued-together grains of sand. Many other larvae are much harder to identify, some building in intricate patterns, and some taking pride in what look like ruined tenements.

When a caddis fly becomes fully grown, it pupates. The "house" is anchored and the opening closed. Pupation is one of the most mysterious processes in the insect world: a total change occurs in the larva's body and, after a few weeks, the developed pupa gnaws its way out. Not seldom, a mature pupa is considerably smaller than the larva was at the beginning of the process.

As with mayflies, there are great differences in how the caddis-fly pupae rise to the surface. Some species creep up onto land, while others swim up through free water. Some hatch right on the surface, but others fight upward and swim to land. Certain species hatch even before they reach the surface.

A typical caddis-fly pupa is surrounded by a thin, more or less transparent membrane, and has a pair of powerful legs in the middle. The membrane can be filled with air, which provides a lifting force to the insect on its way up. The central legs have swimming brushes on their ends, to be used skilfully during the ascent.

Adult winged caddis flies have a hairy coat and, usually, long antennae. Whereas the wings of mayflies are a large front pair and a tiny rear pair, the caddis fly has four equally large wings and is thus easy to recognize in the air, resembling a flapping moth. When it rests, the wings are laid roof-like across the rear body.

Caddis flies are clumsy fliers and often get wet, both while drinking and while laying eggs. Since the adults differ from mayflies in being able to drink, they can comparatively long on land and in the air. Mating normally occurs in the air and, as with mayflies, the species differ in regard to egg-laying. For example, the large *Phryganea* crawl down into the water and lay eggs there. Some others drop eggs into the water, or fasten them to reeds and branches that hang over the water.

After mating and laying eggs, the caddis fly has finished its work and dies – doing so on land, in contrast to mayflies.

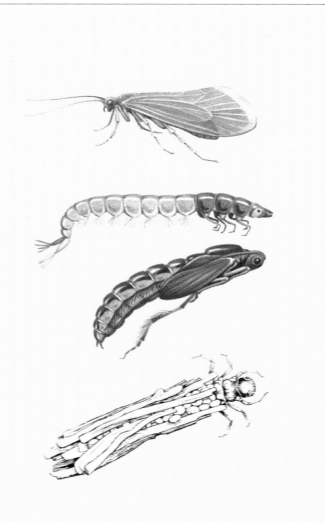

Caddis flies have become ever more important for flyfishing, since they are relatively tolerant of water pollution. They undergo complete metamorphosis before turning into winged insects, so they also have a pupal stage. All three stages appeal to fish – the larva, pupa and flying insect. Shown at top is a winged caddis fly, typified by its hairy body and long antennae. Below this are the larva, the pupa, and (at bottom) a "case worm" larva (Hydropsyche).

So there is no "spinner fall" in this instance. Yet caddis flies are the flyfisherman's dream insects, because all three of their stages provide food for fish and are, in addition, easy to imitate when tying a fly and fishing with it.

Stoneflies
(Plecoptera)

The stonefly is an age-old, exceedingly primitive insect. Like mayflies, it undergoes incomplete metamorphosis. The nymphs are readily identified by their long antennae and, in particular, the two on their tail, where a mayfly normally has three. Further characteristics are the stonefly's flat body and its powerful legs, which enable it to hold firmly on stony bottoms in strong currents, similar to the creeping mayflies.

Many stoneflies hatch during early spring, when no other insects are about. One can often see them sitting inconspicuously with a grip on poles and tree stumps while an icy wind rushes along their surging stream. Not without reason, some of these winter bathers are known as "February Reds".

Stonefly nymphs, instead of climbing to the surface and hatching there, crawl up on land to undergo metamorphosis. During extensive hatchings, fish are attracted and hunt eagerly along the bottom for wandering nymphs. Once on dry land, the nymph cracks its skin and an adult stonefly crawls out. Like caddis flies, it has two almost equally large pairs of wings – but when resting, the wings are laid flat over the back, which makes them easy to distinguish from caddis flies. Besides, the latter are hairier than stoneflies.

A winged stonefly has little talent for flying, and prefers to stay on land among reeds and grass. No doubt it realizes its limitations in the air. For it also mates on land – often preceded by a kind of foreplay, in which the females call the males by drumming on a tree trunk. Sophistication indeed!

Like caddis flies, the adult stonefly can drink and is able to live for some time on land. After mating, the male dies and the female flies upstream to find a stretch of suitable water. There she lays eggs by dipping her rear body in the water. At that time, she naturally faces a great danger of being gobbled by a fish.

Stoneflies are bound to flowing waters, and many of them are very demanding about the water quality. As a rule they are good indicators of clean water, although some robust species can survive in mediocre waters. On the whole, stoneflies are most important in waterways with stony bottoms as well as pure, cold water. Here they also constitute a key food for trout and grayling, which enjoy both the nymphs and adults.

Most prominent of all are the stoneflies in northwestern America. A couple of very large species, belonging to the family *Pteronarcidae*, provide the local basis for exciting and productive flyfishing – partly when the nymphs, several centimetres long, approach land in order to hatch, and partly when the big females return to lay eggs. Since the adults have pale orange bodies, these giants are known in the region as "salmon flies".

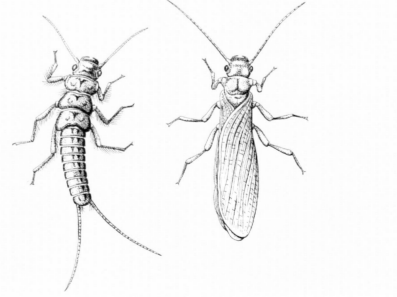

Stoneflies are primitive insects which undergo incomplete metamorphosis. They need relatively high water quality in order to thrive, and are definitely of interest to both fish and fishermen in waterways thet are not too polluted. Shown at right are the nymph – with its typical flat body, two tail antennae and long feelers – and the winged insect, which characteristically lays its wings flat on the back.

Damsel- and dragonflies (Odonata)

The insects to be discussed here are large and, like may-flies, have an ancient and primitive origin. Dragonflies are among the biggest insects that ever flew – prehistoric giants with a wingspan of from 30 to 40 cm (12-16 inches)!

Today's dragonflies are not huge, but they still resemble their ancestors in appearance. Their significance is greatest for fish in lakes and ponds, even if several species also occur in or near running waters. They are greedy predators and all can fly well. Like a helicopter, they may stand motionless in midair and then be gone. Thus, they are difficult to catch, being most vulnerable during the early morning hours when it is still cold and the insects are somewhat lazy.

The dragonfly undergoes an incomplete metamorphosis, going through no pupal stage. After up to three years in the water, the nymph crawls up on land in order to become a winged insect. As a nymph, it moves quietly and calmly in the mud and between plants, where it is hard to observe. It is a greedy, rather clumsily built predator, which moves slowly but can go very fast when necessary. It then uses the "jet" principle, ejecting water with great force from its rear body.

The adult dragonfly is unimportant as fish food, being an all too skilful flier. Its nymph is therefore the target of fish. This is also generally true of the damselflies, which are less well known than dragonflies. They are often mistaken for small dragonflies, but the difference is clear. Adult damsel-flies are distinctive in laying their wings back along the body when resting, whereas dragonflies hold their wings straight out from the body at rest.

Dragonfly nymphs are short and thick in shape, while damselflies are slim and elegant. Since damselfly nymphs pursue an active life, they are very often found on the menu of fish, and are important insects for the flyfisherman and flytier. They have long, thin legs and the rear body is provi-ded with three gill leaves, which function like sculling oars.

Just like dragonfly nymphs, the damselfly nymphs go up on land to become adult insects. However, the latter are poorer fliers and often land in the water, or in a fish's stomach. On the whole, these nymphs are an important source of food in lakes and ponds – much more significant than dragonflies.

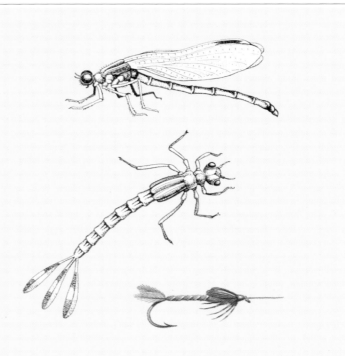

(Above) Damselflies and dragonflies are enjoyed as food by fish in many waters. They have no pupal stage, undergoing incomplete metamorphosis. As the middle picture shows, the nymph is slender with three "gill leaves" on its tail. Beneath it is an imitation nymph.

(Below) Dragonflies, too, undergo incomplete metamorphosis. The short, thick nymphs are an important food for fish in lakes and ponds, where they live in the mud and among plants.

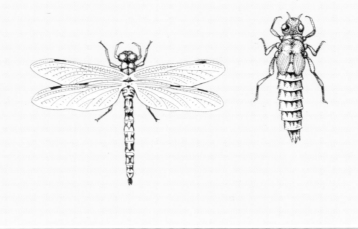

Two-winged insects (Diptera)

This group includes such different insects as crane-flies, houseflies, mosquitoes and dung-flies. Here, though, we shall discuss only the two-winged water insects of the families *Simulidae* and *Chironomidae*, namely the buffalo gnats and the midges. Both are very important for fish. Buffalo gnats live in running water, while midges are most prominent in lakes and ponds.

The buffalo gnat undergoes a complete metamorphosis, with a pupal stage between its larval and winged stages. The larvae are very easy to recognize, having an elongated shape with a flat rear body and, usually, a greenish colour. In waters polluted by organic sewage, such as streams where fish ponds cause pollution, buffalo gnats occur in vast quantities. They sit in thousands upon water plants, and function as a sort of biological purification apparatus. This is because the larvae nourish themselves by filtering bacteria out of the flowing water. In clear, cold water farther north, however, quite different species dominate, placing great demands on clean water.

After several moultings, the buffalo gnat larva pupates. Its case is fastened to a stone or a water plant, resembling a paper cone with the opening turned upstream. When a couple of weeks have passed inside the case, air is formed under the pupa's skin, which eventually bursts. The winged, developed gnat rises on a tiny air bubble to the surface, where it takes off and flies inland. Thus, the buffalo gnat is hatched, not on the surface like other water insects, but already inside its pupal case in the water. The mature buffalo gnat has a characteristically humped back, which explains its name.

The winged female buffalo gnat must suck blood before mating and laying eggs, a fact which causes great trouble for grazing horses and cows. Mating usually occurs in midair, followed by laying of the eggs on or in water. Particularly during the month of May, the water surface can be almost covered with egg-laying females, and the fish feast on them!

Midges, too, undergo complete metamorphosis with a larval, a pupal, and a winged stage. There are innumerable chironomids, as they are also called, but fortunately they can be grouped according to appearance and way of life.

The midge larva is notably important as food for fish in lakes, ponds and bogs. It lives on or in the bottom, where it eats rotting vegetation. The larvae may be green, brown or red, depending on their locality. Green larvae are naturally bound to plants, while brown ones stay on muddy bottoms. The red larvae, which are probably the best known, remain in the depths on the bottom, often in oxygen-poor water. Their red colour is due to haemoglobin, which enables them to survive even under very oxygen-poor conditions. All midge larvae resemble worms with a cylindrical body.

When the larva has become big enough – the largest are up to 3 cm (1.2 in) long – it pupates. The pupa has a characteristic appearance: its rear body is long, slim, and clearly jointed with small, light appendages farthest back. Its breast is much thicker and has marked, dark wing vestiges. On its head are conspicuous bushy, white gills.

The pupal stage seldom lasts longer than two or three days. As the time for hatching approaches, the pupa becomes ever more active. It swims around near the bottom, where it is often caught by fish. When the conditions are right for the pupa, as they normally are during calm evenings and mornings, it swims up to the surface where it may stay hanging for a surprisingly long time. This is obviously the most critical point in the midge's life. The pupa actually hangs with its breast on the surface and its rear body underwater.

In calm weather the water surface is difficult to break through. This is certainly why the midge pupae stay hanging for so long at the surface before they hatch. On the other hand, not very many of them drown during hatching and remain hanging in the water surface film. Suddenly, the adult midge crawls out and flies away inland.

The fully grown midge has a cylindrical rear body with short, slim wings. Males are thinner than females and have large, bushy antennae. Midges create enormous swarms of dancing insects, but – unlike buffalo gnats and ordinary mosquitoes – they do not suck blood. Instead, their wings purr cheerfully, giving rise to the nickname "buzzers". After mating, the fertilized females fly out over the water, often with a thick, bent rear body, to lay eggs.

Midge larvae are extremely important for fish in still waters, and this is true of trout as well as carp and eel. Yet the larval stage has little significance for flyfishing, which profits from the active pupal stage. Trout usually take the pupae when rising calmly for nymphs, with both their back and tail fins showing over the water surface. However, the egg-laying midge females can also be of value to fish and fishermen. When the heavy females find their way down to the water and lay eggs, they become easy prey for fish.

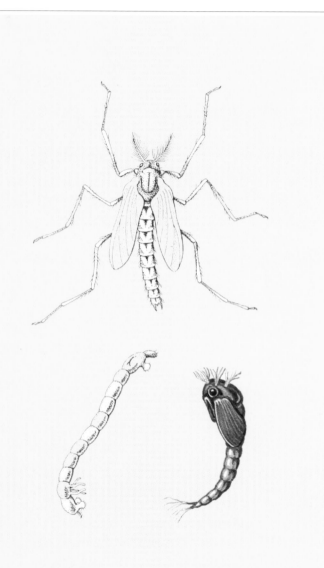

Midges are by far the most important insects in lakes and ponds. They undergo complete metamorphosis, and thus have both a larval and a pupal stage before acquiring wings. The elongated larva (above left) varies in colour depending on where it lives, and can grow up to 3 cm (1.2 inches) long. When large enough, it pupates (above right). After two or three days, the pupa swims up to the water surface and hangs there until it hatches. The pupae are extremely important for flyfishing, since the fish at times feast on them just when they are hanging in the surface film.

What often occurs is a hectic attack on the buzzing insects in almost total darkness.

It can be frustrating when midges hatch and swarm, frequently in incredible numbers at the same time. In spite of that, midges are probably the insects of greatest importance to trout fishermen in most lakes – followed closely by the damselflies.

Water boatmen (Corixa)

The last of the water-living insects to be mentioned here are the water boatmen. Unlike "back swimmers", which have light backs and dark bellies, the water boatman stays on the right keel and, similar to other animals, has a light belly and darker back.

For some reason, back swimmers are seldom found in the stomach contents of inland fish. But water boatmen are apparently quite popular to fish. Moreover, they are exciting insects in themselves. A water boatman can fly as well as live in water – an ability which it shares with very few other insects. Its spoon-shaped front legs are used for eating, its claw-shaped middle legs for holding on, and its powerful oar-like rear legs for swimming. Water boatmen are very good swimmers and rise quickly to the surface, where they take in air and may then return to the bottom, on which they spend most of their time.

When a water boatman needs oxygen, it swims up to the surface and surrounds itself with an air bubble – which it holds tightly with small, water-repellent hairs. As the oxygen in this balloon is used up, more oxygen is pressed in from the surrounding water. So the air membrane operates as a kind of external gill for the water boatman, which can therefore hold itself down in the water for long periods at a time.

Although they live in water, most water boatmen are superb fliers. When they return to the water and dive in again, they make an ample splash! These are heavy insects and can grow to 1.0-1.5 cm (0.4-0.6 in).

Trout is one of the flyfisherman's most common and popular quarries.

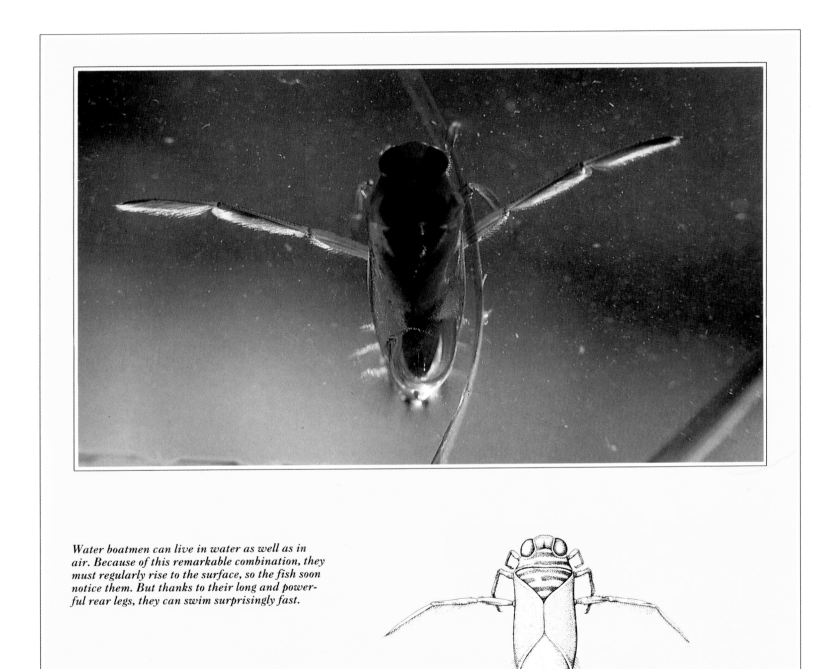

Water boatmen can live in water as well as in air. Because of this remarkable combination, they must regularly rise to the surface, so the fish soon notice them. But thanks to their long and powerful rear legs, they can swim surprisingly fast.

Terrestrials

Formerly, flyfishermen and flytiers spent little time on land-based insects, which occasionally fall into the water and become food for fish. There were enough water insects for all purposes, especially the classic mayflies.

Today things have changed, and many insects – not least the mayflies and stoneflies – have faded from our trout waters because of pollution and other damage due to man. Massive hatchings of such insects are thus only a memory. Interest has therefore naturally concentrated upon "terrestrials", and not only since they occur at periods when no water insects are hatching. One can also often tempt fish with imitations of terrestrials when there are no insects at all on the water. The fish know by experience that a tasty insect may tumble down at any time on the water surface, so they are always prepared!

There are thousands of different land insects able to fall into water. As flyfishermen, however, we can content ourselves with noticing four groups: the ants, beetles, crane-flies and grasshoppers.

Since long ago, flyfishermen and flytiers have been pre-occupied with the so-called "flying ants", a term that is often misunderstood. In fact, only a tiny proportion of all the ants ever acquire wings. Ants are community-building insects in the same way as, for example, bees. An ant community consists of a queen and a large number of workers. The queen normally lays unfertilized eggs which turn into workers. When a new community is to be founded for any reason, the queen begins to lay fertilized eggs. These will become males, whose sole purpose in life is to fertilize the queen. Only the queen and the few males have wings – the working ants never have them.

Once they have come that far, the males and queen leave their old community, and the queen mates with one of the males. The ants are then said to be swarming. After mating, all the males die, while the queen begins to found the new community. If any males fall into the water, the fish go crazy. This usually happens a few times each season, and it is obvious that such "ant falls" can seldom occur. Nonetheless, imitations of ants are frequently good as bait. The reason is that worker ants are diligent, active insects, which commonly fall into the water. The fish thus see and eat both the winged and wingless ants.

Beetles are an important insect group for flyfishermen. On the one hand, they are extremely widespread. On the other, they are clumsy fliers and often need to land on the water surface. When things go wrong, these heavy creatures come down with a splash, which always arouses attention in the water. Imitations of beetles, therefore, are always worth having in your fly box!

Although crane-flies are only occasionally caught by fish, they are interesting insects for both the flytier and flyfishermen. Fish indisputably adore eating them, as can be experienced every year on the great inland lakes in Ireland. There, during late summer, a literal "crane-fly season" occurs, when many of these big insects blow out across the water. They flutter helplessly about, a pattern of behaviour which appeals enormously to the hunting instinct of fish.

American flyfishermen have had great success with grasshoppers, and not surprisingly. Hardly any other insects can get trout to take as easily as do grasshoppers. They are large and nutritious, representing almost pure "energy food", and fish gladly swim several metres to take them. The strike is therefore violent and the fishing quite exciting. This type of fishing is most popular in the American Midwest, where grasshoppers are abundant on the wide prairies.

(Left) A number of land insects are exposed to the hunger of fish at times when other food is scarce. The fish are then quick to take an insect that happens to fall in the water. Examples of such popular terrestrials are shown here: ants, the crane-fly and the grasshopper.

Crustaceans

Crustaceans are among the most important of all fish food. Often plentiful, they are what gives the flesh of trout its beautiful red colour. In fresh waters, we are referring to the groups *Gammarus* and *Asellus*.

Gammarids are recognizable by their high, compressed body with downward-pointing legs. They occur in both still and flowing waters, but need rather clean water in order to flourish. In waterways, they live freely between and on the water plants, at the margins of the current. Their colour is usually greenish with grey and brown markings.

By contrast, the members of *Asellus*, which are broad and flat with outward-pointing legs, tolerate quite a lot of organic pollution and acidification in the water, so they can exist in lakes where not much else survives. Staying in quiet muddy places, they are dark brown with light spots – a fine camouflage on muddy bottoms with rotting vegetation.

Only a few species of these groups exist in fresh waters. Yet both groups are particularly abundant in salt water, where *Gammarus* includes about 200 species and Asellus around 100. There too, they are very important as food for trout and other fish. Other crustaceans live in the sea, not least the large shrimps. These stay buried in sandy bottoms, or circulate near water plants. Most abundant is the group *Crangon*, but more exciting are the *Palaemon* shrimp which undertake regular migrations from shallow to deep waters and back again. At such times, the fish stuff themselves with shrimp!

Finally we have the small but numerous mysids – almost transparent "opossum shrimps" which are not bound to the bottoms, but float freely with the currents. Large quantities of mysids in the water can make it murky. We may not be able to see individual mysids, yet the fish do so with ease and they place high value on this source of food.

Drift

Drifting is a well-known habit at least in the United States, where many flyfishermen drift with the current in boats along the fine trout rivers of the Midwest. This, however, has nothing to do with the "drift" which occurs underwater. The latter phenomenon was discovered rather recently and is very important for both the flyfisherman, the fish, and the animals eaten by them. Such drift is a downstream transfer of insects and crustaceans, often in huge numbers.

There are several forms and causes of drift. At regular intervals, insects and crustaceans lose their grip on their usual habitations and are swept away by the current. This kind of drift happens all day round, and is normally not extensive. Sometimes it increases, as when violent changes occur in the environment, for example during the intensive meltings of ice in spring, or when other events take place that may be experienced as real natural catastrophes by the small animals in waterways. Drift can then be so great that most animals are literally washed away.

In these cases, of course, drift is involuntary. But in others, it occurs more or less by choice. This can happen when the activity of small animals is suddenly heightened: they may be seeking more open water with stronger current, and then the drift will naturally grow. Increasing drift may be due to the daily rhythm, to crowding, or to imminent hatching.

The daily rhythm is the main cause of drift. Nearly all animals exhibit some sort of daily rhythm, being more active at certain times of day or night than at others. Insects and crustaceans are no exception, and most of their species are distinctly nocturnal, making the drift greatest at night. Their drift increases sharply just after sunset and after sunrise. Generally speaking, drift is greatest after sundown when the darkness provides good cover for small animals – and for fish!

Some waters support so many insects that there is just not enough room for them all. Crowding occurs over the best living sites, and this involves a degree of emigration among the surplus insects. They drift downstream in hopes of finding places with more space.

At times immediately before hatching, insects tend to be very active. They regularly leave their residences among water plants and stones, and swim around in more open water until they climb or migrate to land. This means an increased drift, which the fish are quick to exploit.

If these different forms of drift were not somehow counteracted, all of the insects and crustaceans in a waterway would eventually end in the sea, with the final result that no more animals would exist in flowing waters. But obviously this does not happen, and the drift is actually opposed in two regions – the water and the air.

Many species work against the drift by actively travelling upstream. Their journeys occur on the bottom, and in places where migration is possible in spite of the curent – often along the shores in rapidly flowing waters. Crus-

Diverse crustaceans are abundant in both fresh
and salt waters. As a result they rank high among
fish foods. Illustrated at right is a Gammarus
shrimp, which occurs in flowing and calm waters
alike. Usually greenish in colour, it lives on or
between the plants in streams with relatively good
water quality.

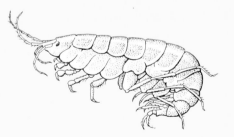

taceans are not the last to oppose drift in this way, as it is the only method available to them.

The insects do likewise, but have a further alternative. They always fly upstream in order to lay eggs. Thus they compensate for the unavoidable drift downstream, to which they are subjected during their larval and nymph stages. Water insects never fly downstream to lay eggs – that would mean sheer suicide for the species.

All small animals in a waterway drift, but some are naturally more prone to drifting than others. The most active ones expose themselves to greatest risk, and the more active they are, the greater their chances of being taken by the current. Gammarids are nocturnal creatures and drift in large numbers. The same is true of the swimming mayfly nymphs and a few of their crawling relatives. The digging mayfly nymphs and the case-building caddis fly larvae, as might be expected, seldom drift. Yet the net-spinning caddis fly larvae often do so.

Natural drift is important in many respects. On the one hand, it provides a distribution of any surplus of animals over a large area. On the other hand, it means that empty areas can quickly be repopulated. The last fact has great significance in view of pollution, which kills the life in a waterway. Drift ensures that a rich variety of animals can re-establish itself in such places.

Finally, drift is also of clear value to the fish in a waterway. Much of their food consists of insects and crustaceans which come drifting down to them. Even if all fish profit by drift, it is most important for the smaller fish. Big fish are nourished to a greater extent by sizeable bottom animals, which rarely drift, and by smaller fish.

Drift is, nonetheless, so important for all fish that they generally choose to stay in places where the current concentrates the drift and, therefore, the food. A good example is the inlet of a fast current to a calm hole. The rapid flow brings many small animals which the fish can easily eat in the calm water. Studies have shown that more small animals drift into such a hole than out of it, and the difference must therefore have been eaten by the fish!

In conclusion, drift is of enormous value to both fish and fishermen. The fish seek places where the drift is greatest, and it is there that we can tempt them with our flies.

A stubborn trout has at last been outwitted. The choice and presentation of the fly were evidently correct.

Small fish

As mentioned earlier, there are no insects in the sea, so marine fish direct their hunger toward crustaceans and smaller fish. However, the latter are also an important part of fish food in fresh waters, especially for the biggest fish. It is therefore necessary for the flyfisherman to know a little about the small fish which are regularly on the menus of other fish.

Small fish are of less significance as fish food in running waters than in still waters. Our trout in running waters gladly eat minnows *(Phoxinus phoxinus)*, small colourful carpfish which need clear, oxygen-rich waters. Elsewhere it is often habitual bottom-fish that are eaten, for example the American sculpins *(Cottidae)* which, with their flat body form, are adjusted to life in flowing waters.

The relatively great importance of small fish in still waters is seen in both lakes and the sea. In both of these, one can distinguish between fish which are bound to the bottom or to water-plants near the shore, and typical school fish which travel pelagically in the free water masses.

To the first group belongs the stickleback, an abundant fish in both fresh and salt waters, which is important as food for trout among others. So are the year-old fry of perch and various non-predatory fish in lakes. The latter normally spawn in late spring, and the fry stay hidden during the summer in vegetation in very shallow waters. Towards summer, the smaller fish wander out to deeper water – as far as the underwater plants which, at that time, often reach up to the surface. Out there, the smaller fish are commonly attacked by larger predatory fish that drive schools of fry to the surface. The small fish leap for their lives, resembling a virtual rainstorm on the surface.

In coastal seas and coves, there are frequently large numbers of gobies. These small bottom-fish closely resemble the above-mentioned sculpins, having broad heads and breast fins. Farther out, one can meet the big sand lances, which are quite valuable to predators. The long, thin, silvery sand lance is easy to recognize. It spends much of its time buried in gravel and sand, but cannot feel secure even there. Sea trout, in particular, enjoy swimming around and sucking up the sand lances on sandy bottoms.

Other food

If we pass to greater depths in lakes and the sea, we find pelagic school fish which are a key source of food for big predators. Larger and deeper lakes with cold water are inhabited by smelt, a thin little salmonoid, almost transparent, which swims freely in sizeable schools. It loves cold water and, during the summer, moves out to deeper water – followed by inland lake trout and other predators. On the other hand, these typical cold-water fish are active until well into the autumn. In melt-water lakes, it is therefore not unusual to observe a "perch picnic" with diving gulls and leaping fish as late as November and December, when other small fish in lakes have long since gone out to overwinter in the depths.

The bleak is another important school fish in lakes but, unlike the smelt, it is a warm-water carpfish that breeds in shallow waters during June and July. This often occurs in large schools, which naturally attract the attention of predators.

In the sea, it is herring that dominate the diet of predators. The great herring is known for long migrations into and out of coastal waters, but the sprat – which is smaller – does not travel so far. Both of these fish live on animal plankton and fish fry, so they journey in free water. There they follow the planktonic organisms' daily rhythm, which is controlled by the sunlight: up towards the surface with waning light, and down into the depths with waxing light. Thus, the greatest chances of finding active herring-hunters are at the surface by dusk.

In addition to the insects, crustaceans and small fish discussed above, several other foods are eaten by fish. Actually most fish are opportunists, consuming whatever they can get. Only seldom are they so selective that they feed on a particular animal species.

In fresh waters, there are often small snails among the more mobile prey. This is something which the flyfisherman hardly needs to know, and bottom-dwelling snails are almost impossible to imitate anyway. However, some snails occasionally abandon their life on the bottom and rise to the surface, where fish gladly take them. Why snails behave in this manner is unclear, but it is certainly a faster means of getting about.

Leeches are frequently found in the stomachs of fish caught in fresh water. Obviously the fish enjoy these fleshy creatures, which swim by wiggling through the water. Leeches can become very large and are also liked by bigger fish. They are easy for both the flyfisherman and flytier to imitate.

In salt water, it is often ragworms that are found in fish stomachs. Notable are the large *Nereis* species, and particularly during early spring when these blue-green worms "swarm" in shallow coastal waters. They leave their holes in the bottom and swim up to the surface in order to mate. Numerous and commonly 10 cm (4 in) long, they offer the fish an easy meal which, in the still cold water, may well be the first one of the year.

There are many examples of fish food other than insects, such as the small fish in lakes and seas. At left are shown two species of importance to bigger fish: the sculpin in North America, and (beneath it) the minnow in Europe. The bottom-living leech (above) often occurs in fish stomachs. It can grow rather large and, just like small fish, is therefore quite popular to the bigger fish.

The flies – our deceptive imitations

There are many thousands of fly patterns around the world. Every day new materials and patterns appear. The range is so wide and difficult to survey that a newcomer may well feel confused when he or she is choosing flies for the first time.

However, flies and fly patterns are often two different things. Fly patterns are what you use as a model for tying; flies are what you fish with. All too many flyfishermen and flytiers overlook this distinction. They place excessive faith in the fly pattern itself, and think more seldom about how the finished fly works and whether it is suitable for fishing.

Among us flytiers are plenty of "pattern fanatics": flytiers for whom a fly is acceptable only if tied exactly according to the rulebook, and then only with the correct materials. Thus they become slaves to the pattern, and are unable to tie a particular type of fly if they lack any of the often exotic materials which are prescribed.

It ought not to be that way – at least from the viewpoint of a flyfisherman. The fish are indifferent to tiny details and conceits; they are far more interested in the actual presentation of the fly than in the pattern. What counts for a fish is the total impression, not the absence of a few fibres or a peculiar feather.

Imitations or fantasy flies

If you tie flies for the sake of flytying, you obviously have to stick to the correct patterns and materials. Then it becomes a hobby in itself. But fishing has for many years suffered from the fact that authors are often more inclined to flytying than to fishing. The available literature has therefore given, at least to beginners at flyfishing and flytying, the mistaken impression that fly patterns are something sacred and inviolate.

Fortunately a clear change in this situation has taken place during recent years. New materials and tying methods have arrived, banishing the old classics into oblivion. These materials are easier to work with than the original ones, and are much more durable too.

Plastic tinsel does not break down like the old metal materials, even in the saltiest water. Stainless steel has shown the same advantage in regard to hooks. Polypropylene has revolutionized dry flies, for example, where it is lighter than water and, moreover, is water-repellent. On the

A deceptive imitation and its prototype.

of fishing situations. Just think of the "muddler", which can be tied in all conceivable circumstances – from the smallest to the largest – and is fished both wet and dry. It is a good instance of a true classic: a fly type rather than a fly pattern.

Consequently, a fly pattern should be regarded mainly as a proposal, rather than as a prescription. It ought to be a starting point for individual interpretations. A pattern which has been thought out or developed in order to suit the discerning trout in a quiet English chalk stream cannot necessarily be transferred to other parts of the world. It must be adapted to the fish's size and the water's current speed, depth and clarity, to mention only a few local factors.

Lastly we should consider the way in which a particular fly pattern came into being. Often the fly's inventor has been in a situation where he or she was forced to get along with the materials at hand. Perhaps quite different materials would have been used if available at the time, and perhaps the finished fly would have been even better. So the flytier ought to have a relaxed attitude towards the pattern. Flies are primarily intended to be used for fishing and, if one does not happen to have the prescribed material, one replaces it with something similar – maybe even better than the original material – for one's own fishing water!

A fly pattern can be created from various points of view. It may be a pure fantasy fly, or an exact imitation. The fly can be imagined to imitate the fish's natural prey, or it can be designed as a provocation. Thousands of fantasy flies have been conceived through the years, but very few have stood the test of time. England's bright red Cardinal, for example, has survived precisely because of its beautiful appearance and classic name. The same is true of a fly such as Silver Doctor, which is equally popular for brown trout, sea trout and salmon. It is obvious that the pretty colours are what have kept these flies in the fly-box, even more than their ability to catch fish, which is no better or worse than that of many other flies.

Things are different with the imitation flies, many of which have lasted remarkably well. This is especially true of dry flies and nymphs from the age of Halford and Skues. Although first tied around the turn of the century, they have nevertheless managed to retain their status for decades. It was, in fact, first when Swisher and Rickards created the famous "no hackle" dry flies that Halford's original dry flies became obsolete. Among other innovations, that of synthetic polypropylene – then called "phentex" – set the development in motion. Until then, natural materials had enjoyed a monopoly.

whole, synthetic materials have made life a lot happier for both the flytier and flyfisherman.

In spite of that, many classics are still in our fly-boxes. They are flies which have been around for longer than most of us can remember – flies so simple and ingenious that they still fish as well as on the day when they were first conceived. Often it is not a question of the actual pattern. These eternally young classics are types which be varied according to the conditions and can therefore cover a range

Good and bad imitations

On the whole, the classic English dry flies are incredibly poor imitations of real mayflies. Their dense hackle, which was needed to let them float at all, was enough to make them bad imitations. That they still could, and can, defeat shy and selective trout in the southern English chalk streams may tell us more about the fish than about the flies.

We usually say that dry flies float, but they very seldom do so. In order to float, a fly must be lighter than water, and this is far from true of ordinary dry flies. A conventionally hackled dry fly is heavier than water and cannot float. It does not sink simply because it is held up by the surface tension. It actually stands on the surface with its many hackle fibres, just as the real insect does with its legs. Both rest on an unbroken water surface and are so shaped that the surface tension supports them. As soon as the surface tension is broken, the fly or insect sinks.

Left: Many flyfishermen think that conventionally hackled dry flies float – in other words, that they are lighter than water. But the truth is that they rest on the water's surface tension.

The surface tension of water, however, varies a lot from place to place. The cleaner the water is, the stronger its surface tension, and therefore the greater its ability to support insects and dry flies. When the water is polluted in any way, the surface tension immediately decreases. Then dry flies have difficulty in staying afloat. But what is worse, the same applies to the real insects. Many of them become unable to complete their life cycle, since they are "caught" hanging in the water surface and remain hanging there while they hatch.

Flytiers should take account of this phenomenon. It means that dry flies must be hackled more densely for polluted than for clean water. Actually we may get along well enough without hackle, as the above-mentioned "no hackles" indicate. As their name implies, these flies have no hackle at all, but consist of a tail, a body, and a pair of conspicuous wings. They can still be made to rest superbly on the surface tension, although in an impregnated condition. At the same time, they are silhouetted to the fish, and this is far better than the hackle fibres' imitation of characteristic mayflies. Especially typical of these insects are their upright wings.

Dry flies can be tied in numerous ways. Here we see a traditional example (upper left), a "no hackle" dry fly (lower left), and (at right) the two steps needed to tie a parachute-hackled dry fly.

Sparsely tied flies are, as a rule, best for selective fish in clear, calm water. They imitate their natural prototypes better than do densely hackled flies, which merely give the fish a confused picture of something that might be edible. Even so, in many situations we are forced to depend on the latter kind of flies – for example in fast waters, where flies with little or no hackle sink instantly.

For such fishing, therefore, special dry flies have been developed, which can stay afloat even in a whirling current. Instances are Wulffs, Kolzer Fireflies, Goofus Bugs and various Irresistibles. These flies are all equipped with strong wings and tail, as well as dense and bushy hackle of the highest quality. This structure enables them to stand high on the water, and keeps them visible to both the fish and fisherman. In the case of Goofus Bugs and Irresistibles, a further step has been taken: they are provided with a sort of "life jacket", an air-filled body of deer hair, which gives them volume and floating force when it really counts.

These ample "floaters" seldom resemble anything in particular, but rather resemble a morsel which the fish are reluctant to pass up. In fast waters, it is nevertheless unnecessary to use the exact imitations which are required in clear, calm water. Fish in a rapid current do not have time to study the fly – they must react fast, or else it is gone again!

But densely hackled flies can also be needed in still waters, for example when fishing with imitations of caddis flies. This often involves large insects that cause commotion when they flutter about, especially during egg-laying. Such behaviour can be imitated by allowing a dry fly to drag on the surface, a technique which calls for densely hackled flies that do not sink immediately.

Today it has become ever more common to tie certain types of flies with foam rubber such as "polycelon". In this way the finished fly is made to literally float, in contrast to normal dry flies which simply rest on the surface tension. Such an ability is used for flies that have to float on the surface – typical hatching nymphs, or heavy land insects like beetles and grasshoppers. The latter can often be served up to notable advantage with a clear, loud splash that draws the fish's attention to the fly. And this is a technique that demands self-buoyant flies: those with a body of cork or foam rubber, which is easier to work with and also lasts longer. Here is still another proof that synthetic materials have revolutionized flytying and given us completely new opportunities.

Colour can trigger strikes

But what is it about our flies that gets fish to strike? An ethologist can provide some insight into this fascinating subject. Ethology is the science of animal behaviour, and conducts research on why animals act as they do.

In one of the most classic ethological experiments, it was investigated how the stickleback reacts to different stimuli. As is well known, the male becomes extremely aggressive during the spawning period. He defends his territory and nest against all intruders, especially competing males.

During spawning, the males are coloured bright red on their bellies, while the females have a large, distended stomach full of eggs. It was studied how the sticklebacks reacted to various decoys. Some of these were exact imitations of males and females, whereas others bore little or no resemblance to them.

The experiment yielded interesting insights into the fish's ways of reacting. Not unexpectedly, close-imitation decoys with bright red colours triggered a violent reaction in the males, which naturally thought that the decoys were competing males. Moreover, decoys with a distended belly attracted great interest as if they were real females.

Yet the truly fascinating result was that perfect imitations did not release stronger reactions than did the less close imitations. It was the colour which proved decisive for the males, and the shape for the females. Colour and shape were the so-called "key stimuli" which triggered reactions – the factors that determined whether there would be any reaction at all. As long as the decoy was red, and preferably bright red, the males showed violent reactions, ignoring all else. Even a red car which drove past outside the window was enough to excite the male; and a red car cannot be said to have much in common with a stickleback!

One might think that sticklebacks are more primitive than the salmonoids which we try to catch with flies, but such is not the case. From a purely evolutionary standpoint, salmonoids are more primitive, and the stickleback is among the most advanced fish. The experimental results with sticklebacks can thus very well be applied to salmon and trout.

When fishing in cold water, colourful flies are often the best choice.

What can we learn from this as flytiers and flyfishermen? Quite a lot. It is natural to attempt to imitate, as closely and detailed as possible, the animals which constitute fish food. The more a fly resembles its prototype, the better it fishes – for fish are not stupid, are they?

Well, fish are indeed stupid, at any rate by human standards. They cannot think in the sense of adding two and two. They learn from experience, but do not reason. They have no perspective on their situation and, instead of thinking, react to external influences. Whether we like it or not, a fish is a primitive machine, controlled by its environment. The frequent difficulty of catching it is due to various factors which we are seldom able to govern.

This logic serves simply to bring down to reality the controversial "imitation principle". Certainly it may be interesting to tie very exact imitations, but unfortunately the fish rarely set much store by them. From the experiment with sticklebacks, we saw that the colour is the decisive key stimulus. If we look at our own flies with the eyes of a fish, things become more complicated.

Fish can see colours – this is a fact. But in regard to dry flies, for example, colour is by no means as important as was once thought by flytiers and flyfishermen. The fish see a fly from below, outlined against the sky in backlight, so they can hardly distinguish beween different colour tones. In practice, it often turns out that we can do quite well with a small range of dry flies in a few colours.

Down at the water, of course, the fish can study our wet flies. Still, exact colour nuances are seldom decisive. This is because there are large individual differences between natural insects. For instance, nymphs which have to moult their skins are very dark, while those which have just done so are very light. Thus the fish see both dark and light insects at the same time, which means that they are not fastidious about exact colours. After all, they only want something to eat!

Colourful flies can be attractive

When we speak of colours and fish, we must remember that colours above the water surface are not the same thing as colours under the surface. The water absorbs some of the light which enters it. The murkier the water, the less light can get in, and the less significance a fly's colours have. We should also keep in mind that red is the colour which fades soonest, and blue is the colour that penetrates deepest. The red part of the visible spectrum is least energetic, and blue is most energetic. If you need a visible fly in deep water, it is thus a bad idea to choose a red one, which will look black to the fish and be hard to see. Instead, choose a fly with blue or green colours – ideally with plenty of tinsel, which can reflect the little available light.

Fluorescent colours have always been of great interest to flytiers. For many of us, fluorescent flies have seemed to be something magical, which now and then can save an otherwise fruitless day of fishing. But there is nothing magical about fluorescent colours. Fluorescence is due to energetic ultraviolet light, which is invisible to us. It is the same kind of light that gives a suntan or sunburn. When ultraviolet light, which is especially predominant on gray and cloudy days, hits a fluorescent material, this is activated by the light's energy and shines with unusual strength. Consequently, fluorescent colours are most clear on dark days, although they should not be confused with phosphorescent colours, which can emit light even in darkness. If there is no light, there is no fluorescence either!

In fly patterns for salmon, particularly the so-called "egg flies", fluorescent colours have made notable progress. Here they are quite superior, although of more doubtful value in smaller flies with quieter colours. Fluorescent colours seem to have the greatest effect when they are used in flies that provoke the fish to strike – in other words, flies meant for fish on spawning migrations. But they should not be forgotten if we are fishing in the cold months, when the water contains little food. Then the fish are hungry, and not especially discerning. In such situations, a fluorescent fly can attract great attention and curiosity, yielding surprisingly good results. Later in the year, when food is abundant, fluorescent colours often lose their ability to attract strikes.

A colourful fly like the classic, eternally young "Mickey Finn" is regarded as a natural attractor – that is, a fly which draws the notice of fish with its strong colours. But it is a fly which can also be very effective during the warm months, when there is plenty of food in less bright colours. Strong red-yellow hues are, perhaps, not so impressive after all. Considering the colours of a minnow or stickleback, one can see that almost every colour in the spectrum is represented. So who knows? Maybe the fish believe that a fly like "Mickey Finn" is an ordinary small fish.

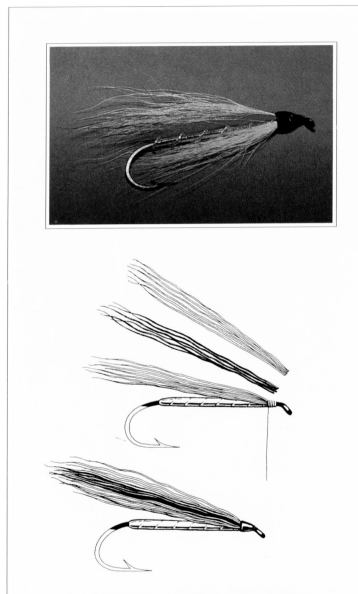

Streamers may be very effective when the fishing is slow. They are easily visible and are frequently good imitations of small fish. Mickey Finn is undoubtedly a classic streamer that can lure fish to strike even when the water is relatively warm.

MICKEY FINN
Hook: streamer hook No. 6-12
Body: silver tinsel
Wing: three sections – yellow, red, and yellow – of hair from polar bear, calf tail, or goat

The fly as a caricature

The experiment with sticklebacks showed clearly that exact imitations are not necessarily the best. Other scientific studies indicate that it can even pay to exaggerate the key stimuli. A good imitation therefore need not be a fly which most resembles the prototype. It may instead be one that overemphasizes typical characteristics of the prototype. We have to think like a caricaturist who instantly hits upon the quirks of his "victim" and exaggerates them. Then there can be no doubt of whom the picture represents. It might be said that the caricature is more realistic than reality!

If the insect to be imitated is, for instance, a mayfly – which has big wings – the fly should have extra large wings. This is actually true of the so-called "no hackle" flies, already mentioned. Usually regarded as exact imitations, they are actually faithful caricatures. Their wings, which are not veiled by any hackle, tell the fish immediately that this is a mayfly.

The "no-hackle" introduced by Swisher and Rickards imitates the mayfly in its "sub-imago" stage, that is, the newly hatched insects. This very stage has caused the fly-tier much trouble through the years, and has given rise to a number of different proposals for the best way of shaping and tying flies. Already at an early date, flytiers began to provide their dry mayfly imitations with upright wings – which were difficult to tie on, were not very durable, and gave the fly the wrong balance. Besides, the wings became almost completely hidden by the dense hackle.

The classic dry fly is slowly disappearing from our fly-boxes and being replaced by new, better and more durable imitations. Not least the parachute flies, whose hackle is wound around the wing root, have become popular. They are easy to tie and rest low on the water, just like the real insects. At the same time, their horizontal hackle adds extraordinary buoyancy. Moreover, the fly lands as light as a feather and always correctly on the water. This is certainly not true of normally hackled dry flies with upright wings, which readily topple over and lie down on their sides.

A mayfly's last winged stage, the spent spinner, is very easy to imitate. This again is due to the modern synthetic materials, which do not absorb water. With them, we can make the flies rest in the surface layer without using hackle. The "polywing spinners" are outstanding imitations with a particularly simple structure – a pair of long tail antennae, a polypropylene body, and a horizontal wing of poly yarn. They can hardly be simpler, and the fish love them!

All these imitations rest on the water, while the hook tip and the whole hook bend protrude down under the surface. Ultimately such a fly does not closely resemble its natural prototype. Insects do not break through the surface – they stand on it. Nevertheless, thousands of very selective fish have been tricked by our flies, despite the quite unnatural iron clump which hangs beneath the surface. This could be seen as another proof that exact imitations are not very significant for the fish's view of our flies.

There are flytiers who make complicated "upside down" flies, with hook points and bends that do not break through the water surface. But these have never been widespread, since they are too hard to tie. As we have seen, even the most selective fish are only seldom able to appreciate our exact imitations, which are primarily for the flyfisherman's own sake!

Function and movement

In the long history of flyfishing there are some examples of amazingly simple flies, so simple that it might be doubted whether they can be used for fishing at all. Frank Sawyer was showered with praise when he created his now classic Pheasant Tail, a fly that consists solely of pheasant cock tail fibres and copper wire. The latter serves partly as binding thread, and partly to weight the fly so that it can sink fast.

Sawyer had noticed that mayfly nymphs of the genus *Baetis* hold their legs close to the body when swimming. He therefore saw no reason to put hackle on their imitations. With sparse material he was able to contrive the right form and colour, while relying on the rod end to give the fly correct movements – an "induced take" which has since become famous.

Oliver Kite, one of Sawyer's disciples, further reduced the Pheasant Tail nymph. He went so far as to use only copper wire on a bare hook, and his Bare Hook Nymph caught plenty of fish. Most of his fishing for fastidious trout took place in the English chalk streams. So much for exact imitations!

Function is a key word when it comes to flies for practical fishing – and regardless of whether they are exact imitations or fantasy flies. The fly just has to work. Dry flies must float, being tied with water-repellent materials; wet flies must sink, absorbing water so as to break through the surface tension. The latter rule is crucial for non-weighted flies: light nymphs, spiders, or wet flies made to be fished high up in the water.

The current speed also influences our choice of material and flytying style. For instance, wet flies for use in still water must be tied with soft material that can look alive and move correctly. Such flies normally fish best when they are sparsely clad. Good illustrations are the classic spiders and soft hackles – their material pulsates at the slightest excuse. Superb in this respect are flies tied with marabou feathers.

The opposite rule holds if wet flies are to be used in fast currents. Here a fly tied with soft material would soon collapse and lose its originally intended shape, becoming just a dead lump of no interest to the fish. One should employ stronger material like cock hackle instead of hen hackle, bucktail rather than marabou, and so on.

If the fly must reach down to fish in fairly deep water, there are two alternatives: using a sinking line to pull the fly down, or weighting the fly and fishing it with a floating line and a long leader. Both methods have their pros and cons. With a sinking line you do not need to weight the fly, which thus behaves more lively in the water. But when fishing nymphs upstream with a floating line, there is only one solution: weighted flies. Then, of course, you must remember that heavy flies are dead flies with no essential life. In sum, clear limits exist to how much the fly can be weighted

Fish often let themselves be tricked into taking, even though the fly is really a rather clumsy imitation of natural food.

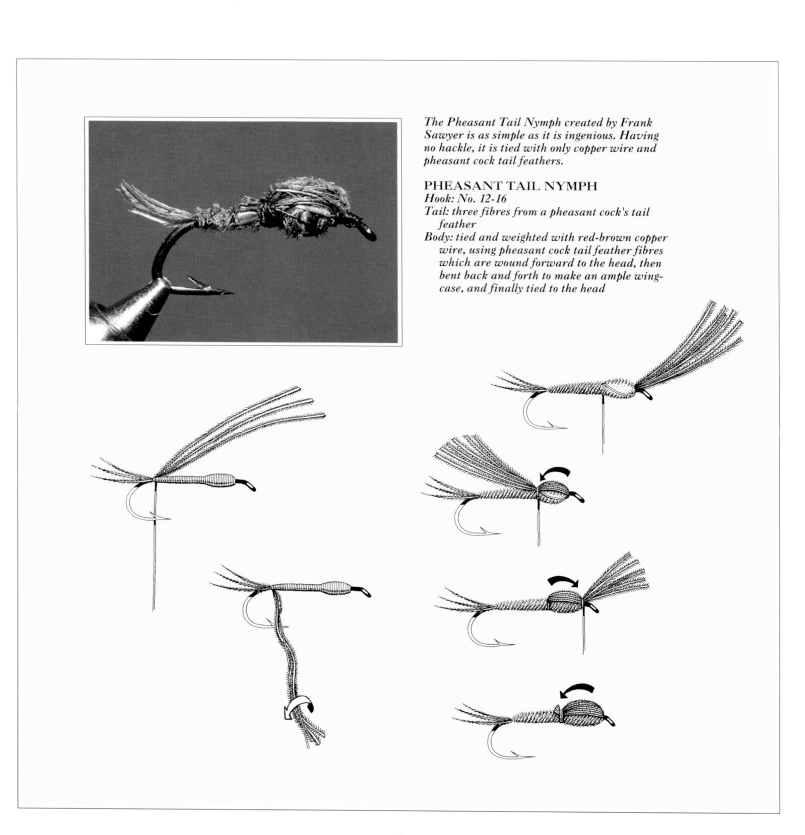

The Pheasant Tail Nymph created by Frank Sawyer is as simple as it is ingenious. Having no hackle, it is tied with only copper wire and pheasant cock tail feathers.

PHEASANT TAIL NYMPH
Hook: No. 12-16
Tail: three fibres from a pheasant cock's tail feather
Body: tied and weighted with red-brown copper wire, using pheasant cock tail feather fibres which are wound forward to the head, then bent back and forth to make an ample wing-case, and finally tied to the head

without hurting its ability to catch fish. The important thing is always to tie it with soft and vital material.

Recently we have acquired fast-sinking leaders, provided with built-in weights. They allow use of a floating line and non-weighted flies. The leader enables the fly to come down to the fish anyway, while also presenting it with a light and lively fly.

From the casting viewpoint, there are definite limits to how heavy a fly can be. Strong fly lines can carry heavy flies better than light flies, but every line obviously has its limitations. Big, densely hackled dry flies create a lot of air resistance and need relatively strong lines to be laid out against the wind. This is familiar to salmon fishermen who try their luck with big dry flies of the Wulff type. But light flies can also be very heavy. Good examples are the "zonkers" and "puppies" tied with thin strips of rabbit fur. The latter have an amazing ability to absorb water, and a wet rabbit is a very heavy rabbit in terms of casting!

The flyfisherman often needs flies which are really bigger and heavier than his equipment can handle. Such is the case with imitations of many medium-size small fish, and with giant flies for huge game like tarpon and sailfish. If these flies were tied in the conventional way, they would be unduly heavy and impossible to cast.

While tying streamers and bucktails on long-shafted hooks, we usually employ short and light hooks for really large flies. They are provided with a wing which is several times longer than the hook shaft, making a fly that is very large and yet does not weigh much. To prevent the long wing from winding itself round the hook bend, it is frequently tied to the rear of the hook shaft. This is done, for instance, on special "needlefish" flies – and characteristic tarpon flies, where the long hairwing is simply replaced by saddle hackle.

Nevertheless, it is also possible to tie a tiny fly on a comparatively large hook. Not seldom, we go after big fish that need strong hooks to be played on. But the flies must be small, since they imitate small insects. Such dry flies can be tied "double", with two flies on one hook. This offers a great advantage when the fish take midges of size 18-24. There is ample room for two flies on a hook of size 16, and then you can also use a stronger leader tippet which matches the fish's size better. Imitations of individual fish eggs – "Glo Bugs" – can likewise be made small on rather large hooks, and paradoxically at no cost to their fishing ability. Here is yet another proof that fish see flies with different eyes than we fishermen do.

Adaptation to practical fishing

Flyfishermen and flytiers are committed, creative people who work continually to keep their hobbies progressing. Originally flyfishing had a very restricted range. The cast was short and the flies could be fished only on or just under the surface. If the fish were not there at that moment, nothing could be done about it. But today's modern, well-equipped flyfishermen want to fish everywhere and under all conditions.

Thanks to developments in gear, we can now reach farther out and deeper down than our predecessors. With fly-lines that differ in sinking rate, we can scrape the bottom in virtually any kind of water. On the other hand, this has led to new requirements for the flies. We must be able to fish them all the way down to, and even on, the bottom without getting them stuck.

The latter problem has been solved in two distinct ways. Flies can be tied "upside down", or provided with a monofilament eye that covers the hook tip. They may be tied on ordinary hooks – as is the popular "Crazy Charlie" type of fly, which is intended for fish on the bottom – or on so-called keel hooks. These can be bought ready-made, but you can use your own pliers to bend the front part of a hook upward. For instance, the well-known "Bend Back" flies are to be used for fishing near the bottom between weeds and stones.

When Don Gapen invented his Muddler Minnow, he hardly realized how much this fly would come to mean for flytying and fishing. It was a fly that, to great extent, could be used both wet and dry. The hollow deer hairs, of which its head is made, give it a characteristic shape as well as good floating ability and water resistance. Floating ability is a natural advantage when the fly must be fished dry or high up in the water. But when fishing deep, near the bottom as an imitation of a "sculpin", the floating force becomes a problem and must be compensated with some weighting.

As a result, we have recently invented flies with the same characteristic shape but tied with other materials. Widely used today are Wool Head Sculpins, where the air-filled deer hairs are replaced by water-absorbing wool, which is clipped down to the right form. Moreover, thick chenille is substituted for the typical "muddler head", giving the same shape but improving the function greatly. The water-absorbent materials enable the fly to sink more easily, so that

Muddler Minnow can be used as either a wet fly or a dry fly. Its head, of hollow deer hair, makes it both buoyant and water-repellent. The muddler's characteristic shape produces clear pressure waves as well as a conspicuous silhouette. It is thus very suitable for fishing at night, whether in shallow or in deep water.

MUDDLER MINNOW
Hook: streamer hook No. 8-12
Tying thread: black
Tail: a section of brown-speckled feather, for example from turkey
Body: gold or silver tinsel
Wing: squirrel hair covered by two sections of brown-speckled feather
Head: a pudgy shape made of a big bunch of deer hair, tied in just behind the eye, then bent backward, secured with tying thread and trimmed

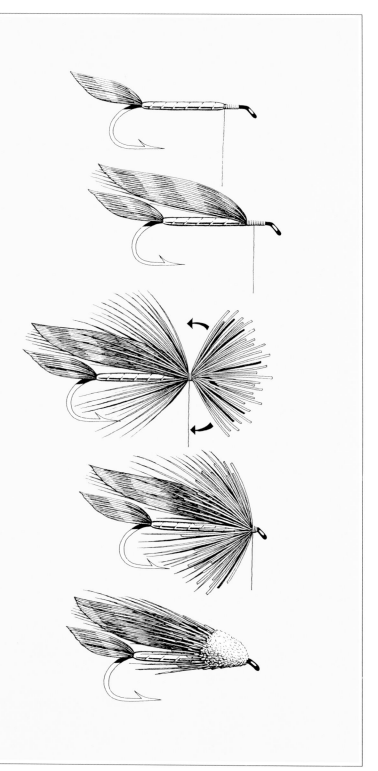

much of the weighting can be avoided.

Besides giving the fly its shape, a "muddler head" has the effect of producing pressure waves in the water. These waves can be sensed by the fish and help them to locate the fly under adverse conditions. Thus, it is no accident that "muddler flies" are particularly suited to night fishing. They present a clear silhouette against the less dark sky, while also sending out plain pressure waves that enable the fish to make exact strikes!

Not seldom, "dragging" flies are also very good for night fishing. They pull up ripples in their wake on the surface, making them easily visible to fish. Notably good in this respect is the original Muddler Minnow with its air-filled deer hairs. Since the fish always see a "dragging" fly from below, its colour is rather unimportant. It is seen in back-light, even at night, so the colour black, being least transparent, gives the clearest silhouette.

Quite different are the "bass bugs" intended for surface fishing in full daylight. Here the colour can obviously be significant for the fishing results, and these flies are tied in all colours of the rainbow – perhaps for the sake of the fish, but in any case for the comfort of the fisherman, who can see the flies more easily on the water. Likewise, "bass bugs" are tied in all conceivable shapes. But they have in common a dependence on the buoyancy provided by their trimmed deer hairs. This keeps them floating on the surface where they can bubble and gurgle, so that even the laziest bass or pike go mad!

Bass can often be provoked by large flies that intrude on their territory, such as a big "bass bug" which is parked among the water-lilies where the fish lurk. Large flies also frequently draw a strike from salmon, at least those that are migrating to spawn. But the fly has to reach down to them – on the bottom, where they defend their territory. When the spawning time approaches, the males in particular acquire an impressive spawning dress, which shines with strong colours. Long jaws with razor-sharp teeth, and a grimly conspicuous jaw-hook, tell competitors to keep their distance. These traits can be exploited by the flyfisherman, if he serves up big flies in bright colours that may release the striking reflex in such aggressive fish. Small dark flies, which made the fish rise to the surface in summer, will have lost their effect in the cold water. Then only big flies can work – and preferably in colours which match those of the fish.

With that, the circle is closed. Flies can be tied as imitations or provocations, dry or wet, and in any sort of shape or colour. Yet the universal rule is that they must fulfil our basic functional needs. They have to be adapted to the fish and the fishing water – otherwise they are worthless for practical flyfishing.

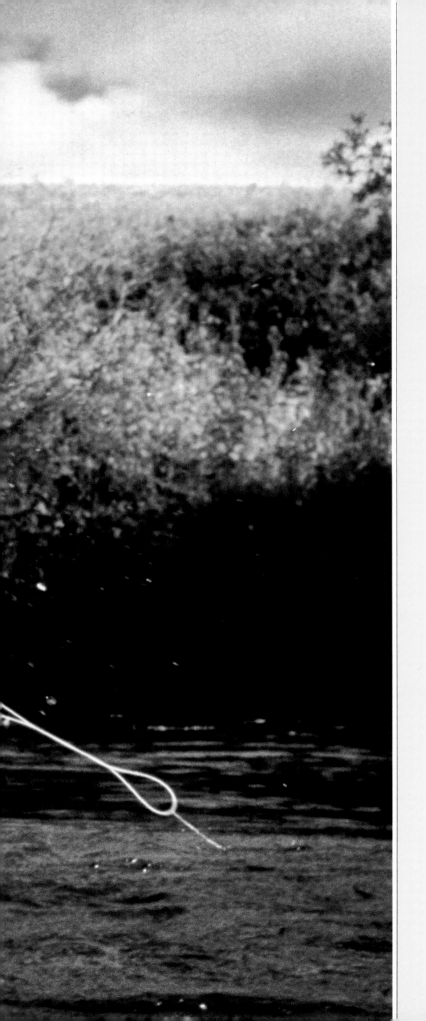

Equipment
and
Casting
Techniques

*It is a fascinating
and beautiful sight to watch
flyfishermen as they present their flies to
the fish with well-timed, harmonious
casts. For the uninitiated,
flyfishing may seem to be a difficult,
exclusive and expensive sport. Yet the fact
is that a fly rod, line, reel and leader are
all you need for learning how
to cast a feather-light fly out
over the water.*

Equipment

The fly line is what determines the casting weight. So it is essential that the rod be balanced against the line's weight during the cast and presentation of the fly. To obtain this balance, lines and rods are classified by a system called AFTM (American Fishing Tackle Manufacturers' Association). Which class or classes you should choose depends on the water you are fishing in – its current, required casting distance, fish size, and other factors.

Rods

Until the 1950s, nearly all fly rods were made of six glued-together segments of bamboo, with triangular cross-section. This is known as the split-cane technique. The unavoidable disadvantages of such rods were their higher weight (much higher for salmon rods), their greater demands for care and carefulness, their relatively high price and shorter lifetime. The advent of synthetic fibre rods was greeted with joy by many flyfishermen, and these rods soon dominated the market.

Carbon fibre rods began to be produced in the late 1970s. Many of us think—perhaps rightly—that their high-tech construction, low weight, fast action, and superb casting ability have revolutionized flyfishing. But it should be remembered that such rods also have drawbacks. Besides being brittle and delicate, they are fine conductors of electricity, which is a serious danger if they come into contact with high-voltage cables. Tube-built glass-fibre rods, although heavier, are thus still on the market, since these are comparatively cheap and durable, as well as often having excellent casting properties.

For technical developments have made quite good tube-built glass-fibre rods available at a fairly low price. In sum, nothing shows that an expensive rod need be better than a cheaper one.

Apart from the AFTM classification, rods are grouped according to their action—that is, how they work. Normally we distinguish between fast action, medium action, and slow action. A rod with fast action has its elasticity mainly at the top. With slow action, the entire rod works during the cast and playing. Medium action is a popular combination of these types, used in many modern fly rods.

When choosing a rod, you must know what it will be used for. The action, line class, and length are determined by the type of water and the fish's species and presumed size. One-handed fly rods are used for fishing in brooks and streams, small rivers and lakes, ponds and coastal waters. Two-handed fly rods are almost exclusively for salmon fishing. Long two-handed rods make it easier to manage a lot of line in the air, but they are heavy and tiring to cast with. A short one-handed rod is convenient when the fishing water is surrounded by bushes and thickets.

The choice of rod depends on further things too. One must check that the handle, reel seat, windings and guides are of good quality and that the rod has enough spine. Generally you can control the line and fly more easily on the water, and achieve a more even casting rhythm, with a longer rod. Rods under 7 ft (2.1 m) cannot be recommended except under very special conditions. For those who need advice when choosing equipment, the following may serve as guidelines.

7.5-9.5 ft (2.2-2.9 m), AFTM class 4-6: fishing in brooks and small streams.

8-10 ft (2.4-3.0 m), AFTM class 6-8: fishing in large streams, lakes, small rivers, and for light coastal flyfishing.

10-13 ft (3.0-4.0 m), AFTM class 9-10: fishing at coasts, large lakes, and for light salmon fishing.

14-18 ft (4.3-5.5 m), AFTM class 10-12: heavy coastal and salmon fishing.

Lines

As the fly line has decisive importance for the cast and presentation of the fly, demands on lines are very high today. They must be supple, light-casting, durable, and easy to feed out through the guides.

Functionally, the fly line helps with its weight in carrying out the feather-light fly. Lines are therefore grouped in twelve standard classes, on the basis of the weight of the line's first 30 feet (9 metres) measured from the line tip. Higher class means greater line weight. Your line class, too,

In order to cast correctly and present the fly elegantly to the fish, there must be good balance between the rod and the line.

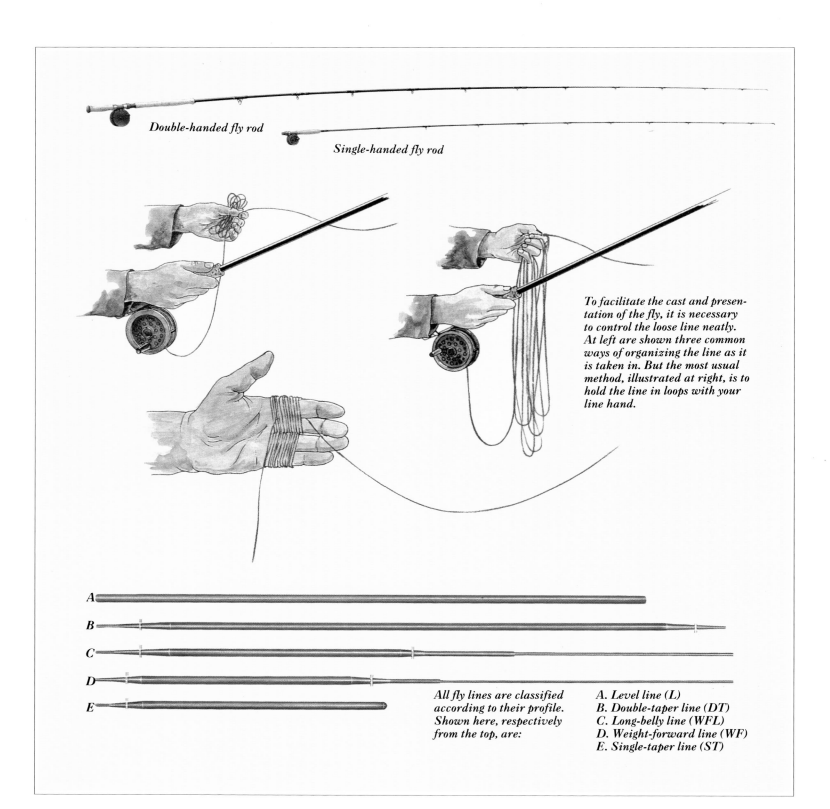

Double-handed fly rod

Single-handed fly rod

To facilitate the cast and presentation of the fly, it is necessary to control the loose line neatly. At left are shown three common ways of organizing the line as it is taken in. But the most usual method, illustrated at right, is to hold the line in loops with your line hand.

A

B

C

D

E

All fly lines are classified according to their profile. Shown here, respectively from the top, are:

A. Level line (L)
B. Double-taper line (DT)
C. Long-belly line (WFL)
D. Weight-forward line (WF)
E. Single-taper line (ST)

is determined by the fishing conditions at the water. Since a light line is harder to cast than a heavy one, only the lowest line classes should be chosen for small and windless waterways. The larger the water – that is, the longer the cast you need to reach out with the fly – and the heavier the fly, the higher the AFTM class which should be chosen. However, a line heavier than class 9 ought to be used only for salmon fishing and arduous coastal flyfishing.

To make the equipment suitable for different types of fish, we have not only the AFTM system but also variations in the tapering of fly lines. This refers to the line's profile, and two main groups exist. A double-tapered line (DT) is thickest in the middle and becomes gradually thinner toward both ends. A weight-forward line (WF), besides its tip, consists of a "belly" about 26 ft (8 m) long – where the weight is concentrated – and a long casting line.

The DT line is used most, because it allows soft and harmonious casts, which are essential for well-aimed and discreet layout of the fly. Its popularity is naturally increased by the fact that it can be turned round when one end has worn out.

The WF line is suitable primarily for situations that call for a longer cast. Depending on the kind of use, the belly length varies. Most marked and short is the belly on the "saltwater tapered" WF line, which serves especially for long casts with heavy flies in bass and saltwater fishing. The "long-belly" line (WFL) has an extremely long clump that makes it behave like a WF line in long casts, yet like a DT line in short casts. A third type of line is the "shooting taper" (ST), also called "single taper", which consists of a short clump attached in a thin casting line, and operates like a projectile when the fishing needs a really long cast.

There is also a distinction between floating and sinking lines. A floating line (F) is used in dry-fly fishing, and when fishing with nymphs or wet flies on the surface. Sinking lines (S) are required when the fish stay deep. Within these groups are also various classes. We speak mainly of slow-sinking (Intermediate), normal-sinking, fast-sinking, and extra-fast sinking lines. In addition, various sink-tip (F/S) types are on the market, and can be preferable to sinking lines – for they give full control over the floating section, and their sinking end can be adapted to the type of fishing at hand. Rapid currents obviously call for heavier (and thus more slowly sinking) line than do still waters, in reaching down to a given depth.

The line's colour is frequently less important than we tend to believe. Fish are hardly frightened by a fly line even if it is very colourful, provided that the leader is long enough. On the other hand, one must keep in mind that light-coloured lines are easier to see when the illumination is poor. Sinking lines, of course, do not suffer by being dark.

Fly lines should always be supplemented with a backing line, or reserve, in case a far-rushing fish takes the fly. A backing line also fills up the reel so that the fly line does not wind up in too tight turns. Such lines are made of monofilament nylon or braided dacron. The latter is usually most expensive, but pays off in the long run since it ages well, is more durable, and tangles less than monofilament line.

Reels

The fly reel is commonly the least emphasized part of our flyfishing equipment. A functional reel must fulfill two requirements: having enough room for backing and fly lines, as well as being able to play big fish effectively. For salmon fishing in particular, it must tolerate long and powerful runs without breaking down. Playing a hooked fish with a loose line lying on the ground is a cause of concern, with the inevitable tangle and lost fish. At least 100 metres (330 feet) of backing line, in addition to the fly line, have to fit on the reel. There must be an adjustable, dependable braking system. The reel should be easy to care for, and soundly constructed with no gap between the spool and housing where the line might get stuck and damaged. Moreover, it should have easily replaceable spools so that you need not carry a reel for each line.

The most usual type of reel is doubtless the traditional one, simply built with no finery. Its handle sits right on the spool, which rotates once each time the handle is turned as the line is wound on – and in the opposite direction as the line is pulled off. When the line is drawn out, the spool is braked by means of an adjustable screw, and you can use your index finger to brake more effectively. This type of reel operates superbly when playing small fish.

Big fighting fish are best chased with a reel whose braking system is more powerful and efficient, such as a slip (clutch) brake or disc brake. These finely adjustable mechanisms also provide soft braking, which can be necessary during powerful rushes so as not to snap the leader. There are also geared reels that wind up several turns of line each time the handle is pulled round.

In general one should always choose high-quality reels. Besides making the fishing more enjoyable, they produce less wear on lines and have a more dependable braking system. It is also worth remembering that the reel should not be too small. It has to hold enough line and backing for the type of fishing you do. And finally, a reel for saltwater use must be corrosion-resistant.

Leaders

The leader's chief duty is to provide an even transition between the relatively thick fly line and the hook eye. A thin leader tip makes it easier to present the fly without alarming the fish, but is too readily broken off by a sizeable fish. Conversely, a thick leader tip can withstand big fish better, yet may be rather clumsy for elegant presentations.

To some extent, the leader's thickness must be adapted to the fly's size. For a thicker leader guides a big fly more accurately than an extremely thin leader tip does.

Leader tips thinner than 0.12 mm (0.005 in) should be totally avoided, and not less than 0.18 mm (0.007 in) ought to be used for medium-sized fish, while 0.30 mm (0.012 in) is a minimum for salmon and other true fighting fish. Large salmon that need big hooks can even call for up to 0.50 mm (0.02 in) at the tip.

The length and tapering of a leader are also important. A good rule is that it should be a little longer than the rod when fishing with dry flies and nymphs, but that 1.5-2.0 m (4.9-6.5 ft) suffices for wet-fly fishing. A leader is built up from its thicker upper end, via a more or less smoothly narrowing transitional section, to the thin tip. About 60% of its total length should consist of the strong upper part, followed by about 20% narrowing and then about 20% tip. The thickest part of the leader, which is tied or glued onto the fly line, must be around 0.5 m (1.6 ft) long with a diametre of 0.45-0.50 mm (0.02 in).

In addition, the leader has to be flexible, soft and easily cast, non-knotting, and able to keep itself stretched in and on the water. A coiled leader can really spoil your sport, not least when dry-fly fishing.

Besides the essential equipment, a clever flyfisherman also needs certain personal qualities, such as an ability to concentrate...

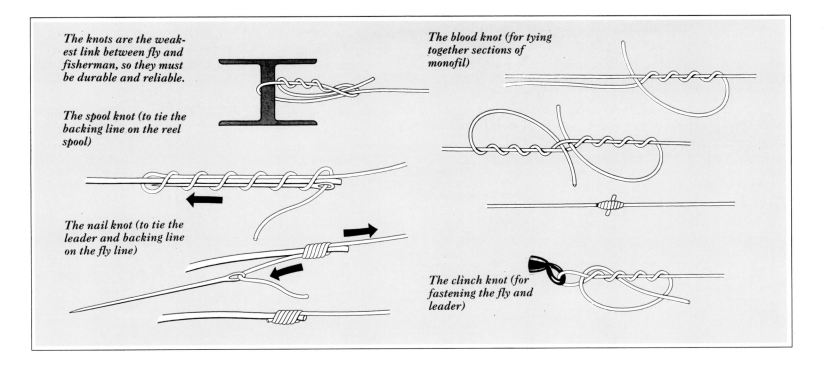

The knots are the weak-
est link between fly and
fisherman, so they must
be durable and reliable.

The spool knot (to tie the
backing line on the reel
spool)

The nail knot (to tie the
leader and backing line
on the fly line)

The blood knot (for tying
together sections of
monofil)

The clinch knot (for
fastening the fly and
leader)

Even if there are ready-tapered leaders on sale in stores, it is not hard to tie them yourself with pieces of monofilament nylon line. The pieces in the leader material should not differ in diametre by more than 0.05 mm (0.002 in), since otherwise the knots are not as dependable.

If you choose to buy leaders ready-made, there is a great range of different types to choose among. Best are ready-tapered, knotless monofilament nylon lines – and braided leaders. The latter, flexible and soft, do not curl as easily when they lie rolled up on the reel for a long period, and they give a generally good presentation of the fly.

Flies

We now come to the equipment which not only gave its name to our kind of fishing, but is the very foundation of this sport's existence – the fly. A symbol that unites the hundreds of thousands of flyfishermen all over the world, it is also a source of arguments. Some maintain that a wide choice of flies is necessary, whereas others are content with a few carefully selected flies. Many of us demand exact imi-

tations, but equally often we consider caricatures to be what attract the fish to strike.

Who is right or wrong in such disputes will not concern us here. Perhaps it is enough to note that our flies and fly patterns are infinitely diverse, and that flies are always a fascinating topic beside the fishing water as well as in the sportfishing stores and magazines.

Internationally, fly patterns are almost uncountable. A lot are pure fantasy flies, while many are precisely tied imitations of particular insects that may live in only one area. There is also a long list of patterns intermediate between imagination and reality. Despite this amazing variety, flies can be divided into main groups: dry flies, wet flies, nymphs, flymphs, streamers, bucktails, lures, salmon flies, and so on.

Hooks, too, enjoy a virtually limitless range of choice. We need only mention the essential differences from a practical viewpoint. Hooks with an upturned eye are generally used for dry-fly fishing; hooks with a downturned eye are for wet flies, nymphs, streamers and other flies that are fished underwater. However, salmon flies usually have an upturned eye although they are fished deep. The hook shaft differs between fly types. A short or medium-long shaft is

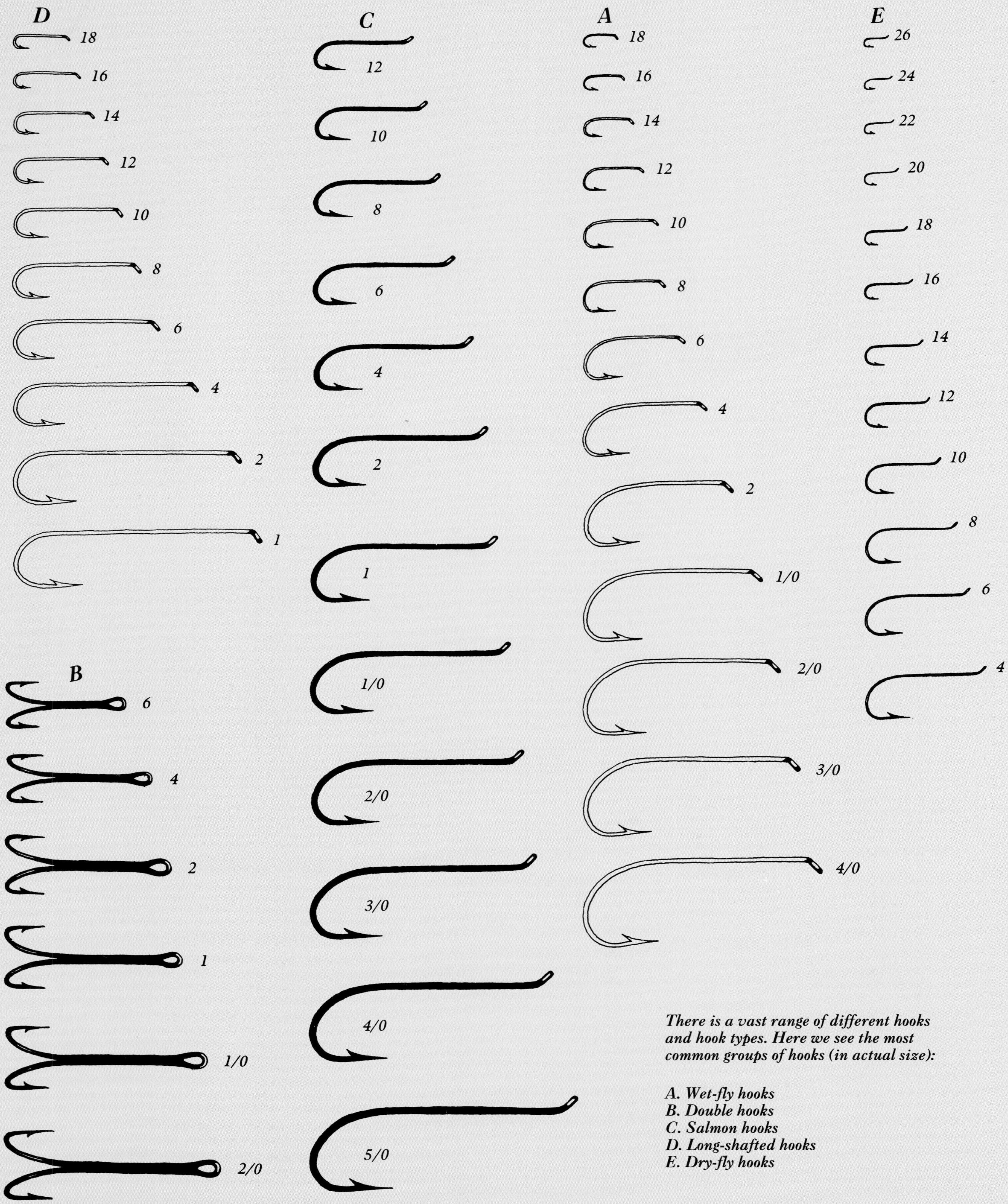

D

18
16
14
12
10
8
6
4
2
1

B

6
4
2
1
1/0
2/0

C

12
10
8
6
4
2
1
1/0
2/0
3/0
4/0
5/0

A

18
16
14
12
10
8
6
4
2
1/0
2/0
3/0
4/0

E

26
24
22
20
18
16
14
12
10
8
6
4

There is a vast range of different hooks and hook types. Here we see the most common groups of hooks (in actual size):

A. Wet-fly hooks
B. Double hooks
C. Salmon hooks
D. Long-shafted hooks
E. Dry-fly hooks

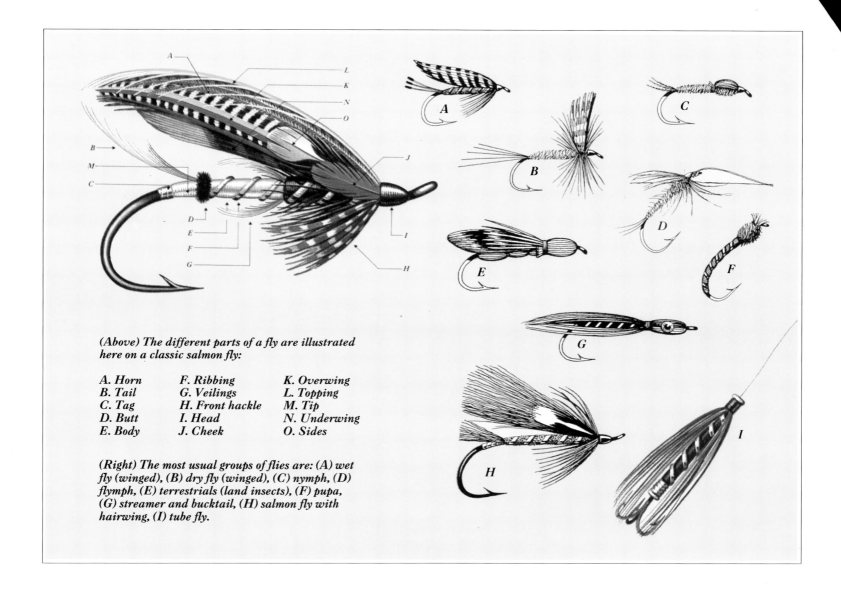

(Above) The different parts of a fly are illustrated here on a classic salmon fly:

A. Horn	*F. Ribbing*	*K. Overwing*
B. Tail	*G. Veilings*	*L. Topping*
C. Tag	*H. Front hackle*	*M. Tip*
D. Butt	*I. Head*	*N. Underwing*
E. Body	*J. Cheek*	*O. Sides*

(Right) The most usual groups of flies are: (A) wet fly (winged), (B) dry fly (winged), (C) nymph, (D) flymph, (E) terrestrials (land insects), (F) pupa, (G) streamer and bucktail, (H) salmon fly with hairwing, (I) tube fly.

used for dry flies and wet flies; streamers, lures and some nymphs are tied on long-shafted hooks.

If flies are to fish effectively, you should always be careful about their quality. This applies to the material as well as to how they are tied. Moreover, hooks should be sharp – and neither so soft that they can bend out during a hard fight, nor so hardened that they can break off. Besides being durable, they must hook the fish solidly. In addition, it is worth knowing that the long shaft of a streamer hook, while allowing very effective imitations of small fish, resembles a lever and gives the hooked fish an excellent

chance of prying itself loose during the play.

Naturally a pattern meant to imitate a certain insect has to portray its prototype in all basic respects. Yet this does not require it to be an exact copy in every detail. Only its similar characteristics need be made clear to the fish – in other words, the fly's proportions and the appearance of its body, hackle, wings, and tail must be right.

In any case, flies obviously have to fulfill their elementary functions. A wet fly should sink to the depth where fish are hunting at the time. A dry fly must be able to float high and lightly, in order to be presented as in nature. A flymph

...ing just in the surface film, or only a ...s under it. The purpose of a salmon fly is to ... provoke the aggressive spawning fish to strike. ...d so on...!

Accessories

The equipment described until now is an absolute pre-requisite for effective flyfishing. But there are quite a lot of items that can make your fishing easier and pleasanter, although not essential to its success.

Clothing should first and foremost be roomy, comfortable and rugged. It ought to give the fisherman proper camou-flage, so as not to frighten the fish unnecessarily. Moreover, it should withstand rain and wind, as well as having plenty of pockets to help you organize your fishing adventures.

A fly vest is probably the most common piece of clothing. Its pockets must be practical and accessible. Before investing in a vest, though, you should check that the pockets will really hold fly boxes and are not so shallow that the contents fall out.

Fly boxes ought to float. A box is easily dropped and, if this happens over deep water, a sinking box can be lost forever. Besides, a good fly box should be clearly arranged and must provide maximum protection for the flies and hooks. Dry flies are best kept in boxes with separate compartments that can be opened and sealed simply, or else in spacious boxes where the flies are fastened in foam-rubber bands. Wet flies are less delicate and can thus do well in relatively flat boxes. The same is true of nymphs, streamers and salmon flies, where it is most important that hooks and barbs do not lose their sharpness. We should therefore be careful with metal clamps and similar fasteners – they must never be allowed to damage the hook point!

Leaders and their materials, too, must be stored so that they are not damaged. If you tie your own leaders, a dispenser is preferable to loose spools, but it must have room for at least five different sizes and the lines should be able to feed without tangling.

Your fly vest or equivalent apparel should also contain a sharp pair of scissors or nail-clippers for purposes such as cutting leader stubs and dressing knots or flies. A sharp knife is necessary for slaughtering and cleaning. Substances that increase the buoyancy of dry flies and floating lines are further examples of essential accessories. A small rotatable

lamp which can easily be attached to a jacket or vest is indispensable for flyfishing at night if you want to have a fair chance of switching flies, tying leaders, and other work that needs some light. Scales and a measuring tape, flat-nosed pliers, a hook-sharpener, line grease, and a line basket can be added to complete the picture of a well-equipped flyfisherman.

Those who do not practise "catch and release" fishing, or land their fish by hand, often need a deep and preferably collapsible landing-net, or one with extension handle. And if you fish much from overgrown shores, a variant is a small collapsible landing-net that can be carried in a quiver. Short-shafted, wooden framed landing-nets are good when wading, while long-shafted landing-nets are more all-round and serve excellently for fishing from low or high shores as well as from boats. The inexperienced salmon fisherman who does not want to risk losing his "dream salmon" when grabbing it by the tail will need a tailer or gaff.

Basic accessories also include some sort of eye-protection. A gust of wind, or a wrong move of the rod, can easily send the fly on a dangerous course and, at worst, into your eye. Ordinary glasses or sunglasses are a cheap guard against permanent eye damage. A clear advantage of polaroid glasses is that they filter out the sunlight reflected from the water surface, and thus increase your chances of seeing what swims under it.

A fishing hat is not only symbolic of fishing success. It also helps to protect the face and eyes from flies that change course during the cast. Besides a broad brim or a screen, the hat should have a deep shape and cover as much as possible of your face, ears and neck.

Sooner or later, one finds that many fine fishing spots cannot be reached without a pair of thigh or body waders. Which of these you choose depends mainly on the water depth. Body waders can take you into relatively deep areas, but they are clumsy to wear in shallow water or on land, and uncomfortable condensation easily forms inside them. Thigh waders are lighter to walk and move in, but limit the depth of water you can enter.

Body waders made of neoprene have many advantages over the "old" rubber type. They are convenient to wade in, provide fine insulation against cold water, and can easily be repaired by the waterside. A drawback is still their expensiveness.

Whether you use thigh or body waders, and whatever the material, certain demands should be placed on their soles. These must primarily be non-slip. The bottoms should be

In addition to the basic equipment, a lot of useful accessories can make the fishing both easier and more fun.

covered with felt or matting, to prevent your slipping on stones and perhaps being taken by the current. Another advantage of silent materials like felt is that they do not scare shy fish as readily when you wade.

As an aid, some kind of wading staff should be used. You can easily make one from any stable length of wood. The important thing is that it does not bend even under heavy force. For this reason, be careful when buying a staff that can be disassembled, as it must be able to support a hard-leaning body. A good wading staff should also have an eye or other device where you can attach, for example, a rubber cord to keep the staff from drifting away with the current if you happen to let go of it. Ideally it ought to have a sound-muffling "shoe", for instance of rubber, as the fish are then not frightened so easily.

Another helpmate for fishing at some distance from shore is a float-ring (belly-boat). This is used almost exclusively in still or very slow waters. You then have every advantage of a boat, and it is a lot easier to transport and launch. But obviously greater care is needed with sharp objects in a belly-boat. A puncture while far out in a lake can be disastrous. One should therefore always make sure that the belly-boat has a two-chamber system.

Such fishing may seem a bit odd to anyone who has never seen a belly-boat fisherman in action. But for those who regularly put on their body waders and flippers, jump down into the inflated ring, and "paddle" out to free water with a fly rod resting on its rubber cover, this is as natural and rewarding a method as any.

Casting with a single-handed rod

As mentioned earlier, the casting weight is determined by the fly line. In other words, the fly is transported out to the fish by means of the line. This undoubtedly looks much harder than it is in practice when the art has been learned. For a beginner, getting the fly and line out while avoiding nearby trees and bushes is almost impossible. Yet only a few hours of intensive training are usually required in order to grasp the basics so well that at least ten metres of line can be cast with no real trouble.

To achieve long casts and complete precise presentations, you often have to spend a long time on different fishing waters. But the fact is that fishing can be effective even with relatively short casts. Long casts are not at all necessary for catching fish, especially in small waterways. It is, however, quite essential to learn correct presentation of the fly, whether you are casting long or short.

Practice and more practice: this is the recipe for learning how to cast harmoniously. A skilful instructor is certainly worth having, but not a prerequisite – the best teacher of casting is the process of fishing itself.

Basic casting technique

When learning to cast flies, you should start in a place with room for the back cast. Many people begin to practise on a grass lawn, but the best location is a lakeside, since laying the line on the water is an essential part of many casts. For the line's friction against the water – which cannot be obtained on a lawn – helps to build up the action in the rod. Certain casts, such as the roll and switch cast, are just impossible to perform except on water.

It is simplest to begin with a single-handed rod of 8-9 ft (2.4-2.7 m). To protect the tip of the fly line, a piece of leader should always be tied farthest out. Moreover, tie on a fly with its barb nipped off. The fly helps to stretch the leader tip, giving better control over the final phase of the cast.

A good cast is based on harmony between the line, rod, and casting arm. One common beginner's mistake is to force the cast, particularly the forward cast. Many are also afraid that the line will hit the ground, and do not wait until the

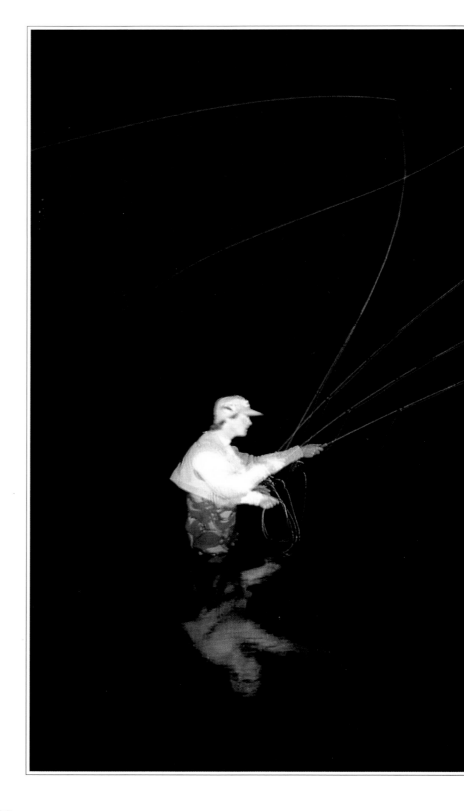

back cast has really stretched out. As a result, the cast collapses and the line falls in a heap. To avoid this and acquire the right rhythm, you should turn your head during the back cast, watching how the line moves and when it has stretched out completely. Only then does the time come to start the forward cast. Calm, smooth movements are the essence of becoming a good caster.

Here we shall briefly describe the traditional casts and their variants. But the continual progress of developments in equipment makes it likely that opportunities will arise in the future for learning new types of cast – tested and adapted to suit modern rods, reels, lines and leaders.

The overhead cast

This is to be recommended as the basic cast. Before beginning the cast itself, pull 6-8 m (20-26 ft) of line from the reel and lay it out on the water. Hold the rod handle with your casting hand just in front of the reel and your thumb pointing toward the rod top. Take the line in your other hand, held at waist height. Stand relaxed with the rod top pointing slightly downward.

Lift the rod upward with a strong but smooth movement. Once it is vertical, stop the back cast. Wait till the line is lifted and stretched out backward. When you feel the out-stretched line's weight in the rod top, it is time to start the forward cast by moving the rod forward to a horizontal position – smoothly but sharply. The line now rolls forward over the rod tip and stretches out before you. Make sure that the line hand always follows the rod's movements.

The next step is to try holding the line in the air, without its collapsing on either the backward or forward cast. These air-casts are made by stopping the rod, during the forward cast, in a position pointing obliquely upward. When the line has rolled forward over the rod tip and is nearly stretched out, the rod is moved backward in a new back cast. The line now flies back and stretches out, whereupon you start a new forward cast. Once this can be done without letting the line touching the ground, you have mastered the air-cast as well.

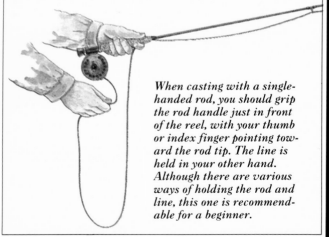

When casting with a single-handed rod, you should grip the rod handle just in front of the reel, with your thumb or index finger pointing toward the rod tip. The line is held in your other hand. Although there are various ways of holding the rod and line, this one is recommendable for a beginner.

The overhead cast is the first cast that a beginner should learn.

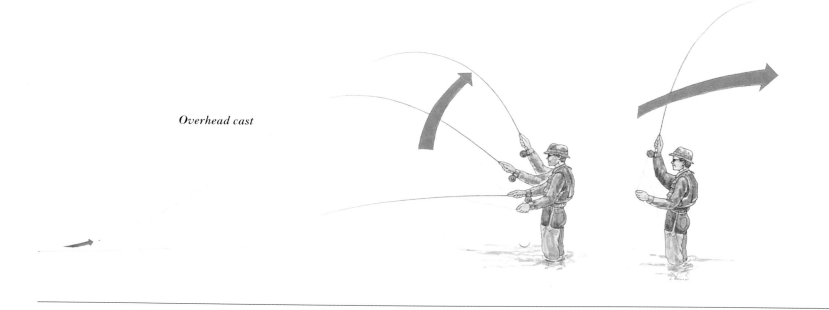

Overhead cast

The double haul cast

Achieving perfect coordination requires some training and many failed attempts. But when you can keep 8-10 m (26-33 ft) in the air with no trouble, practical fishing can begin. At first, you should choose a shore area with space behind you, so that the back cast meets no obstacles. Despite this precaution, you can expect the fly to get caught occasionally on branches and bushes.

Having learned to cast 8-10 metres at the water, you can increase the amount of line in the air by a few metres each time. Hold the loose line in one hand and, when the accelerating backward-and-forward cast has added more energy, release the reserve line in a forward cast. Now the loose line shoots out through the guides to join the airborne line. This step, too, calls for exact coordination which is acquired only through much expert training. Eventually, you can thus lengthen the cast according to your ability, metre by metre.

Shooting out the line in this way is also useful when presenting the fly – not least in fishing with shoot-lines and certain other types of belly-lines, as well as in dry-fly fishing.

A variant of the overhead cast is the side cast. This horizontal, half-high movement follows the rule that a cast should be stretched out where there is enough space. It comes in handy when, for example, fishing on overgrown waterways with limited free space.

Although on most waters we can manage with casting lengths of 10-15 m (33-50 ft), longer casts can be necessary in order to increase the chances of a catch, for instance when fishing in lakes. Even while wading, with the line almost nudging the water surface as you cast backward and forward, the technique of a double haul is very useful, since the cast easily collapses if the line touches the water.

A double haul means that you draw the fly line downward with your free line hand during both the backward and forward casts, thus increasing the line's speed and force. Begin with a strong downard haul at the very beginning of the back cast, then complete it as usual. Just when the forward cast is to begin, make a new haul with the line hand, then release the line when the casting weight is greatest. The loose line will shoot out in the last phase of the cast.

This variant can lengthen the cast by 3-5 m (10-16 ft), but it demands exact coordination between the rod hand and line hand. Since the cast must be calm and harmonious, you should be a relatively good caster before starting to practise it.

Once the double haul is mastered, you can easily feed out a rather long line with some air-casts and finally shoot out the line by 3-5 metres. The double haul's increased line speed can be essential when you are fishing in a powerful headwind and when you need to cast far.

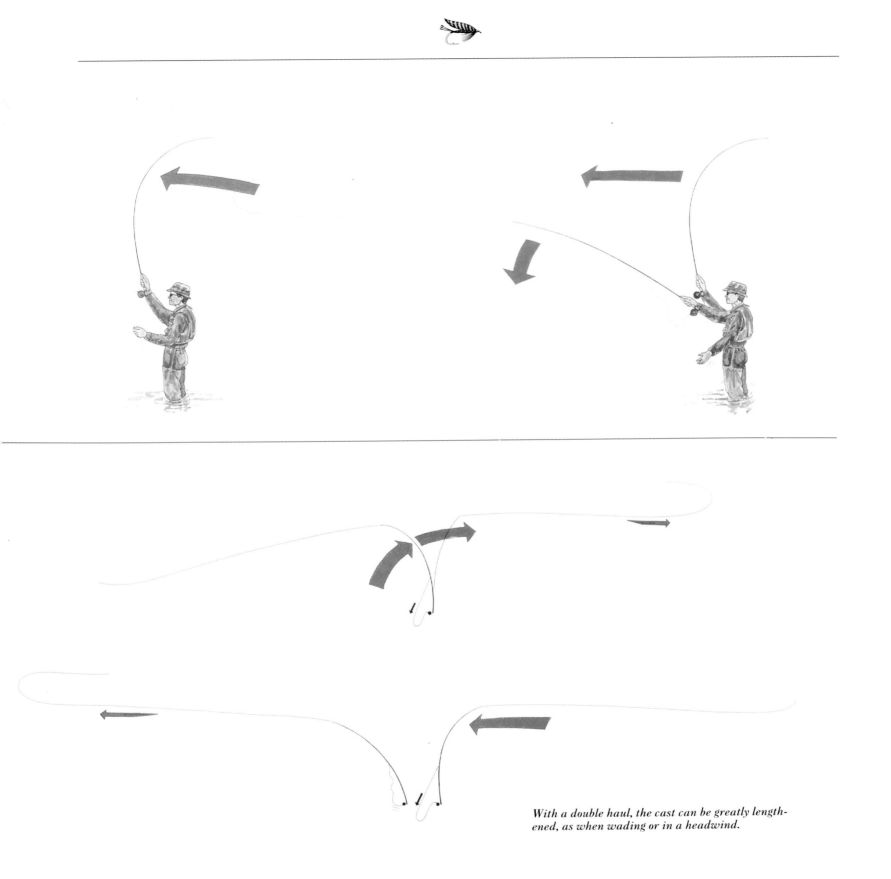

With a double haul, the cast can be greatly lengthened, as when wading or in a headwind.

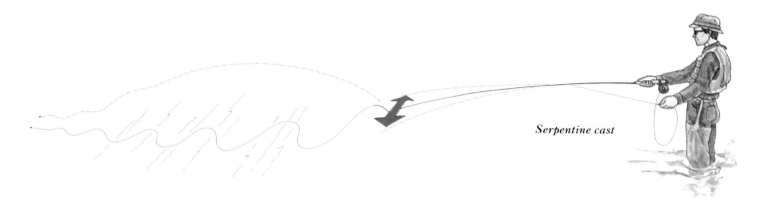

Serpentine cast

The serpentine cast

This cast is employed primarily in dry-fly fishing when the fly has to drift evenly without drag, even if the current is erratic. Your line hand must hold a certain amount of loose line that can be shot out in the forward cast. At the same time as the fly line shoots out, the rod top is moved rapidly forward and backward, parallel to the water surface. Thus the line lands in big curves on the water. The dry fly will gain a little extra time in order to float freely, before the fly line stretches out in the water and the fly begins to straggle. To lengthen the drift, you can also flick the rod top while releasing a little loose line, which glides out through the rod rings and adds to the line already lying on the water. This way of lengthening a cast can, of course, be used in combination with all casting variants, so that the fly will follow the current freely.

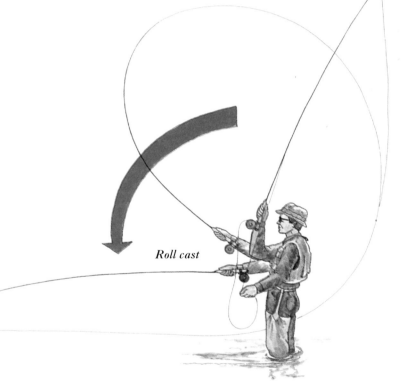

Roll cast

The roll cast

A roll (or switch) cast is used in fishing areas where a back cast is quite impossible to carry out. You can then certainly not cast as far, but with some training a fair length can be laid out.

About 5-6 m (16-20 ft) of line should lie stretched in front of the rod tip. Then the rod is lifted until vertical. Once the line hangs in a curve next to the fisherman, it is cast forward by means of an accelerating whip action – upward, forward and then downward. The line rolls out on the water and the fly lands. By pulling out more loose line and repeating the roll cast a few times, the casting length can be increased to more than 10 m (33 ft).

One can also combine the roll cast with other casts, such as the side cast, for effective results in many situations.

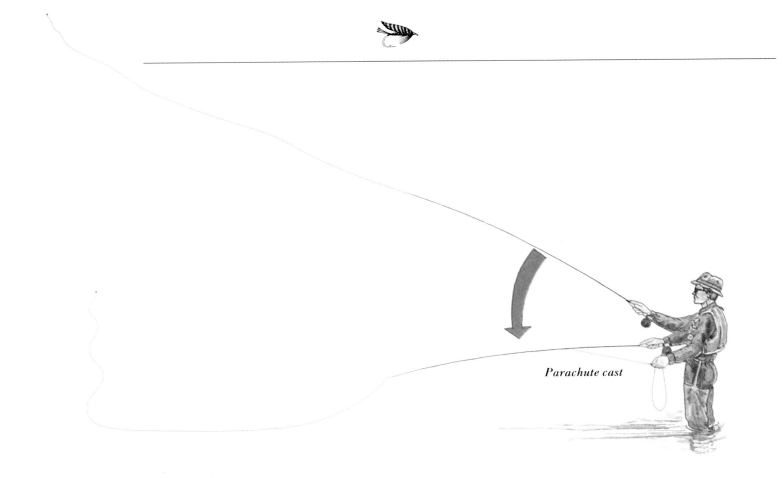

The parachute cast

The difference between a serpentine cast and a parachute cast is that, in the latter, you stop the rod top during the forward cast when it is pointing obliquely upward. The line then shoots away in that direction and stretches out at the same height as the rod top. Then you lower the rod, and the fly jerks back a little before landing with the leader in curves. If the cast is done correctly, the fly, leader, and line end will land after the fly line's rear portion. And the fly can drift somewhat farther downstream without dragging.

Parachute cast

Mending

Mending

The purpose of mending is to prevent flies from dragging or being hindered in their natural drift when the current takes the fly line and drags it along in big curves. You simply float the fly line some distance upstream by mending it, without affecting the leader tip or the fly. Mending is a cast-like movement parallel to the water surface in the current direction. If it is properly performed, the fly line will be laid in a gentle upstream curve. Thus you can considerably lengthen the natural drift – in principle, until the cast is completely fished out and the fly line ends straight downstream parallel to the shore. When fishing for salmon, it is sometimes necessary to mend downstream in order to increase the fly's speed.

Casting with a double-handed rod

Fishing is generally the same with a double-handed rod as with a single-handed rod, but it can be very arduous and energy-demanding because a double-handed rod is longer and heavier. Consequently, a couple of variant casts have been developed specially for this kind of fishing. Perhaps the best known is the Spey cast, which works well in nearly all situations if done right. This cast requires relatively little strength, is effective even in a wind, and does not need any space for a back cast. Moreover, it produces no knots on the leader – which are common in, for example, the traditional overhead cast.

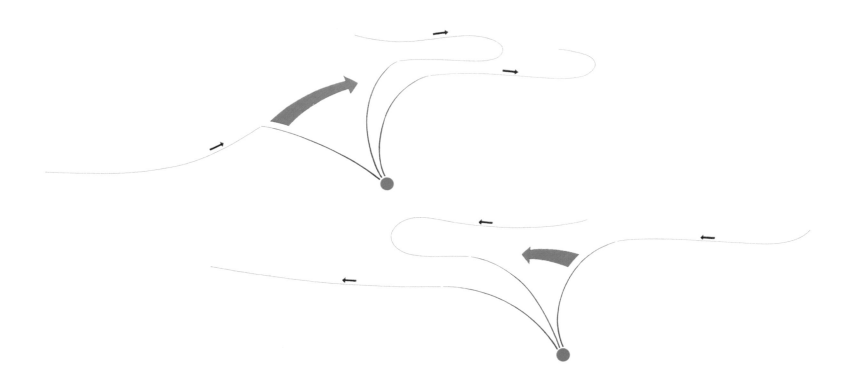

The overhead cast

Casting with a double-handed rod differs in several respects from its single-handed counterpart. But the overhead cast is essentially built up in the same way. Obviously it also has the same weaknesses: you need a lot of space for the back cast, the leader can easily become knotted, and you often have to do an excessive number of blind casts which can be tiresome with a heavy double-handed rod. The aim should be to do only one back cast and then lay out the fly.

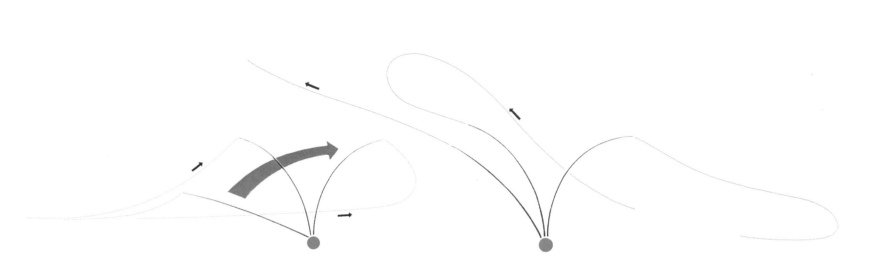

The underhand cast

The hard work of fishing with long double-handed rods is made much more comfortable by modern, light rods of carbon fibre and/or boron. However, it is still important to learn energy-saving methods of casting.

An underhand cast is not only elegant, but also offers the opportunity of fishing for a long interval without getting tired. In addition, this restful cast is quite effective. Using a

back cast, the line is brought under the rod in front of you. When the rod is pointing obliquely backward, the movement stops and the forward cast begins. At this moment the line should not be fully outstretched backward. It must be given the most energy when the rod tip is pointing obliquely forward. With a single air-cast, the line can be laid out nicely in this way.

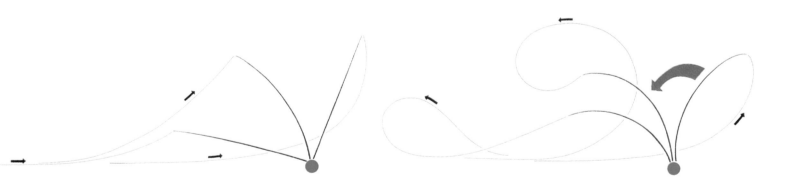

The switch cast

As its name implies, the switch (roll) cast means that the fly line is rolled out onto the water. This cast comes into use mainly on shores with limited space for back casting. It must also be mastered if you want to learn the effective Spey cast properly.

Your rod should have a good spine. During the back cast, it is brought calmly to a position pointing obliquely backward. Now the line must hang in a soft curve alongside you. In the forward cast, the rod is strongly accelerated forward and downward until it is parallel to the water surface. The line then rolls out across the water in a beautiful bow.

The Spey cast has several advantages. It permits a long cast even where the back cast is difficult because of dense shore vegetation; it is not affected much by strong wind; and it demands relatively little muscle power during the actual cast.

The Spey cast

Like the roll cast, this cast is used on shores where vegetation restricts the possibility of casting backward. It also resembles the roll cast in other essential respects. The important thing is that the fly should be placed in the right position before the forward cast, so that the hook does not catch on the line when the casting direction is changed by 45°. Hence, the fly is often allowed to float straight downstream with the current. A "double" Spey cast exists, too, but here we shall concentrate on the single Spey cast, as it also provides the basis for the double one.

Just as with the roll cast, you lift the line from the water by moving the rod to a position pointing obliquely backward. With an accelerating underhand cast, the line is brought backward and upstream on your outer side. But not so much that the fly line's tip soars into the air – it should nudge the water surface, thus adding force to the forward cast. The greatest transfer of energy should occur when the rod is pointing obliquely forward. However, the rod's own action does most of the work. This cast, as well, must be performed gently and harmoniously in a single sweep. It is easiest to carry out with a floating DT line.

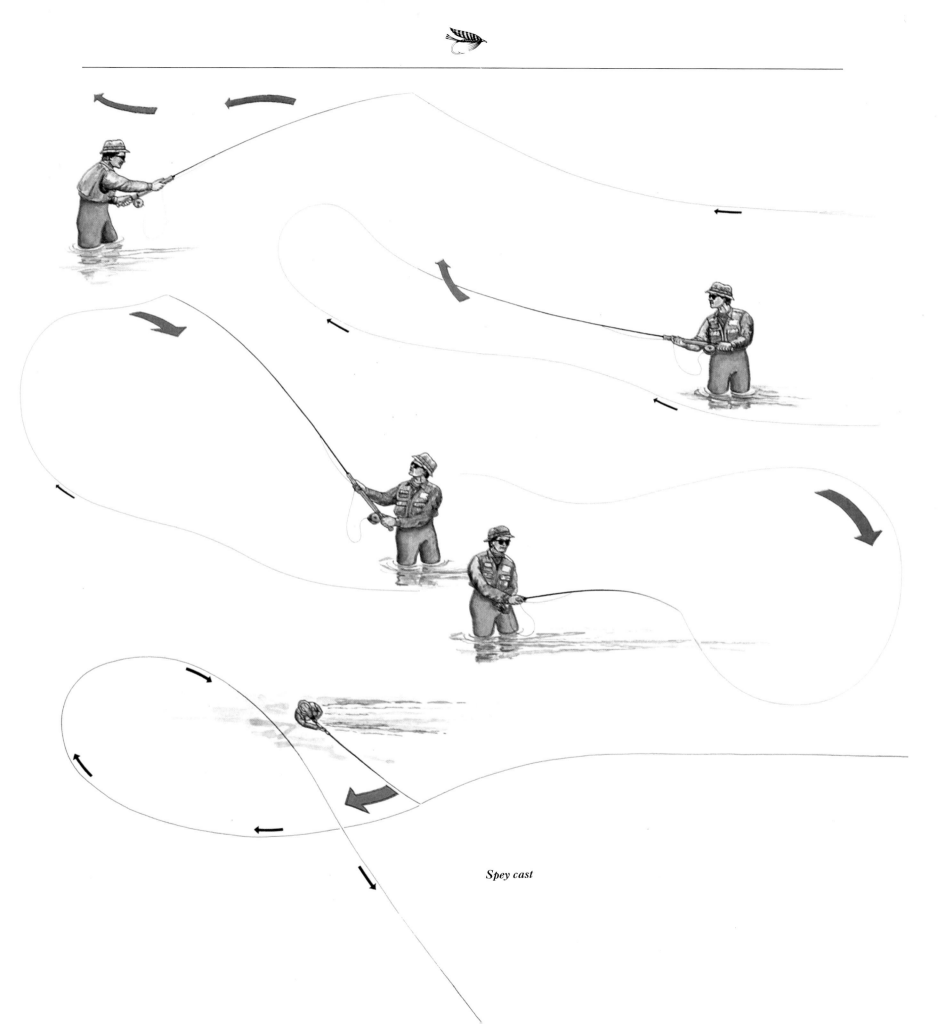

Spey cast

Flyfishing in still waters

Lake flyfishing
is an established and
fast-growing branch of the sport,
even though thousands of streams
are full of salmonoid fish. But most of these
are in remote places where a fisherman
may travel only during the summer
holidays. The early and late fishing
seasons are devoted to the ever increasing
put-and-take areas located only an
hour or two from home.

Rapidly expanding numbers of flyfishermen are well on the way to charting all the earth's flowing waters. While crowding increases on the "classic" streams – of which the sport's pioneers spoke so enthusiastically in books that remain highly readable – the destinations of flyfishermen are becoming distant and exotic.

Unknown territory in the flyfishing world is thus getting scarce and, if Glasnost applies to us too, we may soon learn whether it is true that giant trout exist in the Soviet rivers running north to the Arctic, where fish of 30-40 kg (66-88 lb) are rumoured.

But for those who stay around home, fish have thinned out in the currents of many countries, despite improved management of their habitats. Flyfishing continues to grow anyway, and its practitioners demand the opportunity to fish at a reasonable cost, which also means at a reasonable distance from their origins.

Until now, they have often been satisfied, although most flyfishermen live in urban industrial regions. However, things would be far more difficult if we insisted on pursuing the sport in its "classic" form, along streams with natural stocks of salmonoid fish. The prerequisite has been, and is, that we take advantage of a vast reservoir of fish – in our lakes.

Lakes offer virtually unlimited possibilities of flyfishing, apart from the insistence of a majority of us that our fish should have adipose fins. In Scandinavia alone, for example, there are thousands of lakes with more or less intact stocks of salmonoids, and further thousands whose water quality makes stocking – especially of rainbow trout – a meaningful, indeed profitable, enterprise.

This is a revival of lake flyfishing in the sense that our pioneers, at least in Great Britain, sometimes fished for both sea trout and ordinary brown trout. At any rate, it is the best explanation for the fast growth of flyfishing. In Great Britain, where many reservoirs have been built to collect fresh water for urban needs, a kind of revolution is in the air: reservoirs are stocked with fish and provide recreation for tens of thousands of new and old flyfishermen.

Put-and-take lakes have enabled flyfishing to go on developing in several parts of Europe. Most of the numerous young people who try flyfishing as a hobby gain their first experience on these still waters. And they are right to do so, since one ought to get through the commonest beginner's mistakes before making an attempt on wild waterways, where the fishing is usually much harder.

You cannot learn to flyfish by reading a book about it. But

Two common and popular species for flyfishing in still waters are the brown trout (above) and the rainbow trout (left).

Reading the waters

People who grow up in districts with abundant waterways soon learn to "read" them as fish do. The fish are where the food is, and the most, as well as largest, fish can be found where the underwater menu is marvellous. Here they stand in the current, or scour a small area, since they need not waste energy on hunting. The current brings them all they can eat, like an endless conveyor belt in a free restaurant.

As a result, some places in a river or stream are better than others – especially where several waterways run together, or where backwaters form that concentrate the food. Adult grayling and whitefish, for instance, assemble there, at times in great schools; and it is there that the flyfisherman encounters the biggest fish. Such trout are usually solitary, because trout defend their territory with zeal and they seldom allow smaller competitors to eat at the same table.

These optimum feeding spots amount to only a fraction of the water surface's total area. Certainly much of a productive waterway can provide food during several months of the year, but not enough of it to support big fish, let alone entire schools of adult fish. However, this is sufficient for small fish until they reach a size adequate to compete for the better feeding places.

Thus, a flyfisherman must be able to "read" a waterway for the movements and colour changes that show where its special fish-food resources lie. At times when plenty of insects are hatching, the fish themselves reveal these places by rising greedily. If they do not rise, it can be worth the trouble to watch such places discreetly, as any fish there will give themselves away sooner or later.

Another means of detection is to test a place with a "tempter", one of the favourite dry flies or nymphs that usually yield results even when fish are not rising. Most flyfishermen have, or eventually acquire, a little hoard of such helpmates, which can provoke a fish to strike even if it is temporarily selective – that is, bent on eating a special kind of insect in a particular stage of life.

An experienced flyfisherman has learned his "reading" and soon finds where the fish are feeding, whether or not he is on familiar waters. This is not difficult, at least on small streams. Although it may happen that only small fish take the fly, this does not mean that the water has been read wrongly. Sometimes food is scarce even in the right place – and then the big fish, especially when they are fully grown trout, go back to their hideouts in deep holes under

a good book can provide facts and suggest experiments that pay off. Unfortunately books about lake flyfishing are rare, at least in comparison to those about fish in flowing waters. Once you do manage to learn the correct tactics and strategy for flyfishing, though, you can often catch a lot of fish – and big fish at that.

the main current or the root systems of shore trees.

The large fish in streams are almost perfect economic machines. Hunting has to pay off, in other words to yield more food energy than the hunting consumes. When not enough food exists at their favourite feeding places, the fish do not eat at all, preferring to wait. But when the menu improves, they show up instantly to chase away smaller fish and feast on the goodies brought by the current.

This behaviour is notably typical of large trout, which – during intense insect hatchings – can be seen "swinging" at the surface as they eat: first a part of the head appears, then the back, and finally the upper tail fin, a sequence repeated three or four times in a row. Having risen to the surface when insects are dense, they take an insect at every "swing". After eating as many as five insects, they glide back to the bottom and soon rise again. For a big trout, it is not economical to rise for a single insect: several must be eaten each time to restore the energy that is spent.

Moreover, this behaviour gives the flyfisherman his chance of catching a "dream fish". Such a trout rises so regularly that its return to the surface can often be predicted exactly. A "swinging" trout is also virtually blind, as the movement restricts its field of vision, allowing the fisherman to wade within easy casting distance.

Yet the "reading" of water, and the fishing tactics used at clearly identifiable feeding places, are peculiar to waterways where we can find fish at the same places year after year – and can even catch the same individual fish more than once, at least in the case of trout. For trout are able to spend their whole lives in one limited section of a stream, as long as it contains plenty of food.

In the still waters of lakes, meres and ponds, the same fish species have other habits. Here they seldom meet currents that transport food to particular feeding places. Certain areas do frequently produce abundant fish food, but the fish have to locate those areas at the moments when the supply is greatest. They succeed in doing so, yet how they do it is difficult for us to explain. The fact is that still waters are much harder to "read" than flowing waters.

Standing for the first time on the shore of a wide lake can be frustrating, even discouraging, to a flyfisherman. Where, beneath its vast surface, can the fish be – or are they everywhere? Just as in rivers, the fish do exist at particular places, and these may vary. But long experience on a given body of still water is not necessarily essential to successful fishing, because we have some reliable rules to follow.

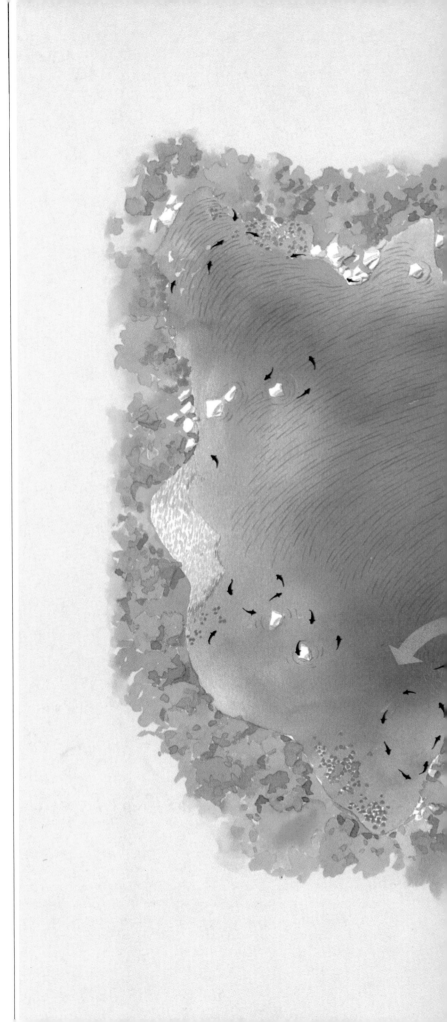

Even for a seasoned flyfisherman, it is sometimes very hard to
tell where the fish are. But just as
in running waters, there are special
places where, for various reasons, fish
can be found: for example, at stony banks
and underwater beds, vegetated shores,
lee edges, deep edges, coves, islets, channels,
promontories, inlets and outlets.

Intercepting the fish

To begin with, you must outwait the fish. It is bound to rise eventually, if the weather is suitable. Rainbow trout which are set out in "catchable" sizes, as is normal, tend to have sharply defined periods of striking, and a few usually break the water surface even if not much food is there. Valuable observations can then be made: risings that are fairly frequent follow a pattern, as though it were a "food patrol".

The rainbow trout in still waters usually appear in small shoals of up to five or so, regularly scouring a particular area of the lake. They take any food on the surface, and thereby reveal their route. Moreover, they show the flyfisherman which tactics are best – where they come closest to the shore and can be reached by a fly cast, or where they can be intercepted by means of a boat or float-ring.

Large lakes contain a lot of these patrol routes, followed by many groups of rainbow trout – so many that it could take years to chart them. In such lakes, the trout seemingly even change routes according to the wind, something that the flyfisherman is wise to note in his diary. But in waters which are less calm and not as windblown, the patrol routes are often identical, day after day and night after night. It may be worth adding that the real heavyweights commonly begin their patrols as the dusk fades, and frequently do so very close to land.

The present author has watched this behaviour in several small rainbow-trout lakes and tried to chart it during long periods of intensive, successful fishing by dusk and night. Groups of up to four big fish could be seen or heard – it was often too dark to observe their rising – long after the smaller rainbow trout had stopped rising. The routes of these heavyweights also passed quite near land; they moved about as fast as a jogger, and one could watch them rise as one ran along the shore.

Conceivably this behaviour of large rainbow trout at dusk and late evening was associated with the threat posed by fishing. In all of the lakes where observations and experiments were made, fishing is very popular. Probably the more sizeable and shy rainbow trout did not dare to begin hunting near land until the lake became peaceful, other fish having given up for the night. It is also likely that food was most plentiful near land during the dusk and early evening; the observations were made in August and early September, when caddis flies were abundantly hatching and fluttering around the bushes on shore.

(Left) Put-and-take fishing in lakes, ponds and meres has become a widespread alternative to the more difficult fishing in streams that are often far away.

Insects that rush back and forth on the water surface, such as caddis flies, often seem to be very attractive for fish, and are thus well worth imitating.

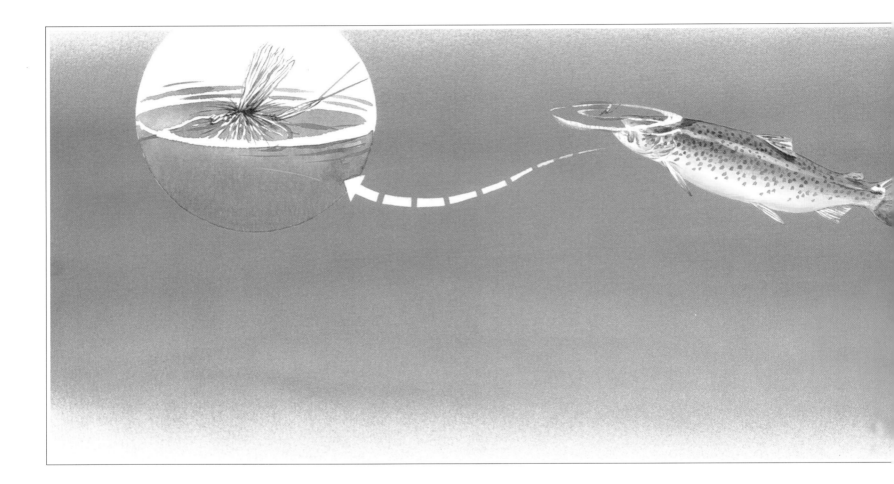

Waiting out the fish can be a profitable tactic. Brown and rainbow trout, for instance, frequently follow a pattern in their rising. By placing the dry fly on the fish's patrol route, you have a good chance of getting the fish to take.

If you are a good caster, you can also try to lay out the fly at the end of a series of rises. After the second rise, showing which direction and speed the fish are moving with, the fly is laid out quickly where the fish are expected to appear next – at the third, and perhaps last, rise.

In any case, patrolling behaviour is typical of all rainbow trout, and the flyfisherman's tactics are clear: wait them out, keeping an attractive dry fly in their path. Sooner or later they return, whether it takes three minutes or more than ten minutes. A dry fly is your best weapon by far, provided that it can wait for the fish – whereas a nymph or streamer must be kept moving, and therefore risks being in the wrong place at the right time!

All of the twenty-odd rainbow trout caught during these experiments took dry flies. Half of them were caught during evenings when not a single rising was seen or heard: there were no caddis flies on the water, yet the fish were patrolling anyhow. If they saw something edible on the surface, they took the imitation – a dry "Nalle Puh" ("Winnie the Pooh") tied on a No. 8 dry-fly hook, and quite a mouth-

The predominant kind of sportfishing is then often trolling.

However, intensive search over wide areas is necessary to find the quarry – at any rate, the trout and salmon. This sort of hunt is scarcely possible with a fly rod. What can be done is to try an established trick, namely hanging a big salmon fly in the swirls that form behind an outboard motor running in low gear. The propeller wake attracts fish, as trollers know – and the trout and salmon are as glad to take a salmon fly as a long, thin wobbler.

While trolling with a fly can be rewarding, it is not the sort of fishing that a flyfisherman dreams about during the dull winter months.

In smaller lakes, a profitable approach is often to wait out the brown trout. But these behave differently from rainbow trout. Commonly they are loners, as also in flowing water. They oversee and defend a territory which is usually much more limited than the patrol routes of rainbow trout, although considerably wider than the feeding grounds of brook trout. Turn after turn, they can mark an area of only 15-20 m (50-65 ft) in diametre, or patrol a shoreline for just 50 m (165 ft). This tends to occur in the evening as dark falls.

Consequently, flyfishermen find brown trout less accessible than rainbow trout, where both exist together. There are many such small-lake territories where no brown trout have ever been caught, since the trout always feed beyond range of the fly. On the other hand, we often succeed with the trout that patrol back and forth along the shore. They usually begin to appear late in the evening, yet are then relatively easy to catch on flies, if the fisherman is discreet: what he needs is not a long cast, but a good hideout behind a bush or boulder.

The shore patrols of brown trout at dusk are especially characteristic in small forest meres, of the kind that Scandinavia has in tens of thousands. Their quagmire shore waters are often far more extensive than the visible surface indicates. Trout hide there by day and sneak up for supper at dusk.

These trout, too, must be waited out. Whoever comes stomping into the quagmires at dusk is sure to have a fishless evening. The fisherman should be there much earlier in order to avoid scaring the trout, and should stay quiet. Making coffee and smoking a pipe are allowed, as long as one keeps one's feet under control. In sum, waiting out the fish is a highly reliable method, especially at times when abundant insects are being produced and attract fish to the surface.

ful, originally used in dry-fly fishing for big sea trout in Norway's river Aurland.

Waiting out the fish is thus a very handy rule of thumb, especially for rainbow trout. If they do not show by day, they often do so towards evening, notably just after sunrise if the weather is calm and the air rather warm.

Limited territory

In huge lakes, it can be extremely hard to locate the trout, and even pointless to try waiting them out. They simply do not show themselves, frequently because they eat almost nothing but small fish in large schools, such as vendace.

Wind direction
and lee edges

Even quite small lakes have a wind side and a lee side –
and therefore, when the wind blows, a lee edge. This is the
boundary between the smooth water and the water with
waves stirred up by wind. In larger lakes, particularly those
with islands and many coves, such lee edges are numerous.
They function in the same way as current edges in flowing
water. The fish food which is transported by the faster
water in currents, and by the wind-driven water in lakes,
eventually ends up in the lee edges, and the fish know it.

The phenomenon is clearest towards the close of the
fishing season, when insects begin to be scarce. Then the
remaining insects may form small drifts, often made of midges and other "small fry". They attract even big fish to
patrol along the lee edges.

The latter behaviour is especially typical of rainbow trout
– and in some mountain regions, of landlocked Arctic char,
which are also great consumers of small insects. But one can
frequently see rainbow trout patrolling back and forth along
lee edges, though they evidently catch very little. The
explanation might be that they, like brown trout, are eager
to have a "roof" over their heads if any can be found, in this
case the rippled water from where they can look out at the
smooth surface and notice even morsels of food on it.

Thus, the lee edges are well worth trying, particularly if
the fish refuse to show themselves and suggest some other
fishing tactic.

*On really large lakes, a boat is often essential in order
to get out to the fish. Moreover, on some big lakes in
Great Britain, "dapping" is a common method. It
makes use of "blow lines", which are very thin and
light, enabling the fly to be carried across the water
by the wind.*

Charts and bottom topography

Bottom charts can tell us more about the fishing water than what we see with our naked eyes. Every lake has its own landscape beneath the surface, and even a simple chart can give the flyfisherman good indications of fishing spots. In some countries, when you buy a fishing licence, you usually also get a chart of the lake and its depth curves, sometimes actually printed on the fishing licence.

Such a chart is invaluable for flyfishing. The invisible boundaries between shallow and deep waters are often areas where rainbow and brown trout, char and grayling, and other salmonoids gather to seek food. The same is true of channels that unite larger lakes. When the wind blows along a channel, it functions like a funnel, collecting and concentrating the fish food, which makes it worth a try.

There are, of course, times when none of these thumbrules will work. For example, in the spring it is frequently useless to wait for a rise. No fish show up, the water is too cold, and the scanty food stays in the bottom's slime and gravel – where the fish stay as well. Nor may the wind give any good indications.

But a flyfisherman has to do something even without help. One clever option is to find a headland between two coves, and try a sink-tip or a slow-sinking line, with a big shaggy nymph or a little Muddler Minnow on the leader. You may guess that there are fish in the coves, while knowing that they are hard to catch – yet you also know something else. Fish are like people in at least one sense: they often get the idea that "the grass is greener on the other side". So they decide that the other cove contains more food; and to get there, they must pass the headland, where your nymph is dangling...

Still-water fly fishing equipment

Something like ninety percent of all the fish caught on flies in streams are taken at a distance of 8-12 m (25-40 ft). Farther away than that, it is much harder to see what the fish is doing with the fly, and more difficult to hook the fish. At over 20 m (65 ft), we seldom succeed.

When fishing in still water, it is much more important to be able to cast far, especially with nymphs and streamers. These depend on the fly being kept in motion all the time, which means that the line is straight.

There is also something that makes longer casts profitable when fishing in still waters: the mere fact that the water is still, and occasionally quite smooth. It is then difficult to get near the fish without frightening them. Currents make it easier for the flyfisherman to hide – he can sneak or wade very close, even to large shy fish, by exploiting the disturbed water's camouflage and the "dead angle" of the fish's field of vision.

Water troubled by waves and gusts of wind can also be used to advantage when fishing in still water, but the "dead angle" seldom can be. For the fish are moving and it is rarely possible to sneak up on them from behind.

Still-water fishing therefore imposes certain demands on the flyfisherman's casting ability, and consequently on the equipment. A long rod of 9.5-10 ft (around 3 m) is adequate, able to cast a light line such as a WF 5 when the wind permits, as it often does when fishing in still water. With a long rod and a light WF line, you can cast farther than 20 m (66 ft) if necessary, yet fish discreetly – which is much more important on calm lake water than in the rough waters of streams.

Another reason for choosing a long rod is that many lakes, not least in the Scandinavian mountains, are relatively shallow and call for wading. But wading at any depth makes it hard to cast with a short rod – the fly tends to hit the water during the back cast, so that the forward cast scarcely resembles what you intended.

Body waders should reach up to the armpits. Thigh waders, which reach only to the crotch, are used less often and only in calm stream waters. Otherwise you might miss many fine fishing opportunities by being unable to wade far enough out to reach underwater precipices which fish usu-

ally prefer, notably the tricky and very easily frightened Arctic char.

In regard to other details of equipment, besides flies for still-water fishing, you should be warned against the advice in many fishing books about the length of the backing line. More than 50 m (165 ft) may be needed at times, and to lose your first four-pound trout because the backing line is too short would be infuriating, to say the least. A proper length is 100 m (330 ft), though there are times when even that can be too short.

When fishing in lakes, a long rod and light line are preferable. With this combination, you can cast long and also present the fly discreetly, as is often necessary in order to induce the fish to take. A landing net, of course, makes it easier to land the fish calmly and securely when the fight is ending.

Fishing at the right depth

Sinking lines are used more often in still waters than in currents, except for salmon and sea-trout fishing in deep, cold rivers. There are many situations, and many lakes, where the fly must be fished deep in order to make any contact with the fish. This is especially true in the early part of the season, when the water is cold and the fish seek food on the bottom. But frequently also during the season's warm periods, the fish become hard to reach, fleeing from the warm surface water to the cool bottom-layer. Then, too, a sinking line can come in handy.

However, even if the fly must descend to, say, 10 m (33 ft), it is wise to avoid fast-sinking lines. They maximize the risk of a very troublesome bottom-snag. A better method is to join a floating level-line of class 3 or 4 with a heavy "belly" of only 7-8 m (23-26 ft) made from a sinking line in the middle class range.

Such a line arrangement means that the sinking-line belly's tip will go deepest. The floating shooting line lifts the belly's other end, so that the belly cannot get snagged except, perhaps, at the tip. But nine times out of ten, only the fly gets caught and, if it does not pull loose, you can quickly tie a new one on the leader tip – which, if made properly, has broken nearest to the fly.

For deep fishing, a sinking belly in the middle class range is a good choice. It descends fast enough – that is, it stays at the same depth if you take home the line at the most suitable rate for fishing with nymphs or with small streamers. A fast-sinking belly (or the type called super-fast sinking) has to be pulled home too quickly to avoid a bottom snag, and then the fly will attract fewer fish.

But for moderate depths, say 2-3 m (6-10 ft), a sink-tip line is recommended. It has a sinking tip 3-5 m (10-16 ft) long, while the rest floats. Such a line is often a bit tricky to cast with – the heavier tip "slings" in the cast – and an alternative is a floating line with sinking leader. Nowadays there are braided leaders, from floating to very fast-sinking, and

the sinking ones yield the same results as the sink-tip line's tip. They are rather expensive, but many flyfishermen prefer them anyway. One does not, after all, need to change the reel or line, but simply changes the leader to fish deep.

Even a floating line with a sinking leader can get caught during the cast. This effect seems very hard to avoid, if you want a line arrangement that protects against too many difficult bottom snags. An old trick is to put a few cloven lead-shot balls on the leader to the floating line. This works well, though the shot balls sometimes fly off in their own direction during the cast!

According to an ancient sportfishing rule, the fish is usually caught either at the surface or on the bottom. The same largely applies to still-water flyfishing, where experience tells us that 95% of the fish are caught with flies on, in, or just under the water surface – and the rest are caught by fishing as close as possible to the bottom.

Certainly there are exceptions. The most important thing, of course, is to fish so that your quarry can see the fly. A fish feeding in the bottom gravel may well rise to a fly that passes 1-2 m (3-6 ft) over its head, if only it glimpses the goodie – and so may a fish swimming at a depth of 1 m (3 ft) if it discovers an attractive dry fly. But the general rule, at the surface or on the bottom, remains a good fishing tactic.

Several other tricks make it easier for the fish to find the fly, even if you do not hit the centre of the rise-ring exactly when the fish creates it. One trick, when the fly – either wet or dry – has landed, is to wait a couple of seconds and then resolutely pull in the line by 30-40 cm (12-16 in), before taking a new pause of two or three seconds. If the fish saw the fly when it fell on or into the water, and wants to take it, the strike will usually come instantly. Otherwise the fly may have fallen in the "dead angle" behind the fish. But the fish will sense the first distinct pull, and as a rule it will turn round and take the fly like lightning.

In a word, letting the fly make noise can be profitable. A good recipe is to supplement reliable wet-fly patterns with a little Muddler head, so that the fly stays hanging in the underside of the water surface. When you carefully retrieve the fly, every little tug will form a ripple around its head – and these "bow waves" seem to attract fish, or at least enable them to detect the fly more easily.

We thus return to the subject of still-water flies. The fly is the most important piece in a flyfisherman's equipment – the only item in the collection that the fish are allowed to see, if the fisherman is handling his gear in the right way.

The float ring has created new opportunities for still-water flyfishermen to cover their waters effectively. Aided by flippers, you can move silently and calmly without scaring the fish.

Flies for still water

Every rule does have an exception, and there are quite a few instances in the rule-book of flyfishing. Yet on the whole, two clear differences exist between still-water flies and the flies that have been proven most effective in flowing water.

On the one hand, still-water flies are all bigger by two or four hook numbers. On the other, dry flies are predominant in flowing water, but play a secondary role in still water, where wet flies hold sway and, indeed, "lures" and streamers earn a much larger share of the credit – as reckoned in number and size of fish caught.

This contrast is hardly surprising. Most dry flies imitate mayflies, whose family has far fewer species in lakes, meres and ponds than in flowing water. Caddis flies are equally plentiful in all of these, although their species, too, are definitely fewer in still waters.

However, still waters frequently offer abundant fish food of another kind: the damselfly nymphs, water boatmen and other beetles, leeches, snails and molluscs, a rich assortment of land insects such as ants, sloebugs, wasps and crane-flies, as well as billions of midges in various stages of life. Not to mention, of course, a lot more fish fry – the kind of food that is often essential if trout, in particular, are to grow really big.

Stoneflies are a family which tends to be strongly represented in waterways that are clean enough, and which sometimes enables us to fish with dry flies as soon as the ice melts. In Southeast European waters like the Austrian and Yugoslav chalk streams, stoneflies may dominate the insect life during much of the season, but they do not occur at all in still waters.

These differences – and there are many more – lead rather inevitably to a choice of fly patterns only some of which are usable in both still and flowing waters, and are then also tied on hooks bigger by two to four numbers if used in still waters.

Occasionally I have tried with American models to compose a "deadly dozen" flies for fishing in streams. Eight or nine of them have been dry flies in sizes from No. 10 down to 18 or 20, while a dozen for still-water fishing have included only 3-4 dry flies. The rest have been wet flies, such as some ample servings of Muddler Minnow, Wooly Bugger,

and Bitch Creek Nymph. Nor have still-water dry flies been of negligible size. The successful Swedish dry fly Streaking Caddis, which imitates a caddis fly and is tied by muddler techniques, has also been included in the dozen for stream fishing, in size No. 8 – besides a wasp No. 10 and a flying ant No. 12.

An exception here is to have a dry midge of size No. 18 or 20 for the golden chances that arise towards the end of autumn, when food is getting scarce in small lakes and the rainbow trout are feverishly hunting what is left – especially midges.

Only two flies have been common to both of these "dozens", apart from the above-mentioned Streaking Caddis. One is Hare's Ear, an imitation of big mayfly nymphs and hatchers as well as big caddis-fly pupae. The other is a Muddler Minnow which sometimes can be an effective lifesaver in either flowing or still waters. But I freely admit that it is difficult to limit the range of favourite flies to just a dozen when fishing in still water. There, the fish are so diverse in diet that I often think every lake deserves its own "deadly dozen".

So a recommendation is that all still-water flyfishermen, when touring several different kinds of waters, take along a field kit in their baggage – namely a reduced set of flytying tools that makes it possible to improvise imitations of those insects and other goodies which the fish prefer at the moment. A collection of ready-made flies that can fully cover all fishing opportunities in all lakes would scarcely be transportable!

Nonetheless, we shall now try to pare down the list of favourites for still water, while also identifying – as far as possible – the insects that they imitate, and which fishing tactic is suitable to them.

The flies described here are a standard range for salmonoid fish. Very seldom do you need to dig deep in the box for "odd" flies, since all of those in the standard range are sometimes disappointing. This applies to fishing trips in many countries such as the United States, England, West Germany, Austria and Yugoslavia.

Choosing a fly can be difficult – sometimes very difficult indeed. But there are several reliable favourite flies that will tempt the fish in most types of still water.

But the rules of thumb for flyfishing in rivers are also valid in still waters, and to an even greater degree. Especially at times when the fishing is best, the fish may alter their food preferences repeatedly during a single day. You have to keep up with them and go on experimenting. This is just what makes flyfishing so inimitably exciting!

Large mayflies

The largest mayfly species in Scandinavia's still waters is *Ephemera vulgata*, the "green drake". Its colour, from dirty yellow to deep chocolate-brown, is darker than that of the "drake" in flowing waters, *Ephemera danica*. Yet many of the classic mayfly patterns are applicable to it. The kind found most effective by experienced flyfishermen in still waters is tied with burnt feather-wings, parachute hackle and a free rear body, on dry-fly hooks of sizes 10-12.

These imitations are used during early summer in north European waters. It generally takes a couple of days before the hatching starts to excite the fish – but then they often hunt the newly hatched mayflies with a frenzy, splashing almost violently as they rise. One can even see rainbow and brown trout jumping half a metre above the surface in attempts to snap up the flies, and their acrobatics frequently succeed.

During this period the fish are easy enough to catch, if you manage to place your fly on their beat. At the same time, a still-water flyfisherman has fine chances of hooking a real heavyweight – for the feast is shared by all the fish, big and small.

However, as a rule it does not last long. It may occur during several periods of varying intensity, depending on the weather. But the fish soon discover greater rewards in trying to snap up these mayflies before they hatch – particularly when they are just about to hatch, and are floating helplessly in the surface layer.

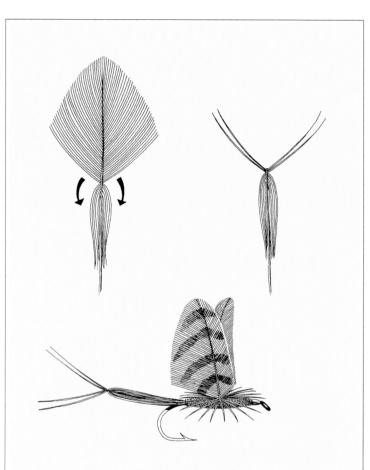

Large mayflies can be tied in numerous ways. This imitation of a "green drake" (dun), tied with parachute hackle, is quite effective – but the pattern must naturally be varied in colour and size, depending on which mayflies occur locally.

GREEN DRAKE (DUN)
Hook: dry-fly hook with downward eye No. 10-12
Tying thread: brown
Tail and reversed hackle: "wonderwing"-tied badger saddle hackle feather, with four fibres left and bent backward as tail antennae
Front body: medium-brown poly dubbing
Wings: two burnt pheasant breast feathers, 13-15 mm (0.5-0.6 in) long, tied back to back
Hackle: light brown cock, parachute-tied around the wing root
Head: black

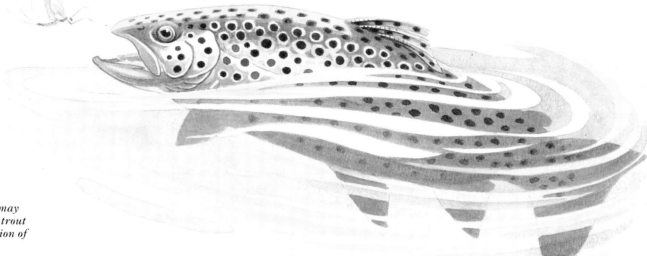

The challenge may be to tempt the trout with an imitation of big mayflies.

The mayfly nymph

This nymph can be imitated quite well with a large Gold-Ribbed Hare's Ear, whose tail you may want to build with 4-5 fibres from a cock pheasant's tail feather. The result, though, has one drawback: unless greased, it does not float very long if at all.

Therefore, assuming that the same nymph is not to be used also as an imitation of large mayfly pupae (in that case without tail-strands, since the pupae lack such a tail), you can replace the nymph's front section with a more or less equally thick thorax of deer hair, and leave a little bunch of hair tips on each side while dressing it. These bunches imitate the wing rudiments of a hatching "green drake". But the most important thing with this tying method is to obtain an imitation hatcher which floats ungreased – and floats in the underside of the water surface, just like its real prototype.

One seldom needs other mayfly imitations, or for that matter any special version of the "green drake" such as a spent spinner – the form which falls onto the water with outstretched wings. It does happen that the fish feed wildly on spent spinners, but even then your dun imitations can be applied with great success. A slight trick is enough to make them work wonders: jerk the line to give them a bit of life. Experience shows that the fish, however hungry for dead mayflies, will always prefer them alive if the choice exists.

This nymph can be fished either weighted or unweighted. If greased, it floats and provides an excellent imitation of large, hatching mayflies and caddis-fly pupae.

GOLD-RIBBED HARE'S EAR (NYMPH)
*Hook: long-shanked wet-fly hook or streamer hook
No. 10-14*
Tying thread: brown
Tail: a sparse bunch, 5 mm (0.2 in) long, of pheasant cock tail feather fibres – or, for small hook sizes, a little bunch of brown cock hackle fibres
Rear body: dubbed brown, gray, and black fur from a hare's ear, ribbed with round or oval gold tinsel
Front body: somewhat darker and thicker dubbing from a hare's ear, with longer hairs "pushed out" to imitate legs and wing cases
Head: clear varnish over the tying thread

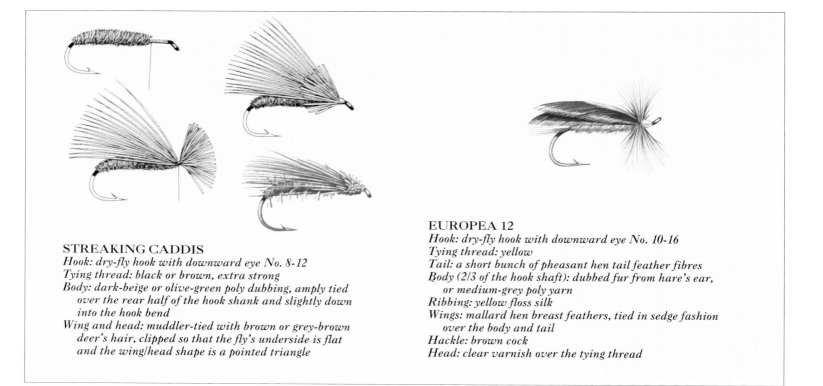

STREAKING CADDIS
Hook: dry-fly hook with downward eye No. 8-12
Tying thread: black or brown, extra strong
Body: dark-beige or olive-green poly dubbing, amply tied
    over the rear half of the hook shank and slightly down
    into the hook bend
Wing and head: muddler-tied with brown or grey-brown
    deer's hair, clipped so that the fly's underside is flat
    and the wing/head shape is a pointed triangle

EUROPEA 12
Hook: dry-fly hook with downward eye No. 10-16
Tying thread: yellow
Tail: a short bunch of pheasant hen tail feather fibres
Body (2/3 of the hook shaft): dubbed fur from hare's ear,
    or medium-grey poly yarn
Ribbing: yellow floss silk
Wings: mallard hen breast feathers, tied in sedge fashion
    over the body and tail
Hackle: brown cock
Head: clear varnish over the tying thread

Large caddis flies

Imitations of caddis flies, whether the complete winged ones or the larvae and pupae, play an enormous and indeed predominant role when it comes to flyfishing in still waters. This is comparable to the significance of mayfly imitations in flowing waters, although caddis-fly imitations are responsible for much of the catch there as well.

Caddis flies are abundant in virtually all waters. There are several hundred species, ranging from very small flies that require imitations on No. 16-18 hooks to gigantic ones with a body length of 30-35 mm (1.2-1.4 in).

The best-known imitation in Europe is No. 12 in the French Europea series. Tied in various sizes on hook numbers 8-16, it imitates a wide range of caddis-fly species. For some years there has also been a Swedish pattern, now extremely popular in Scandinavia and spreading beyond Europe – the Streaking Caddis. This is simple but ingenious: a fat banana-shaped body of poly yarn, with a muddler head which is dressed so that the deer-hair tips on the hook's upper side form the fly's wings, creating the characteristic "roof" of a caddis fly at rest.

Streaking Caddis is an unsinkable imitation, and this is important. For the fishing technique that makes it so effective is based upon adept manipulation of the line, which enables the fly to copy the slithering movement on the water surface that is typical of the big, egg-laying caddis flies and is apparently quite provocative to large rainbow and brown trout.

The most successful time for Streaking Caddis is at dusk and night – when the fisherman can no longer see the fly, but will surely hear the noise of the fish striking at it! A Streaking Caddis should then be kept moving with long, distinct pulls of 30-40 cm (1.0-1.3 ft) on the line, at intervals of 5-6 seconds. It should also be big, and tied on a dry-fly hook No. 8 or 10. Yet this clever fly is equally excellent for fishing in daylight, and it has proved able to tempt even huge grayling that are otherwise unreceptive.

The original version of Rackelhanen has brown wings and body, but many variants have been created. The most popular are one with an olive-green body and beige wings, and another with black body and white wings on hook size No. 16.

RACKELHANEN
Hook: dry-fly hook with downward eye No. 10-16
Tying thread: brown
Rear body: dark-brown or cinnamon-brown thick poly dubbing, amply tied over the rear 3/4 of the hook shaft
Wings: dark-brown or cinnamon-brown poly dubbing, which forms a backward- and upward-pointing V over the rear body
Head: a ball of dark-brown or cinnamon-brown, thick poly dubbing

Rackelhanen should be fished on a sinking leader, with half-metre-long pulls on the line so that it dives continually, then pops rapidly up to the surface.

Medium-sized caddis flies

This group of caddis flies was once imitated almost always with Europea No. 12. But that universal fly has recently met growing competition from a new favourite, Rackelhanen. Its Swedish name refers to a hybrid of two large wild wood-hens, the black grouse and capercaillie. The fly thus named is also a kind of hybrid – it imitates both the hatching pupa and the complete winged caddis fly.

The original Rackelhanen fly was invented by the well-known Swedish flyfisherman and rod-maker Kenneth Boström. It was made entirely of thick dark-brown poly yarn, apart from the hook and tying thread. This material gives the fly – especially if greased – an outstanding buoyancy which is important for its fishing technique. Rackelhanen must be fished with a "wet", slowly sinking leader, and with pulls of about 15 cm (6 in) on the line, which make the fly dive and then pop up again. It thus imitates a hatching caddis-fly pupa and, when you stop pulling, a newly hatched caddis fly that floats on the surface in readiness for its first flight.

Such a series of dives and pop-ups is evidently irresistible, in particular to grayling. Rackelhanen is tied today in all sizes and in endless colour combinations. Notably popular, besides the original colours, are an olive-green body with beige wings and a black body with white wings. The latter often comes on very small hooks, perhaps also imitating reed smuts and midge.

Good imitations of caddis flies are innumerable. Scandinavian flyfishermen experiment constantly with new patterns, but they have some reliable general favourites. In addition to the Swedish smash hits, there is Nalle Puh from Finland, composed by Simo Lumme in Helsinki and originally tied with bear-hair. Modern versions employ contemporary poly material, which seems to make the fly even better. Consequently, on hook sizes 8 and 10, it is a superb dry fly for sea trout in, among other places, the rivers of Sognefjord in Norway.

Caddis-fly pupae

There are a lot of imitations of the pupae as well, and the same patterns are used in lakes as in streams. We have already mentioned one of them, Gold-Ribbed Hare's Ear, which seems to work as nicely when imitating pupae as when the fish are hunting mayfly nymphs about to hatch.

Nalle Puh from Finland, too, has a pupa version – tied in sizes from hook No. 10 to 16, with the rear body usually dirty-orange or with olive-green dubbing. These imitations have rough, very shaggy bodies which, during the fishing, retain plenty of air in small glittering bubbles, thus adroitly copying the gas-filled coat of a pupa.

In the past two or three years, however, Nalle Puh has competed increasingly often with something called the Superpupa. This is a series of six or seven patterns, in sizes from hook No. 8 to 16. They have traditional shaggy bodies of rough poly dubbing or natural underfur. The trick is their body hackle, which winds over both the rear and front of the body, and is clipped over and under the hook shaft.

The Superpupa becomes a floating pupa imitation if it is greased – otherwise it sinks slowly. Like other pupa imitations, it can be tied in a great number of colour combinations. The best fishing results have been obtained with three versions: No. 16 with dark grey body and dark-blue dun body hackle, nicely imitating small caddis-fly pupae as

well as all sorts of other nymphs that are eaten especially by Arctic char; No. 14 with olive rear body and a very dark-brown thorax; and No. 8 with cream-coloured rear body, dark-brown thorax and light-brown body hackle. The last of these is fished primarily as a dry fly, either motionless or with short, cautious line jerks. It seldom arouses the fish in streams, but in still waters it has been a terrible killer.

Not only did the Superpupa become a new favourite – it also ushered in a whole new kind of flyfishing. That is, it turned out to be the best fly known until now for catching whitefish, usually a nerve-wracking ordeal. In many waters, whitefish are specialized to eat the drifting insects, largely caddis-fly pupae, which hover some centimetres beneath the surface. An ungreased Superpupa is cast upstream of the whitefish by 3-4 m (10-13 ft) in a stream, while in lakes it is placed 5-6 m (16-20 ft) in front of foraging schools of whitefish so that it can sink to the right depth before they see it. Moreover, it is enjoyed not only by whitefish: you will often get a "bonus" catch of sizeable trout and Arctic char.

All of this pupa fishing has been done with imitations which are presented in, or just under, the water surface. But caddis-fly pupae begin their journey to the surface from the bottom, and throughout the trip they are attacked by greedy fish. Commonly only a few percent of the pupae escape being taken and manage to hatch on the surface in order to reach their fourth and final stage. Yet these few are enough to ensure the insect family's survival.

Imitating a caddis fly that climbs out of the bottom gravel to start its adventurous voyage, though, is hardly easy. Indeed, it may appear hopeless to make a deep-sinking imitation work naturally. This has been done, but mainly in flowing water and by using Frank Sawyer's awfully ingenious Killer Bug. In lakes we should stick to the surface layer, where the fish also certainly come, sooner or later, in their quest for rapidly rising pupae.

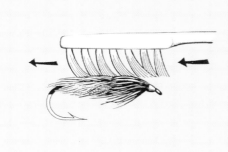

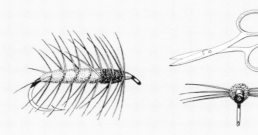

The Superpupa is a terrific pupa imitation which, besides the original (below), also comes in variants: one with an olive-green rear body on hook No. 12-14 and, for Arctic char, one with a dark-grey rear body on hook No. 16.

SUPERPUPA

Hook: dry-fly hook with downward eye No. 8-16
Tying thread: same colour as the rear body
Rear body: cream-coloured, light or dark olive, or dark-grey poly dubbing, amply tied over 2/3 of the hook shank
Front body: dark-brown or black poly dubbing
Body hackle: cock hackle over both the front and rear body, light brown (if the rear body is cream-coloured) or blue dun, or (if the rear body is dark grey) dark blue dun. The hackle is clipped down over and under the hook shank.
Head: clear varnish over the tying thread

KILLER BUG

Hook: wet-fly hook No. 8-14
Tying thread and weighting: thin red copper wire
Body: three layers of copper wire, under an ample body of red, brown, and grey wool yarn (Chadwick No. 477)
Head: three or four turns of copper wire

Killer Bug was invented by the well-known English flyfisherman Frank Sawyer. This fly sinks fast and can therefore be made to imitate a caddis-fly pupa climbing from the bottom toward the surface. The copper wire is attached where the hook bend begins, then wound tightly forward to just behind the hook eye, and finally wound backward. When it reaches the hook bend, it is used to attach the Chadwick yarn, then wound forward again to just behind the hook eye. Lastly the yarn is wound forward and fastened with the copper wire.

NALLE PUH (PUPA)

Hook: wet-fly hook No. 10-16
Tying thread: beige, brown or olive green (according to the rear body colour)
Rear body: beige, dark orange or olive green, synthetic dubbing of rough, glittering materials. The rear body is tied amply, then "combed" so that it can retain tiny air bubbles (the above illustration shows, too, a variant with a silver-ribbed rear body).
Front body: thick, ample dubbing from hare's ear with pushed-out hairs
Head: clear varnish over the tying thread

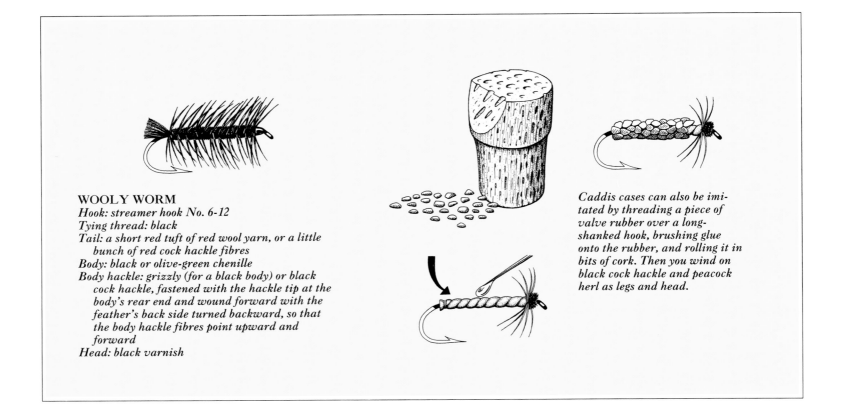

WOOLY WORM
Hook: streamer hook No. 6-12
Tying thread: black
Tail: a short red tuft of red wool yarn, or a little
*   bunch of red cock hackle fibres*
Body: black or olive-green chenille
Body hackle: grizzly (for a black body) or black
*   cock hackle, fastened with the hackle tip at the*
*   body's rear end and wound forward with the*
*   feather's back side turned backward, so that*
*   the body hackle fibres point upward and*
*   forward*
Head: black varnish

Caddis cases can also be imitated by threading a piece of valve rubber over a long-shanked hook, brushing glue onto the rubber, and rolling it in bits of cork. Then you wind on black cock hackle and peacock herl as legs and head.

Caddis cases

Many caddis flies are at the larval stage of case-builders, which put together a tube-shaped dwelling that covers and protects their rear bodies and part of their front bodies. When they move – slowly and clumsily, since they drag the case with them – you can see their heads and legs projecting from the case's front end.

Some birds strip caddis cases before eating them. Fish cannot do this, but swallow them whole, and this unavoidable "house consumption" explains all the rubbish – pine needles, wood bits, grains of gravel – which is often found in the otherwise empty stomachs of rainbow and brown trout.

Caddis-fly larvae are easy to imitate. The case-building larvae use whatever materials are nearest, and these are often pieces of vegetation, which enable us to imitate the worms with a weighted version of an American favourite, Wooly Worm. This fly has the right caseworm profile, being made of chenille – the best body material and available in

numerous colours (mainly dark olive and black). A weighted Wooly Worm can and should be fished deep, with matchstick-long jerks of the line.

In certain lakes and streams, however, caddis-fly larvae choose a different building material: sand and gravel, which make them harder to copy. An old French method was to thread about 2 cm (0.8 in) of bicycle-tyre valve rubber over a long-shafted hook, brush the valve with glue, and roll it in gravel. It is difficult to cast, but its lumpiness can be avoided by imitating the gravel as well – namely with bits of cork, shaved off a wine cork with a rough file! The larva's head and legs on such a valve-rubber fly can be imitated with, for example, a "head" of wound peacock herl, or one or two turns of black cock hackle.

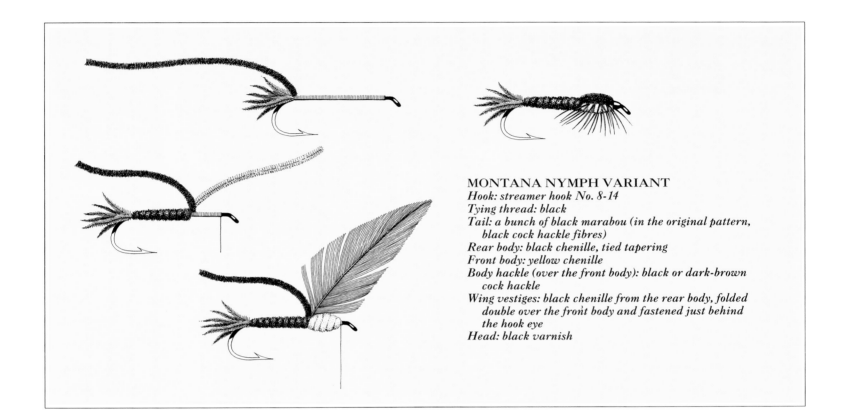

MONTANA NYMPH VARIANT
Hook: streamer hook No. 8-14
Tying thread: black
Tail: a bunch of black marabou (in the original pattern, black cock hackle fibres)
Rear body: black chenille, tied tapering
Front body: yellow chenille
Body hackle (over the front body): black or dark-brown cock hackle
Wing vestiges: black chenille from the rear body, folded double over the front body and fastened just behind the hook eye
Head: black varnish

Damselflies

This is another interesting family of "flyfishing insects". They play little role in flowing waters, but are extremely important – almost always as nymphs – for fishing in still waters. One should, though, take along one or two good representatives of the few exceptions, meaning imitations of complete winged damselflies.

For it happens that one sees fine rainbow trout which have specialized on, and developed a fine hunting technique for, "dry" damselflies. The fact is that damselflies like to sit on leaves, for example of water-lilies. They sit along the leaf edges with their heads bent out towards open water. Since they can see well and react very fast, the trout have to surprise them, from behind if possible. The fish does so by taking aim, flipping itself over the leaf with its mouth open, and catching the damselfly on the way back into the water on the other side.

But the flyfisherman seldom gets such a chance, as the main role is played by damselfly nymphs. These abound almost everywhere in Scandinavian still waters, except in the mountains – and the fish adore them. While they are not hard to imitate, you will have much more success with patterns that are impressions rather than imitations. The best by far is a Montana Nymph Variant, on which the oar-like gills are copied by a 5-millimetre-long tuss of marabou herl, which makes the nymph wave its tail realistically in the water. This fly is tied in two sizes, on streamer hooks Nos. 10 and 12, both weighted and unweighted. The fly is kept moving with short, distinct jerks or twists of the fly line, because a damselfly nymph moves jerkily.

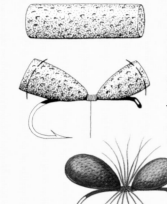

At left is shown the most easily tied imitation of flying ants, which tumble down on lakes and meres while swarming. A piece of punched polycelon is laid over the hook and wound fast at the middle of the hook shank. Then the hackle, of black or brown cock hackle, is wound on.

ANT
Hook: dry-fly hook No. 12-16
Tying thread: black or brown
Rear and front bodies: two balls of fine-fibred black or red-brown dubbing
Hackle: one or two turns of black or brown cock hackle between the dubbing balls
Head: black or clear varnish over the brown tying thread

McMurray Ant is another effective imitation of ants. The fly has superb catching ability, but can be hard to tie – or rather, manufacture – and it seldom lasts for more than one strike. It is made by sandpapering balsa balls and joining them with a stump of epoxy-glued whole nylon line. The balls are varnished and tied onto the hook shaft. Finally the hackle, of black or brown cock hackle, is wound on and fastened with the tying thread.

Ants

Ants, too, play an extensive role in still-water fishing, particularly in the thousands of small lakes in forest regions. Some years ago, a Scandinavian scientist made a study of the food habits of implanted rainbow, brown, and brook trout. It was found that no other food dominated their menu so heavily as did ants during the month of August. This applied to all of the lakes investigated, and the proportion of ants in the fish's food reached 80%!

The explanation is that flying ants swarm intensively at close intervals in late summer. They "rain" down on lakes by the billions – up to several hundred per square metre of water surface – and attract all fish to the surface.

At the beginning of an ant swarming, when the ants fall rather sparsely, the fish are easy to catch, being equally eager and unafraid, so that the competition for titbits of food is strong. But just a few minutes later, it can be almost impossible to hook a single fish, even though they rise madly. The real ants are then too numerous, and a fish is extremely unlikely to take an imitation ant by mistake.

But towards the end of the swarming, ants fall less densely again and the flyfisherman has his chance. Fish in lakes that are blessed with such swarmings become obsessed with ants, so for a long time – often several weeks – imitation ants remain by far the best flies to use, even on occasions when there are no ants or any other fish food on the surface.

Ant imitations are easy to tie. Two examples may be mentioned. One consists of a couple of "balls" of fine black poly dubbing, separated by a sparse black cock hackle. The wings are not important, but sometimes they are added, made of light-grey cock hackle tips and tied in a V shape between the poly balls. These imitations work perfectly – yet another example, the famous American pattern McMurray Ant, is also superb. Its rear and front body parts are of varnished balsa wood; however, it is harder to tie and much less durable.

It is not only in flowing water that fish can be easily frightened. Even when fishing in still water, one should act cautiously and try to keep a low profile.

Ants must be fished as simply as possible, like freely drifting dry flies. Since the fish find them easily enough, no special tricks are required. Nor do you often need any other ant imitations than black ones of sizes No. 12 and 14. Black ants are the most common, and fish take them with joy, even if at times it is actually the much smaller red ants that are swarming...

Wasps

Besides flying ants, a great many other land insects become fish food now and then: crane-flies, sloebugs, bumblebees, wasps, peppered moth larvae, grasshoppers, and all sorts of small flies, beetles and so on.

The most important of these are definitely wasps, which may tumble down in such numbers during the summer and early autumn that they make the fish rise eagerly. A wasp rain can result, for example, from a thunderstorm or a frosty night that renders the wasps almost unable to fly.

It is frequently very hard to see whether wasps are the reason why fish are rising. Wasps themselves are quite difficult to see when they have fallen onto the water. Being heavy insects, they lie deep in the surface layer and may well be noticed only if you look straight down at them. But the fish can indicate what is going on by their powerful, gurgling whirls, like the wake of a energetic paddle.

Wasps are imitated in various ways – for instance, similarly to the simple ants made of poly dubbing, but alternating the black poly with dark orange in order to copy the characteristic stripes on a wasp's rear body. Another method resembles the McMurray Ant, using varnished balsa. Or a muddler technique is applicable, ideally with reindeer hair, which is easy to colour black and dark orange.

The popularity of wasps is greatest among rainbow trout. An insect that can evoke the same response is the sloebug, although this smelly creature is by no means as plentiful, and thus not so worth trying to imitate.

This wasp imitation can, of course, also be given wings, such as light-grey hackle tips that are tied on between the rear and front bodies. But ant- and wasp-eating fish will take the wingless variety just as readily.

WASP
Hook: long-shanked dry-fly hook No. 10-12
Tying thread: black
Rear body: a fat "cigar" of fine black and light red-brown poly dubbing, wound so as to create the typical wasp bar pattern
Front body: a smaller ball of fine-fibred black poly dubbing
Hackle: two turns of dark-brown or black cock hackle feathers between the rear and front bodies
Head: black varnish

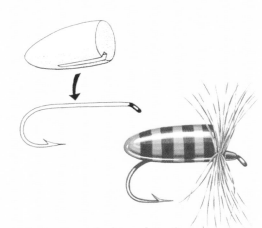

Wasp imitations can also be made in the same way as McMurray Ant – with balsa balls that are sandpapered smooth and varnished in "wasp colours". The hook shank is then glued into a cut-out groove. Finally the hackle, of dark-brown or black cock hackle feather, is wound on.

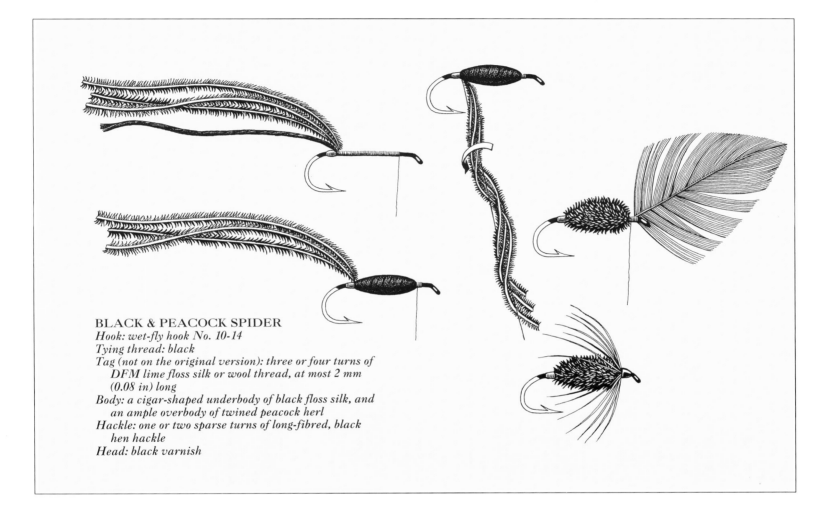

BLACK & PEACOCK SPIDER
Hook: wet-fly hook No. 10-14
Tying thread: black
Tag (not on the original version): three or four turns of
*   DFM lime floss silk or wool thread, at most 2 mm*
*   (0.08 in) long*
Body: a cigar-shaped underbody of black floss silk, and
*   an ample overbody of twined peacock herl*
Hackle: one or two sparse turns of long-fibred, black
*   hen hackle*
Head: black varnish

Snails

The insects discussed above are basically worldwide – their species may differ from place to place, but the families they represent are found everywhere and the behaviour of fish in regard to eating them is surprisingly universal.

One kind of fish food that was described in a pioneering book, *Still-Water Flyfishing* by Tom Ivens, published thirty years ago, was the relatively unknown group of "pulmonate" (lung-bearing) snails which, during the summer, migrate in great numbers through lakes by drifting with the wind and waves.

It was soon discovered that such snails occur abundantly also outside England – in meres and ponds as well as lakes –

and that they are just as appealing to fish there as in the British freshwater reservoirs. In his book, Tom Ivens recommends an imitation named Black & Peacock Spider, whose greatest success occurred during August and September.

Ivens' fly does not closely resemble the snail – or slug – which it is supposed to imitate, but it is extraordinarily effective if fished very slowly in, or just under, the water surface. That the fish, whether rainbow or brown trout, seem to believe it really is a snail, has been well-proved by the present author. Many of the fish in such catches have turned out to be stuffed with pulmonate snails, and nothing else.

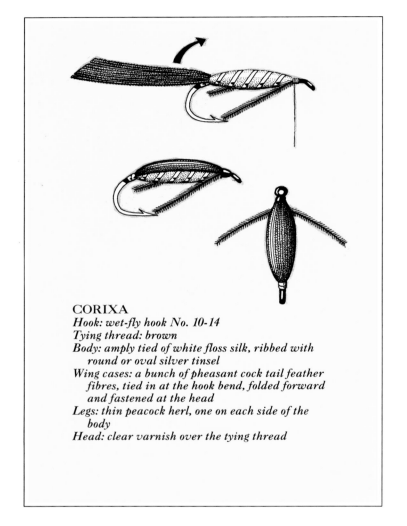

CORIXA
Hook: wet-fly hook No. 10-14
Tying thread: brown
Body: amply tied of white floss silk, ribbed with
round or oval silver tinsel
Wing cases: a bunch of pheasant cock tail feather
fibres, tied in at the hook bend, folded forward
and fastened at the head
Legs: thin peacock herl, one on each side of the
body
Head: clear varnish over the tying thread

Water boatmen

Yet another insect that fish in still waters love to gobble is the water boatman – in Scandinavia and Great Britain alike, as well as in the United States, New Zealand, and several other countries with freshwater salmonoids.

The most common imitation of water boatmen is British in origin. But success does not always follow with this fly on the leader. For these insects do not occur in all lakes, and only on special occasions do the fish concentrate upon eating that particular family. However, such occasions are memorable indeed, arising mainly when the water boatmen are swarming. They normally live underwater, but have to come up at regular intervals to renew their air supply, and then they make miniature "wakes" on the surface. When swarming, they fold out the wings hidden under their shoulder-scales, and ascend from the water like Polaris missiles, heading for dry land in order to mate.

After mating, they return in thousands to resume life in the water, and may then form a "rain" of water boatmen. This recalls a hailstorm, as insects fall all over the surface with short, sharp plopping sounds – and the fish react with the same enthusiasm as when ants are swarming. But you have to be lucky to experience it.

When fishing in lakes and ponds, especially for rainbow trout, "lures" can give very good results.

Lures

Lures are often large and unlike any known insects. In flowing waters they offer little to the flyfisherman, but they can be exceedingly effective in still waters. When fishing the latter, therefore, you should always take along at least three such odd patterns of different sizes: a Wooly Bugger, a Bitch Creek Nymph – both of them heavily weighted – and a Muddler Minnow, which is the one that can also sometimes give good results in flowing water as well.

Wooly Bugger, which has a fine British counterpart named Dog Nobbler, is tied on a streamer hook No. 8, 10 or 12. The other two patterns call for streamer hook Nos. 8

and 10. Nobody knows what a Wooly Bugger or Dog Nobbler is supposed to represent, but perhaps the fish take them for leeches. Anyhow they are frequently murderous, especially when fishing for rainbow trout.

If tying the flies yourself, be very careful about the placement of the weighting. It must lie as far forward as possible, just behind the hook eye. Dog Nobbler, for example, is frequently provided with a head that consists of a divided, epoxy-glued lead shot, varnished and decorated with painted fish eyes. Its weighting is ideal: the fly begins to dive toward the bottom immediately on hitting the water, with

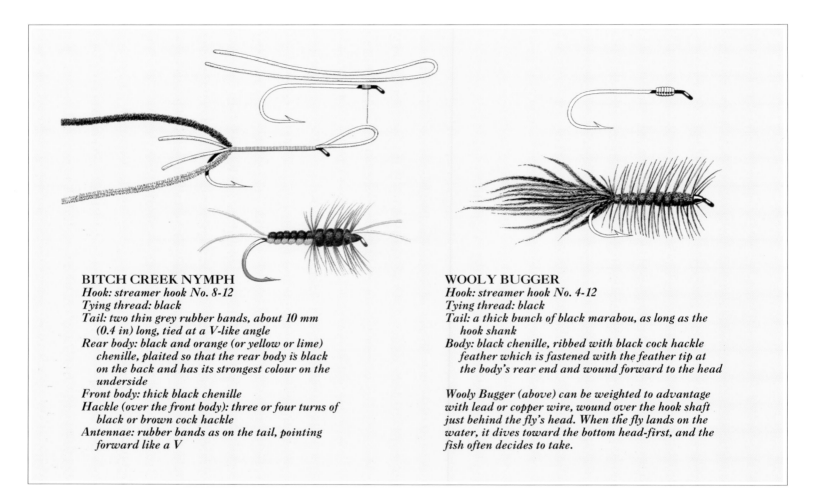

BITCH CREEK NYMPH
Hook: streamer hook No. 8-12
Tying thread: black
Tail: two thin grey rubber bands, about 10 mm
(0.4 in) long, tied at a V-like angle
Rear body: black and orange (or yellow or lime)
chenille, plaited so that the rear body is black
on the back and has its strongest colour on the
underside
Front body: thick black chenille
Hackle (over the front body): three or four turns of
black or brown cock hackle
Antennae: rubber bands as on the tail, pointing
forward like a V

WOOLY BUGGER
Hook: streamer hook No. 4-12
Tying thread: black
Tail: a thick bunch of black marabou, as long as the
hook shank
Body: black chenille, ribbed with black cock hackle
feather which is fastened with the feather tip at
the body's rear end and wound forward to the head

Wooly Bugger (above) can be weighted to advantage
with lead or copper wire, wound over the hook shaft
just behind the fly's head. When the fly lands on the
water, it dives toward the bottom head-first, and the
fish often decides to take.

its head first and its marabou tail fluttering. Thus it attracts the fish instantly, without your needing to move the line. More than a third of the many fish caught by the present author on this fly have taken it on the first dive.

Dog Nobbler, like Wooly Bugger with a solid lead-wire weighting just behind the hook eye, is consequently a kind of jig-fly or fly-jig. The up-down path which these flies follow homeward seems to be much more provocative to fish than the traditional horizontal path.

The best colours are a black or dark-olive body, a black hackle and a black marabou tail – or conceivably even more dangerous, a body of twined peacock herl.

Bitch Creek Nymph has a distinctive type of equipment for provoking fish to strike: four thin grey rubber bands – two at the tail and two at the head, both pairs being tied in V shape – which move vigorously when brought home in jerks. This fly is a wide favourite during heat waves, and is usually allowed to sink to a depth of 4-5 m (13-17 ft) before the line is manipulated.

Muddler Minnow, finally, is fished almost free of weighting, since it needs to be buoyant and pop up to the surface after each pull on the line. It then fishes best, but you can fish it deep with a sinking weight-forward line. It can also be tied in rather light colours, and with a silver body. In the latter form, it imitates many of the small fish that are so common in both still and flowing waters – the minnows.

Unusual fish species

Few fish will refuse a delicious fly if it is served right in front of their noses. Whitefish can be caught on flies, and one of those in European waters is a source of fine sport – the ide. Sometimes it greedily attacks any fly that imitates fish fry, but otherwise it can be tricked only by a dry fly which is presented very discreetly. Today, ides caught on flies in Europe are usually "side-products", notably in Scandinavia where they are occasionally abundant in waters with salmon and sea trout.

Among freshwater fish, the pike and – in Europe – the perch are what, together with salmonoids, persuade most flyfishermen to exchange their angling rod for fly rods. In the United States, on the other hand, it is bass and bluegill, even though perch exist there and so do three species of pike.

Flyfishing for pike requires ample equipment, the same as in one-handed fishing for salmon: rods of 9-11 ft (2.7-3.4 m) and reels that have a durable braking system as well as holding a line of class 8-10 plus a couple of hundred metres of thick backing. Such powerful gear is not for the sake of the wind – unless the fishing is done in a brackish sea like the Baltic, or in large lakes. The problem is that the most effective pike flies are big, lumpy ones, tied on very thick leader tips. Such a tip, of 0.35-0.40 mm (0.014-0.016 in), is essential to prevent the leader from tearing off in a huge pike's toothy grip.

Pike fishing with a fly has become ever more popular, especially in northern Europe. And during one season, early spring, flyfishing is also by far the most effective method of catching pike as a sport. The reason is that pike, when they seek shallow water before spawning, move in a leisurely and dignified manner – they are presumably unwilling to perform any violent manoeuvres, and risk harming their reproduction by spilling eggs or milt. Though not eager to hunt, they do strike.

Consequently, for the spinning and bait-casting fisherman, the best bait is a small or moderate-sized one, which can be pulled very slowly in the water without losing its vitality. But almost no spinning bait can be pulled as slowly as a fly. The ideal fly for pike fishing is a plastic tube, 10 cm (4 in) long, covered or ribbed with silver or gold tinsel, and having one or more wings of soft hair, which "breathe" or

Good flyfishing is offered by many fish species which have no adipose fin. Most of them live in lakes and other still waters, but several can be found in flowing waters as well.

Flyfishing for pike often calls for relatively strong equipment and a thick leader, since the flies are large and difficult to cast – and a pike's teeth are sharp as knives.

pulsate at every little pull on the line.

When several wings or bunches of hair are tied on the tube, they increase the fly's ability to sway in the water, whereas the same fly with only one bunch of hair tends to lose its balance and tip in the direction of its weight – namely back towards the treble hook. Previously, this type of fly was often tied on two or three streamer hooks of size No. 6-8, in a tandem or triple arrangement, with a common "matuka wing" of soft hair. But the simple plastic tube is easier to handle, and the treble hook is at least as effective.

The fly's colours can very well be bright, particularly in springtime. My own pike fishing has succeeded best with a fly that has a bushy white wing, a silver tinsel body, and two tufts of red hair as a beard and tail. Such a fly should be fished with a slowly sinking line, as a fast-sinking line must be taken home too rapidly and does not interest the pike as much. A slowly sinking line can be taken home in leisurely jerks, without the fly either sinking to the bottom or rising to the surface.

When a pike takes a fly during the spring before spawning, it does so almost lazily, gliding forth and closing its jaws around the fly. It then offers unimpressive resistance, and even females weighing 10 kg (22 lb) or more will tire after a few minutes. But once the spawning is over and the pike resume hunting, they take their prey in the true pike tradition – with a lightning leap. How fast the prey move is rather unimportant. A fly which is slowly jerked home can nevertheless be profitable, though hardly better than the well-tried wobblers, spoons and spinners.

As a result, pike can be fished with a fly throughout the season, except for very hot periods when the pike stay deep. Fishing deep with a fly is always difficult, and this includes pike fishing.

Yet pike are also open to dry-fly fishing, unlike most of the other unusual flyfishing species. Certainly they do not make a habit of eating insects, but they gladly attack somewhat larger prey that sometimes stir up the surface – such as frogs and voles. A swimming vole is not hard to imitate,

The popper is a typical bass fly. It is taken home with short, sharp pulls on the line, so that the angled head creates sounds and air bubbles – it "pops". This enables you to catch even perch and pike, for example.

POPPER

Hook: long-shanked, strong dry-fly hook with downward eye No. 2-8
Tying thread: same colour as the body or head
Tail, body and wings: a bunch of hair attached just in front of the hook bend, with sides of one or two saddle hackle tips reaching 2-4 cm (0.8-1.6 in) behind the hook bend
Head: balsa wood, filed down to a rounded cone with its tip backward. A groove is cut in its underside for epoxy-gluing to the hook shank; then the head is varnished and decorated.

either: a bushy, muddler-tied deer-hair fly, mounted on a simple low-water salmon hook, clipped to the shape of a mouse, with a rubber band for a tail, works fine if it is taken home in short jerks. Even big pike, especially in confined waters, can be tempted by such a morsel; and so can big trout that are otherwise quite shy.

Perch fishing with a fly is most successful in high summer, when the water is warm and schools of perch hunt near the surface. At that time, perch can also be fished "dry" with an imitation of, for example, a bumblebee or wasp – insects that are regarded as delicacies by virtually all fish.

Large- and small-mouthed bass, which now exist not only in the United States but also in Spain and elsewhere, are also dry-fly fish, and to a much greater extent. Bass can be fished with many of the traditional nymph and streamer patterns, as well as with special surface flies called "poppers". These have a small head, made of varnished balsa wood, abruptly chopped off in front. It "pops" when jerked in the surface water, and this sound is apparently very attractive to bass – even if an occasional pike, or brown or rainbow trout, also lets itself be fooled.

Poppers can be fished with ordinary light flyfishing equipment. In the United States, however, a special fly line has been invented for just this sort of fishing. It is a weight-forward line with a short head, known as "rocket taper".

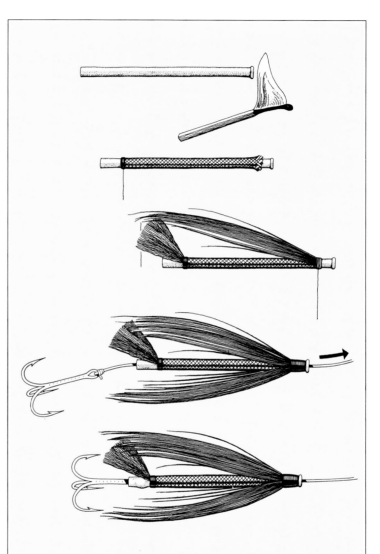

PIKE FLY

Hook: double or treble, with a 63-mm (2.5-in) plastic tube
Tying thread: red
Body: Flash-a-Bou mylar hose, drawn over the plastic tube
Tail: a 15-mm (0.6-in) tuft of red hair, attached to the tube's upper side
Wing: a strong bunch of long white hairs (or a bunch of black under one of white), reaching 1-2 cm (0.4-0.8 in) behind the tube
Hackle: a 15-mm (0.6-in) tuft of red hair, attached like a "beard" on the tube's bottom side, just behind the head
Head: clear varnish over the tying thread

Flyfishing in streams

In small waterways
such as streams, brooks and
tributary rivers, the dominant fish are
often stationary brown trout, grayling
and other salmonoids – even if
they are sometimes accompanied by
salmon and sea trout, which are not feeding
but migrating to spawn. Here, fishing is
done primarily with flies that imitate
the quarry's food of insects,
crustaceans and lesser fish living
in the same waterway. We thus use dry
flies and nymphs as well as wet flies
and, to a lesser extent, streamers
and bucktails.

A waterway's character and geographical location are decisive for the kind of salmonoid fish to be found there. Of course, it has always been difficult for human beings to accept that all fish – especially those in fresh waters – have a limited natural distribution. When we learned the rather simple craft of squeezing eggs from fish and raising trout or salmon fry, we immediately started spreading them into waters where they had not existed. If they were able to spawn and get enough food, they accepted the new environment.

This is why salmonoids occur at all in the Southern Hemisphere – for instance in New Zealand, Tasmania and Australia as well as in South America, where some of the world's best trout fishing is now found. These places have never possessed natural stocks of salmonoids, which originally were confined to our Northern Hemisphere.

The English, in particular, have made a great and laudable effort to implant trout almost everywhere in their former colonies. Residents who had long been away from "good old England" needed at least a few trout to swing their rods at! But the introduction of trout to new waters has not been entirely a positive trend. In many places the new species have prospered enough to completely eradicate the original ones. As a result, several excellent and rare fish species have been lost to posterity. Good examples are the numerous subspecies of the cutthroat trout *(Salmo clarki)*, which spread over North America by adapting themselves to the existing water system and its environment.

The massive stocking of salmon and trout from artificial hatcheries has also "diluted" the valuable gene pool of the few surviving wild fish, an inheritance which has taken millennia of adaptation to evolve and which cannot be recreated once it is gone. Often we know nothing about the gene pool of cultured fish, which are commonly degenerated and domesticated after having lived in confinement for generations. Incurable damage has been caused by the uncritical stocking of such unknown material through the years.

The rainbow trout *(Salmo gairdneri)* has thus come to inhabit most of the world, where conditions are suitable for it. But even the European brown trout *(Salmo trutta)* has crossed the seven seas and can now be found in America as well as Australia. The grayling *(Thymallus thymallus)*, whose farming is a little more complicated and therefore of smaller commercial value, has not travelled so widely, and exists mainly in the places where nature originally put it.

Still more fish than these, however, are encountered in the small waterways. In the far north, besides grayling, brown and rainbow trout, we have Arctic char *(Salvelinus alpinus)*, whose colourful relative from eastern North America, the brook trout *(Salvelinus fontinalis)*, has been implanted similarly in many parts of the world.

Holding places

All of the above-mentioned salmonoids live more or less permanently in the same waterways. Some fish may occasionally make visits to a nearby lake, but they are otherwise bound to the stream where they hunt and reproduce. When we fish for them, we must therefore remember that they have a constant need of cover and of food. So we have to look for them where they can fulfil both of these requirements.

This sounds easy in theory, but is harder in practice, due to the great differences between waterways. Each has its own character, and not until we get to know it can we "read" the water and find the fish. Not only that – there are also significant differences between the fish species. Moreover, the fish seldom occur at the same places in summer as in winter. Consequently, locating them in a new and unfamiliar body of water may strike us as a daunting task.

It isn't, though: with a little common sense, as well as some knowledge of fish and their living habits, we can go a long way. To begin with, there is a vast distinction between a slow chalk stream and a rushing river. For example, the current lee is very important to the fish in a river, but not in a chalk stream. Thus it is easier to find the fish in a fast current, where the holding places are clearly visible in its lee. Such places can hardly be noticed in a chalk stream, whose fish occur virtually everywhere – and may hold in the most surprising spots – so that we have to approach the water with extreme caution.

In the Alps of Central Europe, waterways have long been divided into a trout region and a grayling region. In the former, far up in the mountains where the brooks crash down the cliffs, the red-spotted brown trout is the sole ruler of the cold, rushing melt-water. Farther down as the slopes flatten out, we enter the region dominated by grayling – even though trout can sometimes be caught there as well.

This division is not exactly applicable to other parts of the world, but it tells a little about the fish and their demands on the environment. While brown trout can certainly be discovered in the quietest waterways, grayling never occur up in the mountains.

As was noted earlier, grayling often form small shoals at calm places in a waterway. By contrast, trout are definite loners and do not tolerate other fish in their territory. They also want "a roof over their heads" – being able to hold under a precipice, bank hollow, or overhanging tree. Thus,

Trout – the flyfisherman's classic quarry, and for many of us the prime target in running waters – can be found almost anywhere in the world today.

The same stretch of flowing water is shown here from above and in cross-section. Illustrated in the inset above are some typical holding places: (A) before or alongside stones and boulders, (B) just behind or under rich water vegetation that provides shade and protection, (C) under the protective hanging parts of trees, shore banks, and large roots. Other common places where fish often hold are, in particular, the necks of rapids and the deep calm water which follows a rapid or a stretch of current.

they are closely tied to shores or at least to fixed structures; yet grayling prefer to stay near the bottom in deep water. Further, whereas grayling are mainly active by day, trout tend to be nocturnal, and big ones are notably shy during the daytime, when they stay well hidden in their holding places. At night they may hunt in amazingly shallow water, where they are also easy to frighten!

An intermediate case is the rainbow trout: seldom clearly nocturnal, but not a shoal fish either. The rarer brook trout prefers a solitary life in deep water, but is normally the greediest of all trout species – a characteristic which it shares with the cutthroat trout, mentioned above, so that both of them are vulnerable to overfishing. In other words, they cannot take the same fishing pressure as does the brown trout, which is shy and soon learns to avoid the fisherman's bait.

These are, to be sure, generalizations that must be adjusted to suit the given fishing waters. But all fish have in common the fact that their holding places differ between summer and winter. In summer, when the water is warm, they gladly move to a stream whose water contains more oxygen. In winter the opposite is true, since their metabolism is slower in the cold water. Then they leave the fast streams and gather in calm places, where they can stand in the current lee to save energy.

It is impossible to specify all the types of holding places in a small waterway, so only the real "classics" will be described here. Among them is the calm water in a pool, below a rapid or a stretch of current. The fish stay in the pool's deep, quiet water and benefit from the food that is brought continually by the current. Usually the fish can be found at the deep upstream end during the hours of light. As darkness falls, the fish often retreat to feed in the shallow water at the pool's lower end, where the current is stronger.

The necks of rapids, with deep and relatively calm water just above a waterfall or rapid, are further good holding places. So is the area where water from a fall pours down into a pool, or even simply a pocket of deep water. Frequently the fish stand all the way into the spray! And large stones or cliffs in the main stream are invariably potential holding places, worth being fished carefully. The fish seldom stand behind stones – where the water tends to be too rough – but generally stay in front or along the sides. There and at the front, a current lee provides the fish with a good vantage point to watch for food brought by the current.

In calm waters, the fish are more bound to the deep

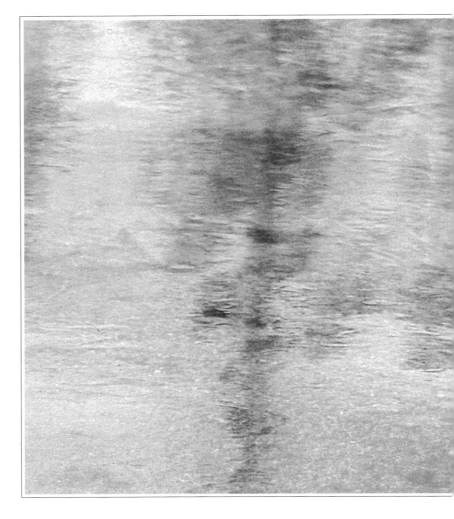

channels, especially at the bends where the current has dug into the banks and often hollowed them out. Brown trout are notable lovers of such dug-out banks. Fish also like to linger near the channels that are formed by areas of vegetation. Here the current collects drifting insects and crustaceans, which thus become easy prey.

Trees that have fallen into a stream offer the fish both cover and current lee. A lot of fish may also be found in large pools with quiet backwaters. Except during the cold season, however, fish seldom hold in the backwater itself, but frequently stay just where the current enters or leaves the pool. The backwater exhibits instead, for example, pike and perch. Unlike the salmonoids, these fish do not really belong there – they merely look for places where the current is weakest.

As a whole, the fish are more shy and cautious in small waterways than in big ones. The more water runs over and around the fish, the more secure they feel. In a small stream, therefore, we must be very careful when getting close to the water and the fish. It is best to keep a low profile, moving slowly and wearing clothes that merge into the surroundings as much as possible.

Then the point of readiness has come to start fishing, which can be quite exciting in brooks and streams. Everything happens at close range, making it essential to have full control over both flies and fish. At the same time, small waterways are good schools for the inexperienced fly-fisherman, who can learn many things about the fish there – and can later apply the lessons to larger, more limitless waterways.

Fish are frequently difficult to see in flowing water, but they may be detectable if you approach the water very carefully.

"Tailing": the fish eats on the bottom and shows only its tail fin above the water surface.

Types of rise

One very important thing a flyfisherman should be able to do is read different "rise forms". When the fish takes an insect at or near the water surface, it leaves rings or ripples on the surface. These serve to show the fisherman what sort of insect, and in which stage, the fish takes. On this basis the fly is chosen to catch the fish with.

The rise form is the visible sign of the fish's activity, and it can have quite diverse appearances – depending on the insect species, the fish's size and the water movement. In any case, the rise itself is the essence of flyfishing: it means direct eye contact with a hunting fish. Hardly any other sight can be so stimulating, or indeed so frustrating if you fail to catch the fish, which either flees in fright or goes on rising nonchalantly.

It has to be emphasized firstly that a flyfisherman should always wear polaroid glasses. They not only protect the eyes from a wildly moving fly, but also filter out many of the irritating reflections that prevent you from seeing into the water. Hence they are at least as important as the rod, reel, line and fly – in fact more important, as they provide the best possibility of watching the fish under the surface even if no activity appears on the surface.

If we look farthest down into the water, a glimpse of the fish's side as it turns in the current is often all we see of it. Yet this captivating "wink under water", in the words of Skues, indicates that a fish is making a quick detour in its hunt for nymphs or other prey – a fish, therefore, which can be caught.

(Above) "Head and tail" means that the fish takes nymphs and pupae just in or under the surface layer. First you see the head, then the back fin, and finally the tail fin over the water. However, big brown trout and steelheads often display only their backs.

(Below) When a fish takes, for example, nymphs just under the surface, the water over the fish moves up and forms "bulges" on the surface. In this form of rise, you very seldom see part of the fish above the surface.

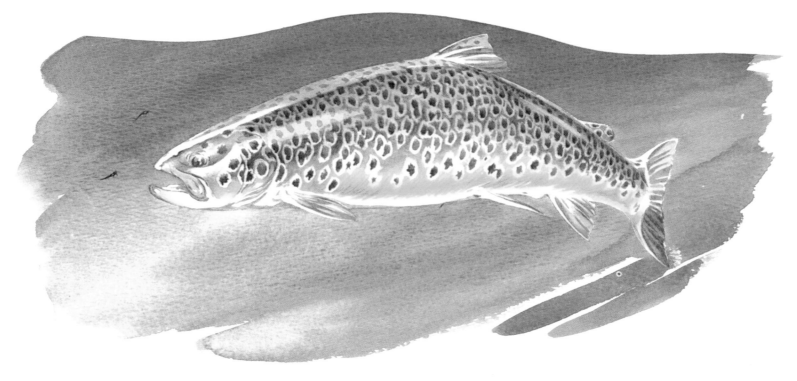

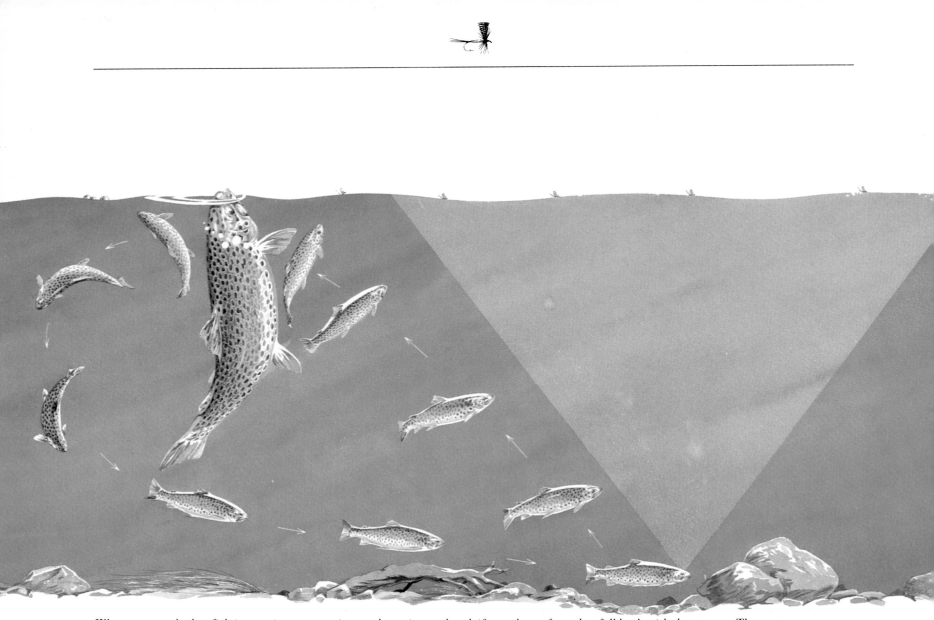

When trout, and other fish in running waters, rise to take an insect that drifts on the surface, they fall back with the current. Thus you see the fish rise downstream of the holding place. To give the fish time to climb to the surface, you must therefore lay out the fly a good way upstream of the assumed holding place. Keep in mind, too, that deep fish need more time to rise than do fish near the surface.

When the water is relatively low, a phenomenon called "tailing" can be observed. In this rise form, the fish almost stands on its head in the vegetation to shake loose insects and crustaceans. It will then stick the tip of its tail out of the water, a characteristic sign. Now and then it moves downstream to pick up the creatures shaken loose, but it rapidly returns.

If the fish is hunting higher up in the water, you can frequently see it flickering in the light or lifting the water. As a result, swells are formed in the surface, leading us to speak of "bulging fish".

Commonly the fish proceeds to take the nymphs and pupae that are hanging motionless in the surface film before hatching. You see the fish "head and tail" – as first the head, then the back, and finally the tail emerge from the water, like a porpoise rolling at the surface. Here we also use the phrase "porpoise rise". When this is witnessed, you know that your leader should still be carrying a nymph, not a dry fly.

A fish takes sizeable prey such as small fish by using its jaws, but it consumes insects and other small animals by sucking them into its mouth, out of the current that flows constantly over its gills. The mouth and gill covers create a pressure drop that sucks the water in; then the mouth closes and the water is pushed back through the gill openings. Any food in the water is sieved out by the gill rakers and is swallowed.

If it is impossible to figure out what the fish are presently taking, trial-and-error is often necessary. Experienced fishermen know that a lot of flies may have to be tried in a day before finding the "right" one for wary trout.

Surface rising

When taking an insect at the surface, a fish usually sucks in some air as well. The air subsequently forms small bubbles on the surface, giving a sure sign that the fish took a winged insect at the surface – in other words, not a nymph or pupa just under it. If so, there can be no doubt that the time has come for a dry fly!

Exactly what happens on the water can be seen much more easily with a pair of binoculars. Moreover, it is always worth carefully studying what the current brings along. By combining the two sources of information, you are as well-prepared as possible, and can really pick out your fish.

We say that a fish "rises" when it takes insects on the surface. The resultant ripples, which spread downstream with the current, were once named "tell-tale rings" by an Englishman. But such rings can look very differently: they may be big or little, violent or controlled. At the violent end of the spectrum, we have fish that are in a hurry to take insects. These may be newly hatched duns, which can lift from the water at any moment and thus evade the fish. Or they may be egg-laying caddis flies that flutter over the surface, or large grasshoppers that are eager to reach dry land. All of them stimulate energetic rises, with big rings and loud splashing.

The same can happen when a fish takes small insects in a

(Above) A splash rise occurs when fish rapidly chase insects that are lifting from the surface or fluttering just above it. A spray rise may occur even when the fish hunts under the surface, if it suddenly swerves at high speed to swim in another direction.

(Left) A sip rise is the commonest form of rise, producing only rings on the water surface. The rings are deceptive as their size gives no clue to the fish's weight.

(Right) "Cruisers" are fish that more or less regularly patrol the relatively calm areas of a current. Just as when fishing in lakes, one can estimate in advance where the fish will rise the next time, and lay out the fly in its path.

strong current, where it must act fast. It may also be a little fish that has difficulty in sucking up insects. Sometimes you then find it jumping out of the water to take the insects on the way down, so that you have to wait a bit for the counter-strike! Conversely, we often encounter very big fish which make no noise, but only leave tiny ripples on the surface, leading us to speak of "sipping" fish or a "sip rise". This latter phenomenon is typical when many small insects are hatching simultaneously on a calm surface. There is plenty of food even for a big fish, which otherwise might not be interested in small prey. It hovers just under the surface to suck in the insects at a leisurely and rather cautious pace. Such hatchings occur among the *Caenis* mayflies, and among the small reed knots that cover the surface at times like a carpet – or what the English call a "blanket hatch".

On very quiet stretches of current, you may meet "cruis-er" fish that methodically patrol their territories to find insects on the surface. Identical behaviour is common in lakes – and there, too, it is necessary to foresee the spot at which the fish will rise the next time. Then you lay out your dry fly and wait with mounting excitement. Normally, though, a fish rises at a particular place in the waterway, giving you a natural target. Otherwise the dry fly cannot be positioned properly – that is, far enough in front of the fish, which must have time to rise to it.

A fish rises to the surface by angling its breast fins so that the current presses it upward. After taking an insect, it turns the fins downward and swims back to the bottom, assisted by a stroke of its tail. Thus, while climbing to the surface, it drops back with the current. So you see it rise a ways downstream from its holding place. And this means you should lay out your dry fly a good distance farther upstream than you perhaps thought necessary at first, or else the fish simply won't have time to rise for it!

As a rule the fish rises from the bottom, but it may let itself come up with the current to just under the surface if there are enough insects, and if the current is not too strong. Trout do so often, whereas grayling always stay on the bottom.

In this connection you should remember that, the deeper a fish is holding, the longer time it needs to rise to the surface. Consequently the fly must be served farther upstream of the rise rings. Moreover, the fish will only rise to the insects within a narrow region, the "feeding lane", which is directly above it. Insects and flies that drift towards it outside this region are ignored. The fish does have a wide "window" and can easily see them approaching from the side, yet it will not touch them. Too much energy would be required to move sideways in a strong current, and the fish may also find it difficult to judge the distance and speed to such food. It therefore keeps its breast fins still, and takes only what passes right over its head.

Essential equipment

Flyfishing in streams is not dependent on heavy or expensive gear. It seldom calls for really long casting, and the fish are normally not so large as to demand costly fly reels with refinements like disc brakes. Neither need the equipment tolerate salt water. In sum, you can start your career as a flyfisherman on a small waterway without investing a fortune.

A single basic outfit can get you far, but serious flyfishermen soon discover that at least some extra gear is necessary. Waterways change during the season, so the fishing does too – from the high levels of springtime to the low, clear waters of summer with their careful, fastidious inhabitants.

The infrequent need for long casting means that the fly rod does not have to fulfil many conditions. A cheap glassfibre rod is good enough, although you will naturally get more enjoyment out of fishing if you buy the best that you can afford. The more expensive carbon-fibre rods from well-known manufacturers cast better than do cheap glassfibre rods. However, they do not necessarily catch more fish. For a fish is caught by the fisherman, not by the equipment! Whether you allow yourself to be seduced by attractive fishing gear, however, is quite another matter.

The rod's length is determined entirely by the kind of fishing water – whether it is large or small, open or overgrown. In general you should always choose the longest possible rod. A long rod has definite mechanical advantages, with a higher back cast and better line control in both the air and water. A good standard length for all flyfishing in streams is 9 ft (2.7 m). This will let you keep the line free from high grass, bushes and trees. It also permits such a high back cast that you can easily keep the line out of the water even if you sometimes wade in deep. In addition, this is a good length for being able to mend and control the line, leader and fly while fishing.

A shorter fly rod is relatively poor at dealing with all these tasks. However, it makes life much easier if you have to fish in fairly small brooks which are overgrown with trees and bushes. Then a long rod can be almost impossible to handle.

The line that carries the fly out to the fish must also match the rod – in other words, have the same AFTM class, in order to be cast properly. If the line is too heavy, the rod will be overloaded and the cast is shorter. Conversely, too

light a line will not load the rod sufficiently and the cast is less accurate.

The AFTM system is based on the weight of the line's outermost 30 ft (9.15 m), since it has been established that this length is what usually strains the rod. When fishing in small waterways, however, one often casts with a shorter and lighter line, which strains the rod less. This line cannot make the rod work as it is designed to do. A good idea is therefore to choose a heavier line class than recommended, if you are fishing mainly with short casts.

For relatively short casts, you can use both double-tapered (DT) and weight-forward (WF) lines. A DT line, unlike a WF line, can be turned round when one end is worn out. On the other hand, a WF line is superior for fishing dry flies downstream. It enables you to easily shake out further loose line through the eyes, something that is almost impossible with a DT line.

Streams are seldom especially deep, so a normal floating line is usually quite acceptable. If fish are holding near the bottom, the fly or leader can simply be weighted. During high spring water, though, it can be worth trying some type of sinking line to get down deep enough. This is particularly true when fishing streamers and bucktails. Then you can use a fully sinking line with an adequate sinking speed, depending on the current strength and water depth. The greater the latter are, the faster the line should sink.

But in many cases a fully sinking line is not very practical. If the stream contains a lot of big stones, the line will easily get caught on them. The alternative is to use a sink-tip, whose end takes the fly down to the fish. Its floating main line does not get caught on stones, and facilitates control as well as mending of the line.

The leader's length, just like the rod length, depends entirely on the conditions. It can vary from as short as 3 ft (0.9 m) to as long as 12 ft (3.6 m). The longest and thinnest

For a flyfisherman, the rod is absolutely the most important piece of equipment. It must not only act as an extended arm when casting and presenting the fly, but also be able to work as an efficient lever when playing a hooked fish.

leaders, of course, are used only in low clear water with shy, easily frightened fish. One must also keep in mind that the leader tippet should be extra long when fishing with very thin leaders. For the longer the tippet, the more elastic it is – a property that can be extremely useful, especially if your strike proves too hectic!

In normal fishing with a floating line, a good standard length is 9 ft (2.7 m). If fishing with small flies, you need only lengthen this leader with an extra-thin tippet. But using a big wet fly, streamer or bucktail, on a fully sinking or sink-tip line, is quite another matter. The priority is then to get the fly down to the fish. Current pressure on a long leader will lift the fly up from the bottom, away from the fish. So here one uses a short leader of at most 6 ft (1.8 m). The deeper the water, the shorter the leader – and the fly will in all probability reach the fish.

Short leaders can also be handy in dry-fly fishing. For example, in small overgrown waterways, a long leader is simply bothersome – just like a long rod. Instead, a leader of 6-7 ft (1.8-2.1 m) should be used.

The fly reel is the least important part of your equipment when flyfishing in streams. It acts only as a storage place for the thick fly line. Although one rarely encounters really big fish in these waters, one should always have at least 50 m (165 ft) of thin backing line innermost on the reel. Then you are safe even if an unexpected monster pops up to take the fly.

Suggestions for equipment

A good all-round set-up for flyfishing in streams will include a rod of 8-9 ft (2.4-2.7 m) in AFTM class 5-6. This rod can not only serve small dry flies and nymphs easily and elegantly. It also has enough strength for fishing with heavy nymphs as well as small streamers and bucktails. A floating WF line will fill most needs, and a sink-tip takes care of the rest. The reel should hold the fly line and 50 m (164 ft) of 20-lb backing line.

When summer is at its best, the water levels are often lowest. The water is then clear and the fish are shy. These conditions can require extremely small flies and hair-thin leader tippets; so you need extra light gear to handle them. A rod of 7-8 ft (2.1-2.4 m) in class 3-4 is suitable. It lays out dry flies of sizes 18-24 like dust grains on the water, and is flexible enough to play fish even on a leader of 0.12-0.14

mm (0.005 in)! No actual backing line is necessary, since the current pressure on a whole fly line will be sufficient to break the thin leader. Still, you should not choose the smallest "midging" reels for such fishing; they look very elegant, but their minimal diametre gives a braking effect that is too strong when the line rushes out. Do not use any reel less than 3 in (7.5 cm) wide.

When fishing with big heavy nymphs, or if you have a big streamer or bucktail on the leader, there is a need for stronger equipment. A rod of 9-10 ft (2.7-3.0 m) is enough, as it can withstand both the high spring water levels and any huge trout that happen to take the fly. For the same reasons, the reel should hold 100 m (328 ft) of 20-lb backing line in addition to a WF sink-tip line.

When fishing with big wet flies and streamers in deep and rapid waters, you should use a short leader, since the pressure of the current lifts up the leader and fly toward the surface – away from the fish, which often holds nearer the bottom.

Techniques and methods

Downstream wet-fly fishing

Fishing wet flies downstream is the oldest and commonest method. The line is cast across the current, or obliquely downstream, and the fly follows the flow freely until it drifts into a soft bend at your own bank. Often the fish takes just as the outward fishing is ending. Also illustrated here is the fly's drift when mending.

Naturally we begin with the most classic of flyfishing's many methods. The first true flies – long before dry ones appeared – were wet flies, and they were fished downstream. This approach involves simply laying a cast across, or obliquely down, the stream toward the opposite bank. As the current takes the line, the fly follows a curve in towards your own bank. You then take a step or two downstream and repeat the procedure. Thus you work your way down through the most promising stretches of water.

Here is a perfect method for the beginner. For if the cast is not laid out well, the current immediately stretches the

line and leader again. Besides, many fish get hooked of their own accord during downstream wet-fly fishing. So the method can hardly be more elementary – and still it is capable of refinements that make it amazingly effective in the right hands.

When·a fly line is laid straight across the current, it will be pulled downstream in a wide curve. If the current is strong, the pull is so violent that the fly travels across the surface. This is not attractive to fish, and you must compensate for the current's effect by mending the line. The technique is to lift the line from the water and to shift it

BUTCHER
Tying thread: black
Tail: red feather fibres
Body: flat silver tinsel
Ribbing: oval silver tinsel
Wings: blue mallard wing feather
Hackle: black hen feather fibres
Head: black

TEAL & RED
Tying thread: black
Tail: golden pheasant tippets
Body: bright red wool
Ribbing: thin oval silver tinsel
Wings: teal flank feather
Hackle: brown hen feather fibres
Head: black

MARCH BROWN
Tying thread: black
Tail: brown-speckled partridge feather fibres
Body: grey dubbed hare's fur
Ribbing: gold wire
Wings: pheasant hen wing feathers
Hackle: brown-speckled partridge feather fibres
Head: black

This hairwinged wet fly – with dubbed wool body, hen hackle, squirrel-tail hair wing and black head – displays no special pattern but is a type of fly that has become increasingly common recently. The USA in particular has a tradition of tying soft-hackled wet flies with hair wings. Even in many of the classic wet flies, it can help to replace the feather wings with thin hair wings, which last longer and make the fly at least as attractive to the fish.

upstream, reducing pressure on the current. You may have to do so several times as the fly swings through the current.

Until now, we have been describing the classic "wet-fly swing", which is as effective for trout and grayling as it is for salmon and for sea trout. The only difference is that, in streams, we try to imitate the fish's food with our flies. Depending on the current speed, the line can be mended either upstream – if a fast current threatens to tear the fly out of the water – or else downstream. The latter applies if the fly happens to drift into calm water, where it will stop and sink rather lifelessly. This is avoided by mending the line downstream so that the current can take the line and fly again. You are then helping the current instead of fighting it.

Thus, when fishing in streams, mending the line is as important as making fine, exact casts. If you can't mend the line, you can't fish effectively either!

The fly may be allowed to drift straight across the current by itself, or it may be jerked now and then with the rod tip. Fishermen disagree as to which of these techniques is best, but this depends basically on the fly's size. Small flies imitate small insects, which obviously lack enough strength to fight a fast current, and will therefore drift away rather life-lessly. But big flies imitate big insects or even fish fry, which can easily travel against the current. Consequently, small flies (size 12-14) should be fished with no rod movement, whereas larger flies (size 8-10) should be given extra life with the rod tip.

Many of the classic wet flies that are fished downstream were originally imitations of drowned or drowning mayflies. Examples are March Brown and Blue Dun, which should thus be fished by "dead drift" – with no rod movement. But it is more sensible to invest in fly patterns that represent fish fry to a greater extent. These are illustrated by Alexandra, Bloody Butcher and Freeman's Fancy, all with bodies of silver or gold tinsel. A downstream wet fly can be made more functional by replacing the original feather-wing with a more mobile and durable hairwing.

This kind of fishing is often regarded with some disdain as a sort of "fishing machine", covering the waterway mechanically and without any real enjoyment. That may at times be so, but never need be. It is up to the fisherman whether the fishing is to be inspired or routine. Those with insight do not fish through the stream inch by inch, but concentrate on the spots or holding places which look most promising – or on fish that reveal themselves in various ways.

If you have noticed a fish or know a good holding place, here is a useful trick. Lay your fly a fair distance upstream of the fish or holding place, with a slack line. This gives the fly time to sink a little, before the current stretches out the line and leader. When the line tightens, the fly moves up in the water and swings out towards midstream. Often the strike comes just then, as though you were pressing a but-

ton – so effective is the trick if done right. The best flies to use are wet ones with a silver or gold body and a thin hairwing. The leader must be thin, of 0.18 mm (007 in), so that the fly can sink and move freely in the current.

When fishing out, you should make sure that the fly always fishes at the proper speed. If it starts to drag in the surface, decrease the force on it by lowering the rod tip; and if necessary, mend the line upstream. But if the fly drifts into calm water, raise the rod tip; and if this is not enough, mend the line downstream. Eventually the fly will arrive at your own bank, or downstream of you. Then you can begin a new cast.

If the water is deep and being fished from a bank, it should be fished thoroughly before taking in the line for a new cast. This can be done by pulling the line in small jerks with your left hand. Sometimes surprising results are achieved by taking in the line a little faster. A fish may rush in to snap up the fly and disappear!

On a taut line with a wet fly downstream, many fish are hooked in the actual strike. They take the fly and travel with the current, but soon realize their error. The fly does not "taste" right and they reject it. Then the strike must be quick – though not violent. It should be a controlled tightening of the line, rather than a literal striking action.

Frequently the fish can be seen taking the fly in a swirl just under the surface, whereupon you must immediately tighten the line. At other times you can only feel, or see, a gentle tug on the line – so you have to react even faster. There is always more time to spare if you see the fish take than if you simply feel it. Keep your eyes open in order to hook the fish solidly!

The fish didn't have time to reject the fly. It was hooked with a lightning-quick strike and landed after a nerve-wracking fight.

Upstream wet-fly fishing

Here is another of the classic methods in flyfishing. It has a lasting association with the Scotsman Stewart and his now legendary "spider" flies. Stewart fished along streams in the Scottish highlands, where the insect life was poor but sudden floods, or spates, were frequent after rainstorms. Thus the fish were seldom large and, though always hungry, they were shy and easily frightened in these small waterways.

As a professional fisherman who lived on his catches, Stewart recognized that downstream wet-fly fishing would not do under such conditions. He began to fish with wet flies in the opposite direction, and tied them so that they were specially adapted to this kind of fishing. His spider flies are simple, with a sparse but very soft hackle, whose fibres truly come alive in the current. They were the fore-

The method of fishing a wet fly upstream is used mainly when the fish is very shy. It is also notably effective, since you are behind the fish and cannot frighten it as easily.

runners of the now well-known "soft hackles", which can be said to represent the fish's food rather than actually imitating it.

Upstream fishing has several clear advantages, but also demands more of the fisherman. This is perceived as soon as you try it. For the current is a real problem here, as it brings the fly right back to you – and frustratingly fast, if you have not yet learned to control the loose line.

Nonetheless, you can then approach the fish from behind, where it is least attentive. And the fly is presented

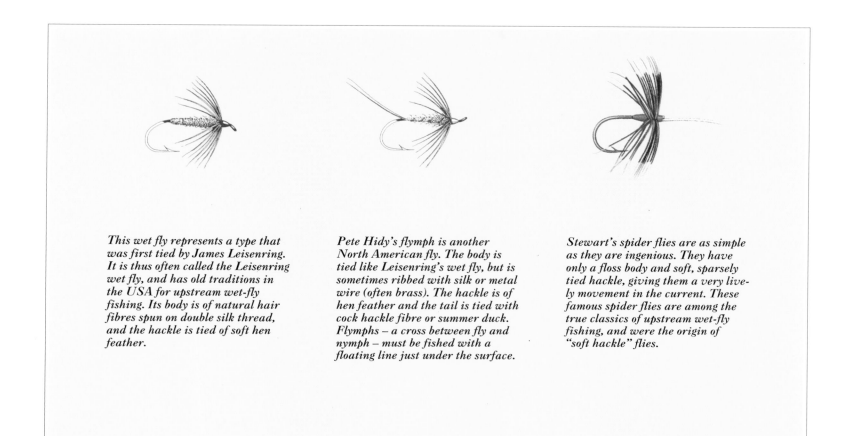

This wet fly represents a type that was first tied by James Leisenring. It is thus often called the Leisenring wet fly, and has old traditions in the USA for upstream wet-fly fishing. Its body is of natural hair fibres spun on double silk thread, and the hackle is tied of soft hen feather.

Pete Hidy's flymph is another North American fly. The body is tied like Leisenring's wet fly, but is sometimes ribbed with silk or metal wire (often brass). The hackle is of hen feather and the tail is tied with cock hackle fibre or summer duck. Flymphs – a cross between fly and nymph – must be fished with a floating line just under the surface.

Stewart's spider flies are as simple as they are ingenious. They have only a floss body and soft, sparsely tied hackle, giving them a very lively movement in the current. These famous spider flies are among the true classics of upstream wet-fly fishing, and were the origin of "soft hackle" flies.

in the same way as the fish is accustomed to seeing food: drifting freely with the current. Even if upstream fishing is more demanding than downstream fishing, it is a far more effective method in trained hands.

The fly is laid with short casts upstream to the presumed holding places or observed fish. As the current brings it back again, you must take in the loose line and raise the rod tip, so that you always have full control over the fly and its journey through the water. With short casts, raising the rod tip while the fly drifts is sufficient – but with longer casts, loose line must be taken in as well. A long, soft rod of 9-10 ft (2.7-3.0 m) in class 5-6 is ideal for this exciting method, since you thus obtain the best possible line control.

The strike is made when you see the fish turn with the fly. Good eyesight is therefore essential. Here you do not have, as in downstream fishing, the chance to feel the fish

strike – for the line is not taut. If you don't see the strike, the fish will almost always have time to spit out the fly. But if you are quick enough, the fish gets hooked even more solidly than in downstream fishing, where you cannot avoid occasionally pulling the fly out of the fish's mouth. So this is another advantage of the present method.

Upstream dry-fly fishing

Althogh it was not Halford who "invented" the floating fly, this Englishman's name will forever be associated with the emergence of dry-fly fishing, which he systematized in order to make it an exact science. The purist members of his imitation school thought that dry-fly fishing with exact copies was the only proper form of the sport.

However, as we have already noted, this view soon developed into fanaticism. Imitations were tied of numerous insects – primarily mayflies – which occur on the southern English chalk streams, and these were imitations not only of the species, but also of both sexes and their stages of development in each species! The school went so far in many places as to ban all other kinds of fishing.

Dry-fly fishing is usually considered the most exciting form of flyfishing, since one can follow the whole course of events clearly. The advantage of upstream dry-fly fishing is that dragging flies can be avoided to some extent. The illustration shows this method with a curve cast.

Although fortunately we are no longer so narrow-minded, it must be admitted that dry-fly fishing is among the most fascinating pastimes imaginable. Here one sees the fish first, then one tries to figure out what it eats. A corresponding dry fly is chosen and presented as correctly as possible to the fish. If everything is done well, the fish rises to the fly and sucks it in – right before the fisherman's eyes, as exciting as can be.

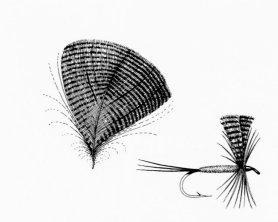

Dry flies of American type have soft wings from the flank feathers of ducks, mainly summer duck. Some well-known examples are the Cahill series, of which Light Cahill is perhaps the most renowned.

"Spent spinners" are mayflies that fall down dead on the water surface with outspread wings after laying eggs. The wings of their imitations can, of course, be tied with feather sections in the time-honoured way, but are increasingly being replaced by synthetic materials, and thus tend to be called "spent polywings". On spent spinners the tail and wing are separated into two equal parts with figure-of-eight tying.

A classic English dry fly. In this type of fly, the wings are made of quill sections. Some good instances are Black Gnat, Coachman, Greenwell's Glory and Blue Dun.

Parachute-tied dry flies have the hackle tied in horizontally, wound around the wing root. Here, too, it has recently become ever more common to use synthetic materials in the wings, making "parachute-tied polywings". They can imitate a large number of species, and are thus quite handy and effective on many waters.

Some people regard dry-fly fishing as a simple, easy method. For the whole sequence of events is visible, in contrast to wet-fly fishing where, instead, you need a sort of "sixth sense" to tell you where and how to fish. Yet dry-fly fishing makes clear demands of good casting technique and line control. Whereas a few fish can often be caught by wet flies even with poor technique, dry-fly fishing is uncompromising in its own way. If you cannot present a dry fly lightly, elegantly, and at just the right spot – and if you cannot make sure that it floats freely over the fish without dragging, you won't get any fish. That's just how simple it is!

Dry-fly fishermen soon discovered the advantages of fishing upstream, and this method is still required on most of the classic English chalk streams. One locates a rising fish and sneaks up on it from behind, to within casting distance. The fly is placed far enough upstream so that the fish will have time to notice the fly and, hopefully, rise to it.

The main problem is "dragging" flies. These are dry flies that do not follow the current freely, but make furrows on the water surface. This is because the fly, leader and line do not drift with the same speed. When the fisherman stands on land or in the water, the current pressure on the line and leader will soon be transferred to the fly. It starts to drag immediately, no longer drifting freely like a natural insect, and is therefore usually rejected by the fish.

If you cast a dry fly straight upstream, this problem tends to be minimal. Then the current pressure is normally the same on the line, leader and fly, so they drift with the same speed as the loose line is taken in with your left hand.

Casting straight upstream to a fish that rises, however, will take the line and leader right over its head. This is bound to displease it and, in most cases, it will be frightened and stop rising. To avoid spoiling the opportunity, you should present the fly a little from one side. Lay it at an angle against the current, so that the line and leader do not hit the water over the fish.

As a result, though, the current will push differently on the line, leader and fly. If you leave it at that, the fly will very soon begin to drag, with greater pressure on the line than on the fly. But this can be prevented in various ways, with more or less advanced "trick" casts.

The simplest solution is to cast out a curved line instead of a straight, stretched one. Then the fly undergoes at least a short delay in floating freely downstream before the current has stretched the line, and hopefully the delay will be long enough for the fish to take the fly. Casting a curved

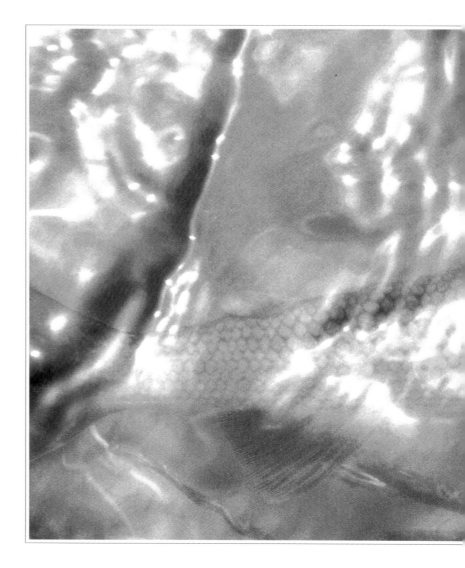

line is fairly easy. Most simply, the rod top is shaken from side to side when the line is stretched in the forward cast but is still in the air. This is commonly known as the serpentine cast.

It is much harder to produce so-called "curve casts". We speak of left-hand and right-hand curve casts, or positive and negative ones. The basic idea, of course, is to give the fly extra time to drift freely. Yet curve casts require such fantastic casting ability of the fisherman that most of us give up. They need training and a good understanding of the dynamics of the cast. Here we shall have to pass over these specialized techniques.

*Grayling is a very popular quarry for flyfishermen
in some parts of the world. In northern Scandinavia
and the Alps, it can be tempted with a dry fly fished
upstream.*

Downstream dry-fly fishing

Fishing upstream with a dry fly can be justified on many good grounds, as we have seen – when the conditions are right for it. But by no means are they always so. Often a better method is to fish the same fly downstream, quite contrary to the classic and puritanical dry-fly school. Halford would turn in his grave if he could watch such a method being practised on his beloved chalk streams.

The English chalk streams, whose banks were the original cradle of dry-fly fishing, are relatively small and narrow waterways. They provide every reason to fish the fly upstream. Yet when fishing in larger and broader waterways, we frequently meet fish that simply cannot be reached by casting a dry fly upstream. It is then necessary to fish straight across the current, or even downstream, in order to get at the fish.

In large, broad streams, it may be hard to reach the fish if you are fishing a dry fly upstream. Then often your only chance is to fish downstream. A stop cast as illustrated here, or the similar parachute cast, is frequently essential to prevent the fly from dragging as soon as it reaches the water.

Henry's Fork Hopper is a typical American grasshopper imitation. Its body is tied with deer hair, and the wing with brown-speckled feather fibres. The deer hairs are folded backward at the head and clipped off on the fly's underside. These hollow air-filled hairs give the fly its excellent floating quality.

Here is another grasshopper imitation, loved by trout especially in the USA. This type of fly is characterized by the Muddler head, tied with deer hair and trimmed to the right shape.

Bivisible is an example of a Palmer-hackled dry fly. The hackle is wound over the whole body, from tail to head. This fly can be tied in many colour variants, but all have white hackle closest to the head.

Dry flies with bushy hackle are definitely good all-round imitations, and float very well even in fast currents. They are also easy to tie and to vary in colours. To be really effective, they are often tied with two hackles, wound in sequence.

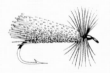

Humpy is still another high-floating fly for downstream dry-fly fishing. It has a big bushy hackle of cock feather, as well as a tail and "body cover" of deer hair. This makes the fly float nicely even in strong current.

Goddard's Caddis was originally tied as an imitation of large caddis flies, but in the USA it is also used on waters where fish eat grasshoppers. It is tied mainly with air-filled deer hairs that make it float high, enabling it to rush across the water surface like a caddis fly or terrestrial insect in a hurry to reach land.

When fishing a dry fly across the stream, you may well have to mend the line upstream at intervals. Still better, though, is to learn the "reach" cast: after the cast has ended, but while the line is still in the air, you hold the rod upstream with an outstretched arm. Thus the dry fly receives a further delay before it begins to drag. Obviously the longer your rod and arms, the longer time the fly will spend drifting freely down towards the fish.

For fishing more directly downstream, the reach cast is not very helpful. Then you should use the parachute cast, whose name tells a lot about how it is done. Quite simply, the forward cast stops too soon, making the line stretch out while high up in the air. Holding the rod tip aloft, you let the fly line fall lightly and elegantly onto the water. The leader, which weighs almost nothing, follows passively along and comes down in a heap. This enables the fly to float freely a while longer, as you calmly lower the rod top and finish with your arms outstretched as usual.

The parachute cast is as indispensable for downstream fishing as the reach cast is for cross-current fishing. In both cases, you can lengthen the fly's free drift by releasing a few metres of loose line through the rod rings. For this to work, the line absolutely must be a weight-forward line, whose thin shooting line is easy to shake out.

As noted previously, fish take only the insects which are on the water surface within a rather narrow region overhead. If the cast is too long, downstream dry-fly fishing allows you to correct it by simply pulling the fly back into place! Once the desired path of drift is attained, you decrease the pressure and release some loose line. This must be done fast, since the line is now taut all the way to the fly.

The same technique can pay off when you need to skate a dry fly across to the fish. Until now, we have tried to make the fly drift as freely and peacefully as possible, and this is certainly the only good rule in most cases. But if, for example, there are big caddis flies, or insects that flutter about on the water surface, then a dragging dry fly is often the only thing that works.

Getting an upstream dry fly to drag realistically is out of the question. Natural insects invariably fight against the current – not along with it. The current threatens to push them downstream, which they actively oppose. This behaviour is best imitated by fishing downstream with a dry fly that alternately drags and drifts freely.

The technique can be guided by raising the rod top with a taut line at intervals to release more loose line. But watch out – the strikes become violent when the fly is fished in

this way. Here you need a controlled strike as well as a strong leader!

Strikes are relatively complicated, in either upstream or downstream fishing with a dry fly. Indeed they vary from fish to fish, and between different fishing waters. Thus, both fast and slow strikes can be useful in dry-fly fishing. Yet this can be quite frustrating to a beginner: the fly may be torn out of the fish's mouth, or will already have been rejected by it, if the strike is respectively too fast or slow. Luckily, there is a kind of system to follow. Calm fish should be hooked with a calm strike, and quick fish with a quick strike.

In downstream dry-fly fishing, you can easily imitate the insects that fight against the current, by raising and lowering the rod tip. This allows the fly to drag against the current at the surface, or to drift freely a bit downstream. The fish may then take violently when they no longer can stand the temptation.

For instance, a trout that is holding in a quiet pocket on the edge of a strong current may be in a hurry to take insects on the surface. It shoots up, sucks in the prey and darts back to the depths. Naturally a dry fly will be taken in the same way, but since the fish is accustomed to a fast pace, it is quick to spit out the fly – so the strike must be made instantly.

The opposite is true of a fish that holds in calm water and sucks in spent spinners and other small insects. Knowing that it has plenty of time, it rises slowly to the surface and lingers confidently, sucking in the helpless insects. A dry fly is taken with equal laziness, and a fast strike would be sure to tear the fly out of the fish's mouth. Consequently, the fisherman must control himself – if possible – and delay the strike until the fish is on the way down with the fly. This can be as difficult as it is exciting!

These two general situations are easy to deal with in practice, as we can decide in advance which type of strike should be used. However, one is often forced to make the choice during the strike itself, and that may be even harder.

In calm waters, the fish sometimes makes a side-detour to take a good morsel which it has seen from a distance. It has to hurry, and its strike is more violent than usual. The same happens if the fish rises at the last moment for a poorly placed dry fly which drifts far to the side. We may have decided in advance that this particular fish requires a calm strike, but now we must make a new decision in a fraction of a second! Similarly, if the fish takes hatching insects that can lift from the water at any time, it may act speedily and require a quick strike.

In general, small fish are fast and big ones are slow. So the rule of thumb is that big fish should be given more time to take the fly and descend with it. This can be difficult to follow in practice – especially if you have been fishing all day for small trout and grayling, which call for quick strikes and may make you unable to change your style. If you then happen to confront the biggest fish of the day, or even of the year, it is worth taking a pause. But once the situation is clear to you, there should be less trouble in adjusting. You can always close your eyes and count to three as the fish takes the dry fly!

Finally keep in mind that, if the fish takes the fly on a long cast, the strike must be made faster than usual. The longer your line is, the longer time it needs to transfer the strike to the fish. Conversely, with a short line you can hook the fish at a more relaxed pace.

Nymph fishing

While puristic dry-fly fanaticism was at its height along the southern English chalk streams, a prominent lawyer strolled by those waters, deep in fresh thought. Professionally he was accustomed to reasons and logical proofs – an ability which he extended to his observations on the fishing waters.

G. E. M. Skues became the next pioneer of flyfishing. He realized that the trout in his chalk streams did not by any means always take the winged insects on the surface – even if Halford wished that they did! Quite often, the fish instead took nymphs just under the surface.

These facts led Skues to tie the first true nymph flies. They not only sank like wet flies, but were also imitations as exact as the dry flies of that time. With them, he fished precisely as though they were dry flies; the only difference was that they were presented freely drifting under, or in, the water surface.

When fishing with a nymph, the fly often must be given time to sink down to the depth where the fish stand. So you have to place the weighted nymph as far up as the current allows, to give a more realistic presentation. But it may be hard to detect when the fish takes the nymph, so you must pay attention and try to see whether the fish suddenly darts away to the side, or if the floating part of the leader suddenly dives.

Such "wet-fly fishing" did not appeal to Halford and his disciples. As a result, Skues had to struggle for years before his method was accepted as a worthy alternative to dry-fly fishing. As luck had it, he succeeded.

The next step towards modern flyfishing was made by Frank Sawyer, a riverkeeper on the River Avon. His job afforded much time to study fish in their natural element. Thus he discovered that the trout were often active along the bottom, when no activity was occurring at the surface. Obviously the fish consumed food, so they ought to be catchable.

This is a type of nymph which imitates stonefly nymphs. It comes from the northwestern USA, where it is very popular in fishing for cutthroat trout, rainbow trout and brown trout. The body is often a combination of dubbed material and plastic strips in different colours. The wing cases are of either plastic or tied-down feather sections, the tail and antennae of stiff fibres. Usually it is weighted or tied on a heavy hook.

This Skues nymph is tied with a sneck-bend hook and shows how Skues himself tied it. The nymph has a small dubbed rear body with a conspicuous dubbed breast section, but also soft antennae and a soft hackle. It must not be weighted, as it is usually fished in the upper water or in shallow currents.

Frank Sawyer's classic Pheasant Tail is a very simple but effective fly. It imitates small, not yet developed, nymphs. The fly is weighted with copper wire to sink fast to the bottom, and is thus well suited to upstream nymph fishing, since it must be fished without any extra movements.

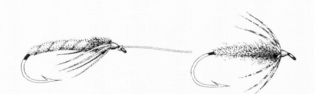

Here are two types of caddis-fly pupae with dubbed bodies. These bind microscopic air bubbles to themselves, giving them a silvery appearance like the hatching insect. The imitations can also be provided with "lively" wing cases or hackle, and the body can be ribbed with wire. Such flies may be fished at all levels in the current, depending on how much they are weighted.

Just as Skues tied his nymphs as imitations of fully developed mayfly nymphs, Sawyer created the astonishingly simple Pheasant Tail Nymphs, representing smaller nymphs that were not yet fully developed like adults. He had noticed that these always held their legs to the body when swimming. For the same reason, in contrast to Skues, he omitted the hackle from his flies. Instead, he weighted them so that they would sink quickly to the bottom and, therefore, to the fish. Sawyer fished his nymphs upstream towards observed fish, without making any extra movements.

Oliver Kite, also a denizen of the Avon, developed this technique further with his "induced take". If the fish will not take a freely drifting nymph, the cast is repeated and the fly is lifted up in front of the fish's nose – like an escaping insect. And not many fish can resist that!

Nymph fishing has long been reserved for the calm, crystal-clear chalk streams, where fish are easy to perceive and the classic upstream presentation is both possible and suitable. Yet these conditions do not always exist elsewhere. In many places the current is too fast for this technique. In most cases, we have no chance of locating the fish before casting to it, either because of the fast current or because the water is too deep and murky. Here, we need new methods, or else modifications of the old ones.

In almost every way, nymph fishing is a cross between dry-fly and wet-fly fishing. You can fish upstream or downstream, with a floating or a sinking line. The flies vary from the biggest to the smallest, and are fished underwater like wet flies, but are tied as pure imitations like dry flies. Such a range of variations is enough to confuse even the most zealous beginner at flyfishing.

There is, however, a certain system in the methods and their use. Pure upstream fishing can be done only when the current is not too strong. Under calm conditions, you can fish with a floating line, long leaders and weighted flies. You cast to observed fish or presumed holding places. At all events, the aim is to place the nymph so far upstream of the fish, or holding place, that the fly has time to sink to the right depth.

Once the nymph is at the fish's level, the problem is to detect a strike. This is easy enough if you can see the fish and fly clearly. If only the fish is visible, you must watch for it to make a quick turn aside, when the fly is presumed to be nearby. The white gape of the fish's mouth is a sure sign that it has taken the fly or a natural insect. Whatever happens, you must tighten the line instantly, so that the fish will not have time to spit out the fly. It may hold a very small nymph in its mouth for a long while, and then it is usually hooked well – all the way down in its throat.

If you see neither fish nor fly, you can only rely on the visible signs at the water surface. The line tip or the leader's floating – possibly greased – section may suddenly be drawn under the water. Life is definitely made easier by using a "strike indicator", consisting of a little cork ball, a piece of foam rubber, or a stub of poly yarn. This works like a float and reacts immediately if the fly is taken. Its location along the leader depends on the fishing depth.

Upstream nymph fishing with a floating line and a long leader can be done with any size of nymph. If you choose to fish downstream, you must remember that only relatively large, powerful insects are able to fight against the current. Small mayfly nymphs have no chance, so it is understandable why the flyfishermen on the classic chalk streams always fish their small nymphs of size 14-16 upstream. Anything else would involve an unrealistic presentation of the fly.

Notably active and strong swimmers are the big caddisfly pupae, which like to oppose the current. Therefore, imi-

When a large trout takes drifting midge pupae in the surface layer, often only its back fin and part of the back appear above the surface.

tations of them can be fished downstream to advantage, meaning nymphs of size 8-12. According to the current, they are fished with a floating, sinking, or sink-tip line. Here a sink-tip is preferable to a fully sinking line, since – like a floating line – it allows regular mending of the line, which in turn enables the fly to fish correctly. Just as in ordinary downstream wet-fly fishing, the fly should not normally drag.

In really strong currents, nymphs must be fished upstream, using strong equipment, a fast-sinking line, a short leader and large weighted flies. The flies are usually imitation stoneflies of size 2-8. As such fishing is a little violent, its practitioners are not very numerous. The fly is transported upstream with short casts, enabling it to sink before it passes right in front of the fisherman. While the line is sinking, the current pulls it away, so the point is to hold as much as possible of the line out of the water as the fly sinks. This is best done by holding the rod top high with outstretched arms.

If everything else has been done right, the big nymph will have reached the correct fishing depth when it is just in

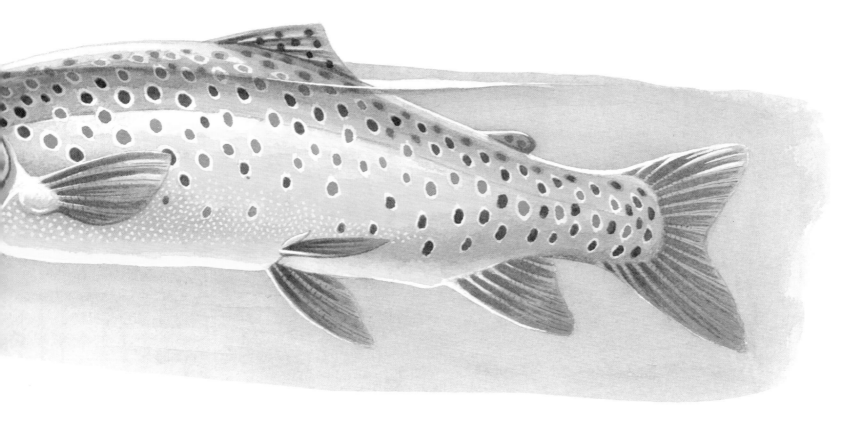

front of you. Only then does it begin to fish. You must therefore let the nymph drift freely over the bottom as far as possible, by lowering the rod top at the pace of the fly's drift. Most fish take when your line and arms are stretched downstream, since the fly then starts to climb and swing out of the stream. The strike feels violent in the hard current, but the fish is often poorly hooked. Thus a certain percentage of fish is always lost by this method, but it is still the only one that works well in strong currents.

Finally, a word about the rather unusual form of nymph fishing which occurs each summer in Alaskan rivers. It uses so-called "roe flies" that imitate, in colour and form, individual fish eggs. During the summer, thousands of Pacific salmon migrate up these rivers to spawn and die. On the journey upstream, they are accompanied by grayling, Arctic char, and rainbow trout – which intend to eat the roe left by the spawning salmon. This annual drama is a fascinating sight. Like small grey-black shadows, the roe-eaters flit among the large salmon at the spawning grounds. When the female salmon releases some roe, they dash forward and partake of it, before the male salmon chases them away.

As the salmon are so plentiful, the roe is a very important supplement to the diets of other fish in the rivers. For the same reason, roe flies are extremely valuable to the fly-fishermen who swing their rods in Alaska during these periods. The round, fluorescent flies should not be missing in any fly box!

Roe flies are fished exactly like the nymph fisherman's other imitations, by "dead drift" right over the bottom. Normally you can get by with a floating line and long leader, but in some reaches of water it can be necessary to fish with a sink-tip line. As a rule, the current is strong just over the spawning bottoms.

These flies can be weighted so that they sink quickly to the fish, but then they do not sway freely with the current. So it is better to weight the leader – by fastening lead shot to one of the blood knot's loose ends, or winding lead wire round the leader just above the lowest knot. The fly will thus come down to the bottom and, at the same time, drift freely with the current. This approach can also be used to advantage with any other nymphs.

Streamer fishing

Fishing with streamers and bucktails is both the easiest way of flyfishing, and the method that yields the biggest fish! This may sound paradoxical, but it isn't. There are two reasons: you can do nothing wrong with a big streamer or bucktail, and the fact is that big fish prefer big flies.

Streamers and bucktails represent various small fish, and are tied on long-shanked hooks. In addition, they may be pure fantasy creations. A streamer is tied with soft feather-wings, of saddle hackle or marabou, and it is intended for fishing in relatively small and calm waters. By contrast, bucktails are provided with hairwing – originally hair from a deer's tail, whence the name – and they are consequently suitable for fishing in broad, fast waters. Historically, streamers belong to the American east coast, while bucktails come from the west coast. But apart from that, they are fished in the same way.

The nice thing about small fish compared with tiny insects and crustaceans is that, to a great extent, they can oppose the current. Being strong swimmers, they commonly dare to enter more open and rapid water. As a result, the flyfisherman can fish his flies almost anywhere he likes: up or down or across the stream, either fast or slow. The fly will be equally attractive in all cases, and you need not worry about whether the fly will drag. At the same time, with big flies, we address the largest fish in the water, which of course are notorious fish-eaters. Really large fish have long ago given up eating small insects in favour of more substantial young fish. Otherwise they would never have reached the size that makes them so desirable to us!

Trout are the commonest guests of our fly rods when we fish with streamers and bucktails. Grayling prefer insects and other small creatures, although this does not prevent large grayling from occasionally taking a small streamer. When it comes to trout, one can get the feeling that not even the largest streamer is large enough.

The great majority of small fish in flowing waters are definite bottom-dwellers. This applies not least to the minnows – already mentioned – and the sculpins, which exist in many fast rivers around the world. They not only live on the bottom, but actually spend most of their time resting on it.

All this means that the flyfisherman's long-shanked flies should be fished as deep as possible, with a sink-tip or fully sinking line. Only in the smallest, shallowest waters can you get by with a floating line. On the other hand, you can fish rather daringly with these big flies: fast or slow, upstream or downstream. There are unimagined possibilities of variation, in contrast to the usual fishing with wet flies or nymphs.

It is more than a matter of using your imagination. If the fish does not take a freely drifting streamer, try instead taking home the line very quickly. Now and then you can even "awaken" a lazy trout by letting the fly splash down right on top of its head. One must admit that this is not an elegant manner of flyfishing, but it can be extraordinarily productive.

Normally we fish streamers and bucktails as imitations of the small fish that exist in the given waterway. They are tied, and fished, with maximum realism. However, the usefulness of these long-shafted flies hardly stops there. They are also effective in provoking the waterway's spawning fish to strike.

As noted in Chapter 2, trout are aggressive fish that defend individual territories in the stream. They are aggressive all year round, but this behaviour becomes ever more manifest as the spawning time approaches and they defend their territory with fury against any intruder. The flyfisherman can take advantage of this situation when the fishing season is coming to an end and the trout's spawning time arrives. Then the fish may be hard to attract with ordinary imitation flies since, having feasted all summer, they are fastidious and well-nourished. Besides, they are ever less interested in food and increasingly concerned with spawning.

It is then time to serve a big, colourful streamer or bucktail – a fly whose size and hue can, by themselves, give the fish an impression that some possible rival is encroaching on its territory.

This method of fishing can be pretty exciting. It is important to have a good knowledge of the locality, so that you know exactly where the fish are holding. You have to seek them out with streamers and bucktails of large size, and present the fly right in front of them repeatedly until they react. Often nothing happens on the first cast, so you must continue stubbornly. For the more glimpses the fish

Big fish gladly take big flies. Towards the end of the season, when trout are no longer so interested in small insect imitations and try to defend their territory more actively, a streamer or bucktail can be quite effective.

In recent years the word "streamer" has wrongly come to mean all flies tied on long-shanked hooks with long featherwings or hairwings. A traditional streamer, however, has only wings made of long hackle feathers, tied in at the head. The body is often of floss or flat tinsel, ribbed with oval tinsel.

Thunder Creek is an American type of fly meant to imitate small fish fry. Since the food of fish can vary around the world, this fly should be tied in the colours that best resemble small fish in your own water. The wings are tied in three steps: a thin bucktail wing on the hook shank, bent backward; then a dark bunch on the upper side and a light bunch on the underside, both pointing forward; finally the bunches are bent backward and fastened with tying thread.

It is typical of Matuka streamers that the wing feathers are wound along the whole body. The fibres on the undersides of two hackle feathers are removed, and the wing is placed on top of the hook shaft and fastened at the head. Then the ribbing is wound carefully forward through the wing and is attached at the head. Finally a false hackle is tied in.

Bucktails, as the name implies, were originally tied with deer-tail hair. But today they are tied with various types of hair, for example from calf tail, squirrel tail, polar bear or goat. The body is tied, just as in a streamer, of floss and/or tinsel – the wing and hackle being tied in at the head. One may also tie in a tail of coloured or plain feather fibres.

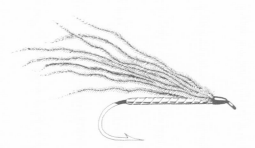

Long-shanked hooks of streamer type, with marabou-feather wings, have become ever more popular. The advantage of this amazingly soft wing material is that it gives a lifelike impression in the water, often attracting fish to take. Such wings create little air resistance, so you can swing out rather large flies even with a relatively light-actioned rod.

The rainbow trout – whose seagoing variant is the steelhead – belongs to those species that gladly take a well-served streamer or bucktail.

gets of the fly, the more irritated it becomes. Finally it cannot endure the temptation and tries to chase away the fly.

At first you frequently feel only a strong blow against the fly, without hooking the fish. The fly has thus only been hit, not taken in the fish's mouth. Yet there is a good chance that one of the following casts will result in a solid strike by what may be the season's largest trout. In any case, such fishing is fascinating once the quarry has been aroused.

In Alaska and British Columbia, every year sees a rather special kind of streamer fishing for large rainbow trout and Arctic char. It takes place when extensive schools of salmon smolt begin their migration downstream toward the Pacific Ocean. They are often smolt from sockeye salmon, which emerge from lakes in the water system – of which the predatory fish are well aware. So the latter gather at the outlets of lakes to feast on the young salmon. If you stumble upon such a smolt migration, you are sure to have exceptional fishing experiences for quite a while. Sparsely dressed streamers and bucktails are the only thing worth putting on your leader.

In several places farther north, trout are regularly caught with mice or lemmings in their stomachs. These small rodents provide the fish with huge chunks of concentrated protein, yielding a colossal spurt in growth. Thus, during good years for mice and lemmings, they are the sole diet of many large trout, and you need to "match the hatch" by serving a delicious deer-hair "mouse" that floats on the water surface. This mouse is fished dragging, and the fish takes it with a savage strike.

An important point is to fish near the banks, where the fish are accustomed to seeing mice or lemmings tumble in. Big flies are required, so you have to give the fish plenty of time to take the fly before tightening up on the line. Otherwise you will only tear the mouse out of its mouth. Whoever has tried this fishing once is sold on it for a lifetime!

If you fish a deer-hair mouse in quiet parts of a stream, it is often attacked by pike, which offer an entertaining sort of fishing. Pike are not distinctive stream fish, and avoid the fast sections of a waterway, but they can be abundant in sections with deep calm water. Here you may also find small schools of perch that gladly take a little silvery streamer.

Catch and Release

Whatever the method of fishing, stocks of fish in streams are fairly vulnerable. The quantities of food, and therefore also of fish, are strictly limited. In addition, every waterway has only enough holding places for a certain number of fish, especially when they are trout. As a result, we obviously cannot catch more than a small number of fish in small streams, and then only if the streams are in their natural condition.

Today, most waterways are far from being in as good condition as they should be. Damming, regulation and pollution have gone mad among them. In many places, this has meant that no natural reproduction exists any longer. A lot of waters contain only stocked fish. Thus a natural waterway with natural fish stocks is an extremely valuable resource that should be treated with great care.

Rational fish management, in the latter case, is not conducted by harvesting any surplus, but by protecting the fish that are there already. The best approach, of course, is to leave the fish in peace – with no sportfishing. But the next best, and most realistic, is to put back the fish that are caught. This policy is what Americans call "Catch and Release", or "No Kill".

"Catch and Release" is undoubtedly the future basis of fishing management. With a steadily rising pressure on our fishing waters, there is no alternative, unless we degenerate to plain "put and take". Sportfishermen simply cannot afford to continue harvesting the last stocks of wild fish.

"No Kill" is not a form of snobbery, as many Europeans unhappily believe. It is a rational form of fishing management that has been used professionally in the United States for the past 10-15 years, and with good results. There, most fishing is open to whoever has obtained a fishing licence in the given state. Only in a few places is fishing subject to private ownership as in Europe.

The fight is over. A tired-out fish slides slowly up from the sea, ready to be landed...

This status has made possible a coordinated, more effective fishing management in large water systems, as well as a test of "No Kill" and its effects on a suitably large scale. The American fishing authorities can, whenever they think necessary, impose new and stricter regulations for a particular fishing area. They can immediately raise the minimum size, decrease the allowed number of fish caught, put a waterway under protection – or introduce "No Kill".

The whole process has been gone through in the United States. It began with virgin waters that offered fabulous fishing to the relatively few sportsmen of those times. There were plenty of fish, and big ones. Yet after World War II, the fishing pressure really began to grow, and many such waters were fished out. The authorities set out quantities of new fish, and once again there was a quarry to catch. This was straightforward "put and take" fishing. Next, however, critical voices spoke up. People did not want to have fish regardless of the price. They wanted quality fish – born in the wild and raised in natural waters, not in fish farms. It took a long time before the authorities reacted, initially with stronger restrictions on fishing, and later by introducing the first clear "No Kill" stretches on special waterways.

These stretches soon became popular, since big fish were still to be found there, offering a real challenge to the more demanding sportfishermen. At the same time, many scientific studies showed that the natural fish stocks were growing healthily under this radical form of fishing management. "No Kill" spread subsequently to numerous other waters.

There is no point in introducing "Catch and Release" if flyfishermen do not know how to handle the fish that are caught. All too many will die after being released. But if the fish are handled properly, they will quickly regain strength – and be able to give some other fisherman a lively experience later on. As Lee Wulff once expressed it: "A trout is too valuable to be caught only once!"

The following rules should therefore be followed when releasing fish:

– Use barbless hooks, which make the releasing much easier. They hook the fish better than ordinary hooks do, and are still a lot easier to remove. Press down the barb, file it off, or use true barbless hooks. If a barbed hook sits deep, clip off the leader near the hook and leave it there; the fish will then get rid of it.

– Fight the fish as quickly as possible. This prevents the formation of too much lactic acid in the fish. Never use a leader which is thinner than necessary for this. Super-thin leaders are not "sporting": rather the opposite.

... and to be put back. But be careful to handle the fish properly and to let it gather strength before you return it.

– Let the fish stay in the water as long as possible when the hook is to be removed. Never touch the fish with dry hands, which can injure its protective layer of mucus. Use a landing net of knotless cotton, which is most gentle for the fish. If the fish is to be photographed, hold it with one hand by the tail and the other hand under its front body. Be careful not to squeeze the fish, and never touch its gills!

– Revive the fish before releasing it. Hold its head upstream in flowing water, or move it back and forth in still water, so that fresh water passes over its gills. Not until the gills pump regularly again, and the fish can keep its own balance, is it ready for releasing. The fish should be able to swim out of your hands by itself.

Fishing for salmon and sea trout

Salmonoids and related
species do not feed in fresh water
after returning from the sea. Therefore, we
can only speculate about what to offer
them in order to entice
them to the hook. Some writers
suggest that these fish have varying
motives for taking a fly – and such factors
as boredom, anger, curiosity,
and memory reflex have been proposed.
Although we shall probably never know the
real answer, it is tempting to theorize
and the present author is
no exception.

Good casting technique, and long experience on the same river under varying conditions, are typical attributes of a successful salmon fisherman.

I would compare salmon and sea trout to a half-sleeping cat which lies down in the sunshine and pays little attention to its surroundings. Of course, unlike the salmon, a cat will feed when it is hungry, but at times it is provoked to attack something that it has no intention of eating – such as a leaf blowing in the wind. Some reflex action is triggered by the sight of a moving object and induces the cat to chase it. This may have less to do with the object's colour than with its movement, and possibly its resemblance to an ailing prey.

However, many wild cats survive by being able to run fast, and must be continually on the alert – even practising when they are not feeding. Fish, particularly salmonoids, rely on their speed of interception to get a meal. Possibly on

occasions they take a fly when their reflexes have been triggered to attack something that they neither want nor need as food.

Thus, before fishing for salmonoids, it may be very important to learn not only how to cast well, but also how to think and act like a hunter, and to study animals in order to acquire a sense of their behavioural rhythms. One can even make notes of the feeding times of birds, fish and animals such as cattle and sheep. With trout and other fish which feed in fresh water, it is worth observing their feeding times and diet. We cannot directly do so with salmon and sea trout, but we must be aware of the rhythms of wildlife – as well as getting to know the water that we are fishing in.

The future of salmonoid fishing

Another general point to remember is that the future of the wild Atlantic salmon species is severely threatened today. Our fishing should therefore be conducted responsibly, which may mean a limit on catches and the methods of catching. The late British king George V summed it all up by saying: "The wildlife of today is not ours to dispose of as we please. We have it in trust and must account for it to those who come after us."

There is still a great magic in seeking salmon with a fly, and the thrill of the take never pales. Yet unless conservation measures are applied, we may have already lived through the golden years of salmon fishing. Surely mankind will not be so foolish as to let this sport slide into obscurity through wanton neglect!

Throughout most of Europe, the two main species of anadromous fish, *Salmo salar* and *Salmo trutta*, are better known by their common names: salmon and sea trout. But the prefix "Atlantic" must be added for salmon, while the European sea trout is perhaps better identified as a sea-run brown trout. This enables us to distinguish them from the five species of Pacific salmon, belonging to the genus *Oncorhynchus*, and from the sea-run rainbow trout known as the steelhead.

The majority of flyfishermen consider the Atlantic salmon to be the leading sportfish. With experience of many species of salmon and sea trout, however, I am not sure that this accolade is well-deserved. The fresh-run sockeye and coho salmon in Pacific rivers are hard fighters, as is the steelhead. And where else in the world would you find salmon that grow to the size of the chinook or king salmon, nearly 100 pounds (45 kg)?

The techniques of angling for salmon originated largely in Europe. Much of the folklore that has grown up around salmon was created by the British. Not only were they in the vanguard as sportfishermen for salmon, but their influence and expertise contributed a great deal to developing the Scandinavian resources.

Large Atlantic salmon are the ultimate challenge for many flyfishermen.

Equipment

As far back as two hundred years ago, it was casually assumed that, if trout take small flies, salmon can be expected to take larger flies. This, of course, we no longer find logical. On their return to fresh water, all salmon species cease to feed, and they stay in the rivers only in order to rendezvous with a partner on the spawning beds. Nature demands simply that one spawning pair produce another spawning pair within five or six years. Although a few Atlantic salmon may survive to spawn again, the Pacific species all die immediately after spawning.

Both Atlantic and Pacific salmon have proved to be a valuable food resource, and have been irresponsibly exploited by commercial fishermen, who have long been legally entitled to catch as much as they can. The laws are slowly being improved and enforced so as to curtail such over-exploitation, but there is also a wide appreciation of the value of salmon as a sporting resource.

Today there are notable developments in the restriction of fishing methods, commercial as well as sporting. Often it is required that only flies be used. Fish farms are supplying more of the market needs, and in North America all kinds of bait-fishing for salmon are forbidden. More of the Scottish, Irish and Scandinavian fisheries are gradually imposing a fly-only rule. Still, it may take time to convert the anglers who think more about the value of a prize than about the method of catching it.

Although fish farming to supply the public is a comparatively new and fairly profitable business, artificial rearing of salmon has been going on for several years. Man has made some attempt to replace fish where he has overfished, but mainly on a haphazard basis without training.

Patience, watchfulness and powers of concentration – these are qualities a salmon fisherman needs.

There are still numerous countries in which many forms of angling are permitted. Nonetheless, many of us feel that flyfishing not only offers a greater challenge, but also represents a better sporting method of catching these lovely fish. It is now several years, for instance, since I have fished for salmon with any other lure than a fly. On many rivers the methods of flyfishing can be very effective, although on a few rivers they are less productive than certain forms of bait-fishing.

It is, then, angling with a fly that will occupy us here. This is a superb way of enjoying sport with worthy fish – and once you have mastered some of the basic techniques, it is much easier than might be supposed by beginners.

Much of the tackle used in flyfishing for salmon and sea trout was invented in England. About 150 years ago, back-breaking rods of up to 20 ft (6 m) were fashionable. Leaders were of plaited horsehair and twisted silkworm gut. The most dramatic changes in tackle have taken place since World War II. Today carbon-fibre (graphite) has ousted glass, split cane, greenheart and hickory as rod-building material, while reels have become far lighter and more effective.

Silk lines and twisted flax are virtually things of the past. Modern synthetics give us every required combination in floating and sinking lines. The Association of Fishing Tackle Manufacturers (AFTM) has standardized much of this tackle, so that specific line sizes and weights can be made compatible with rods. Perhaps the greatest benefit that synthetic fibres have brought is in the field of transparent monofilament. Based on nylon, it has eliminated the need for gut or horsehair casts, and some remarkably high breaking strains are produced with minimal diametres.

Traditionally the fly rod was, and still is, double-handed. It may be anything from 12 ft (3.7 m) for fishing a river of modest size, to 17 ft (5.2 m) for a broad river. Much of the flyfishing in Britain and Scandinavia is done with double-handed rods. But North American anglers, who often fish from canoes, have shown a marked preference for the single-handed rod. At least one noted American angler, Lee Wulff, takes great delight in extracting massive salmon on a toothpick-like fly rod of only 6 ft (1.8 m) weighing less than 3 oz (85 g).

European anglers are still convinced that their way is best, while those in America share an equal conviction that any rod over 9 ft (2.7 m) is quite unnecessary. These prejudices are often deep-rooted and have little other foundation. I am reminded of a Scottish proverb: "Convince a man against his will. He's of the same opinion still!"

There is something to be said for each point of view. I have fished frequently with both types of rod, and firmly conclude that the double-handed rod is sometimes better suited in tactical terms, but that a single-handed rod seems more sensible at other times. On many Scottish rivers I would confine myself to a double-handed rod until the end of the main snow melt. Yet as soon as the rivers start falling to summer level, and for tactical reasons which I shall discuss later, I would adopt the single-handed rod. In the large, strong Norwegian rivers, a two-handed rod of 14-16 ft (4.3-4.9 m) is most common throughout the season.

It will be a happy day when both European and North American anglers discard their prejudices and recognize that, to be an all-round flyfisherman, one should have each type of tackle available during the whole season.

The choice of tackle

In making your initial choice of tackle, however, it is important to decide where you will do most of your fishing, and at what time of year. A lot depends on your location and the size of the river. A Norwegian river in June, for instance, may be nearly at flood level from melting snow – whereas a river of similar size in Scotland or England may already be thinning down to summer level, long after the main snows have melted.

The best choice for spring fishing on Scotland's famous river Spey, and in large Norwegian rivers during summer, is a 15-ft (4.6-m) double-handed carbon-fibre rod. With this I would carry at least two reels: one with a slow-sinking shooting-head line of size 11, and the other with double-taper fully floating line of similar size. The DT line is almost essential in order to do a proper Spey cast, while the sinking shooting-head line may be cast overhead for long distances. I would also carry a range of flies varying from 2.5-in (63 mm) tubes to size 6 or 8 doubles or trebles, without much concern for pattern.

One can also bring a net, gaff or other implement to extract fish from the river. Many prefer to wade the river with as little encumbrance as possible. For early spring or late autumn in Scotland, and during the summer in Scandinavian rivers, good tackle includes the following items:

- A stout pair of felt-soled breast waders, preferably in neoprene.
- The 15-ft (4.6-m) double-handed fly rod.
- Drum fly reels of 3.75 x 4 in (95 x 102 mm) with adjustable drag.
- A 30-ft (9.1-m) shooting-taper slow-sinking line of size 11, and another of fast-sinking type, attached to oval monofil backing.
- A 30-yd (27-m) double-taper floating line of size 11, spliced to at least 150 yds (137 m) of 25-lb test backing.
- A big box of flies, as outlined here.
- Spools of nylon monofil, between 10-lb and 25-lb test.
- A pair of scissors.

Additional accessories could be a wading stick, net gaff, and so forth. Indeed, if you do not know your river intimately, it makes good sense to have a wading stick. This should have a weighted bottom, so that it is always at hand and does not

float on the surface. If floating, it can make trouble and foul up some of the line which you intend to shoot.

As an alternative and back-up outfit, for such fishing in early spring or autumn, I recommend a single-handed rod of about 10 ft (3 m) with a smaller fly reel, and a forward-taper line of size 7 with an 8-lb test leader. This is a much-loved outfit for late spring and summer fishing on the small or shrunken streams of Britain. Moreover, it is fantastic fun to play a salmon on a light, single-handed rod. And there can be little doubt of the tactical value of such an outfit when the rivers have shrunk to their bare bones, with fish that are shy of all but the most slender leader.

An important aspect of tackle selection and use is your mastery of the best knotting techniques. All knots cause a loss of strength in your leader, and bad knots can be so inefficient that they may reduce the strength by more than half. It is a good idea to learn knots so thoroughly that you can almost tie them blindfolded.

Traditional salmon fishing from a boat with a double-handed rod.

One of the worst knots that may accidentally be induced into your leader is politely known as a "wind knot". Sometimes it may occur in very windy conditions, when the leader gets tangled and a single overhand knot is produced. This makes the leader extremely fragile to sudden loads, and might well break it when a fish is being played. Such knots can be termed "bad casting knots", since they can usually be avoided. All you need to do is open up the loop of the line a little, and lower the rod tip immediately after the power stroke in the forward cast.

Selecting flies

A classically tied Butcher.

Most discussion of the effectiveness of salmon and sea trout flies is speculative. Since the fish do not feed after returning to fresh water, they may have no interest in whatever we offer them, and no strict logic will tell us what size or pattern of fly will be the best in any given circumstances.

However, salmon can indeed occasionally be caught on a wide variety of fly patterns. Ancient lore suggests that we use big flies in extensive, deep and cold waters – and small flies in limited, shrunken rivers when the water is warmer and the fish are confined to shallower areas. In practice, there is a whole range of techniques which defy the basic rules, although we should never be dogmatic about them.

It is wise to arm yourself with a wide variety of fly patterns, in varying weights and lengths. Sometimes the weight of the fly is more important than its overall size. At other times you may want as small a fly as you can find. Generally, there is a lot to gain by having as large a selection as can be carried comfortably.

For fishing in early spring on many of Britain's classic rivers, I use a heavy sinking line and a tube fly, mounted on brass tubing to enable it to sink well down in the water. If the river is full with melting snow or recent rain, it may contain some suspended matter and thus lack the crystal-clear quality of a river at normal height. In addition, the water temperature may be a little above freezing, and this could be an occasion for the large fly if fished as slowly and deeply as possible.

Alternatively, the same river in late May or June might need little more than a light floating line, and a single-hooked fly of size 10 or 12 which is lightly dressed and has little weight or drag effect. Still, there are no fixed rules, and I have frequently seen a complete reversal of tactics bring about an unexpected success.

In making your choice of fly pattern and size, it pays off to keep in mind the laws of nature. Nothing in the wild which is preyed upon by other species has a garish appearance. The prey usually has some form of natural camouflage and does not look out of place in its environment. This fact should dictate the choice of fly in very clear water. Do not select a fly which is conspicuous, and it is a good idea to make your flies ever more subdued in colour as they get smaller. In high turbid water, however, you may well need to confront the fish with a more garish lure – and perhaps even intimidate the fish, presenting the lure where it will threaten the fish on an eye-to-eye collision course.

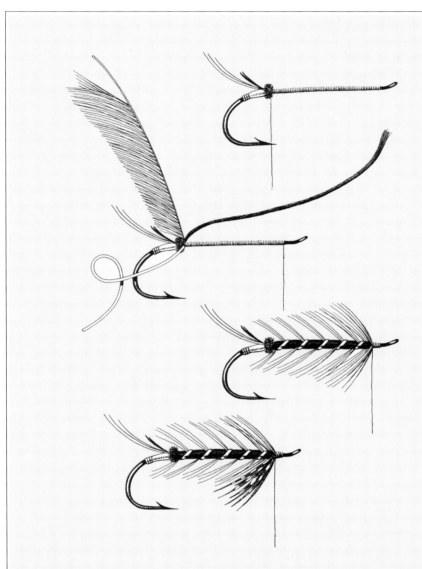

THUNDER & LIGHTNING

Tag: oval gold tinsel
Tip: yellow floss
Tail: golden pheasant crest feather and Indian Crow
Butt: black ostrich herl
Body: black floss
Ribbing: oval gold tinsel
Body hackle: orange cock hackle
Front hackle: blue guinea hen or blue jay
Wing: brown feather sections from brown mallard
Topping: golden pheasant crest feather
Sides: jungle cock
Head: black

This is how a classic salmon fly is tied. Thunder & Light-
ning is a good example of dark flies, which work best by
evening and night or in bad weather (hence the name?)
and when the water is murky.

At right is shown a Silver Doctor. This light fly is most
suitable in fine weather and when the river water is
clean and clear. It belongs to the Doctor series and is also
a good instance of a Mixed Wings fly.

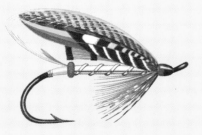

The colour of flies

On the above basis, I find it helpful to use a colour of fly which matches the overall colour of the river bed. Some rivers are generally brown, like weak coffee without milk, and these call for a dark-brown or black fly. The Spey responds well to this type, and patterns such as the Monro Killer, Thunder & Lightning, and Stoat's Tail are all effective. Other rivers, for example those flowing off bare rock or limestone, are often crystal-clear at times of normal flow, absorbing much ultraviolet light. They may have a blue or green tinge, making flies of the same hue more suitable.

During early spring and late autumn, though, your river will probably be higher than normal, and unusually turbid due to rainwater. I would then recommend slightly brighter or garish flies in yellow or orange for very cold days, and less conspicuous flies for warmer days. Good examples of flies for high, cold water are Yellow Dog, Tadpole, Willie Gunn and Collie Dog.

Nonetheless, the final act of deluding a fish into taking your lure is often unrelated to your choice of fly pattern. It may have something to do with the size of the fly, but usually the decisive factor is how you present the fly. Unfortunately, a fisherman who accepts the advice that he is fishing with the wrong fly might become furious at the suggestion that his casting and presentation are poor. In spite of that, the tactical and technical requirements are most likely to cause failure. And if there is a prerequisite in salmon and sea trout fishing, it is knowledge of the best techniques needed for any given situation.

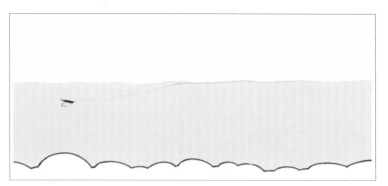

In warm low water, the current is frequently slow. The fish are then eager to rise and take the fly, which can be fished just under the surface with a floating line.

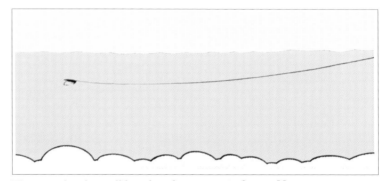

The river level is still low, but the current is faster. Now a sinking line is needed so that the fly will not drag on the surface.

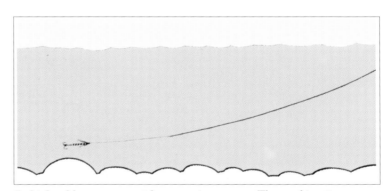

In high cold water, a rapid current is common. The combination of a fast-sinking line with large tube flies is then necessary to get down to the bottom, where the fish lie.

The water's temperature, level and current speed are factors that influence the fish's choice of holding places. A floating line and small flies are useful mainly during the warm months, when the water is low and the current therefore slow. But in the early season, with high and cold water, the current is strong and the fish take the fly at a greater depth. You must then often fish with a fast-sinking line and large flies.

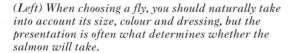

(Left) When choosing a fly, you should naturally take into account its size, colour and dressing, but the presentation is often what determines whether the salmon will take.

179

Casting and presentation

Experience shows that this kind of fishing depends mainly on the ability to cast a long line and on intimate acquaintance with the water being fished. The one-week-per-year salmon angler is severely restricted, and his difficulty is compounded if – like so many of us – he likes to try a different river each year. At no time will he ever fish a single stretch of water and get to know it under all its conditions. Yet he will never be able to fish it to full potential until he has tried for several years on the same stretch.

It is not intended here to teach the complexities of casting. A videotape may be more helpful than a book, but the best way to learn is from a professional instructor – not an enthusiastic amateur, however talented – and to spend as long as is needed to master the techniques under his supervision. Anglers often spend surprising sums of money in fishing rents, travel costs and hotel bills, only to prove themselves incompetent at casting when they arrive at the water.

For double-handed fishing, you must be able to cast at least 25-30 metres (80-100 ft). Such distances may not be achieved immediately, but it should not take long to accomplish them comfortably in the overhead mode. It is then very important to master both the single and double Spey casts. These will enable you to fish areas of water that are obstructed by overhanging trees or high banks, and where the overhead cast is impossible.

Letting the rod work

The novice should learn that it is the rod which must do the work – and that style, not brute strength, will make the cast look good and be effective. Ladies and small men often

An experienced salmon fisherman knows that he must let the rod do the work, if he is to fish for a whole day with a long double-handed rod. Every cast has to be as energy-saving as possible.

seem to be better stylists, while large and powerful men apparently work hard but do not achieve the right distance or style. But if you have both style and strength, you may well be on the way to becoming an exceptional salmon fisherman!

If you have no experience at all, it will pay to begin with a double-handed rod and a floating line. This gear is more quickly mastered than the single-handed rod or a sinking line, although the techniques are basically the same. The rod must act as a spring when casting, and as a lever when playing the fish. Thus, to get the best from your rod, you must use its springiness – and this is where many problems occur.

Some fishermen simply wave the rod about, using more muscle than they need. It is the flex of the rod that propels the fly line. No matter how much energy you expend, if you merely wave the rod and do not load it as a spring, you cannot cast far or with great style. Good casting is not an art, but a craft that any able-bodied person can soon learn.

The next difficulty, getting access to good water, has already been mentioned. Direct access to the best waters is not easy, even if you can afford the rent. But it is wise to get the best you can, and to remain a regular tenant over the years until you know the best times of year and the best places for fishing. Such knowledge is not easily won, either – and that is why many of the classic salmon waters have gillies, or guides, to assist the visitor and ensure that he fishes only the most productive areas.

This problem is less serious for anglers in Canada, Iceland and Scandinavia, where the more severe winters usually delay the first thaw until May. Then the melting snow makes the rivers rise, and the fish start to run. On many of these rivers, the season is confined to June, July and August. But in Britain, Ireland, and some other European rivers, one can fish in open season throughout the year by moving round a bit. The classic British rivers tend to open in February and close at the end of October, yet some open in January and others do not close until the end of November or even in mid-December. This poses tactical issues for the flyfisherman, although it does give him a longer season, and perhaps a better chance of finding some good water at modest cost.

It might be expected that an experienced salmon angler like myself would be most frequently asked about the tactics needed to catch salmon. Surprisingly, the commonest question is: "Where can I go and when?" It is also the hardest to answer satisfactorily.

The holding places

Another familiar puzzle is the definition of a pool. This may seem literally obvious, but not everyone knows what it means in the average salmon river, rock-girt and rain-fed. Usually we must see a river at fairly low level in order to identify these areas – where water rushes down from one cataract, levels out in a calmer and deeper section, and then speeds up before tumbling into the next pool below. A pool may be anything from a few metres long, on a small spate river, to several hundred metres long on a big river. It starts at the neck as the water cascades down over a firm riverbed. The top portion of the neck is called the stream or run, while the portion that trails away is the glide. The very bottom of the pool, before the river rushes away to form the neck of the next pool, is the tail.

It makes sense to fish most rivers from the inside of a bend. But there are notable exceptions. The flows and depths of a river vary as it progresses seaward. Water tends to flow in a straight line under the force of gravity, and its influence on obstacles will increase with the volume of water and the height of its fall. Therefore, at any bend in a river, the ground tends to be least solid on the inside bank. The main stream is usually forced down the outside of a bend, while the inside curve contains the calmer water.

Where a river turns sharply, and unless it flows over bedrock, the continuous floods may scour out a deep depression near the inside bank. This area may well harbour good stocks of migratory fish. Thus, as a rule, many rivers do fish better from the inside of a bend. You can cast into the fast water with certainty that your fly will then swing into the calmer water where the fish tend to lie.

With experience on one stretch of water, you will learn the precise places where the fish lie at any given height of water. In many cases, you can predict the chance of success from your knowledge of the ideal water height for any specific pool. This knowledge is extremely important in fishing any water to its full potential. In times of flood, of course, the fish tend to lie under the bank where, at other times, you find dry land or can wade out.

While the bends and curves in a river help us to "read" the water, we still have a lot to learn about its depth – the portion that we usually cannot see. Many rain-fed rivers vary tremendously in depth, and are also influenced by the type of riverbed. Good rivers for flyfishing are often comparatively shallow. Solid rock may take thousands of years to erode, whereas gravel may be shifted by each flood.

The best way to learn the geography of a river, or of the section which you want to fish regularly, is to put on a wetsuit and explore it underwater at different heights. The next best way is to study its contours at a time of very low water. Even then, unless you can move or think like the fish, you are not likely to sense how subtle changes in the flow will determine where the fish lie at various heights of water. Such knowledge could help in the presentation of your fly, although not dramatically altering your catch.

A knowledge of where the fish are, in a river or pool with a given water depth, tends to be what distinguishes the successful salmon fisherman from the "always unlucky" ones. This knowledge is attained almost exclusively by fishing regularly in the same river for a long time.

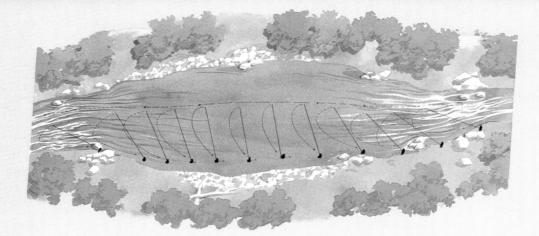

A pool with varying current speed is fished according to a certain system. Where the current is strongest, at the beginning and end of the pool, the fly is cast obliquely downstream and followed immediately with a mending upstream. In the pool's calmer middle, the fly is laid out straight across the current, and possibly followed with a smaller mending. In a very slow current, it may even be necessary to go against the flow, step by step and cast by cast, to make the fly travel better.

In shallow flowing parts of a river, fish often lie before or beside large stones or cliffs, where they can find lee from the current.

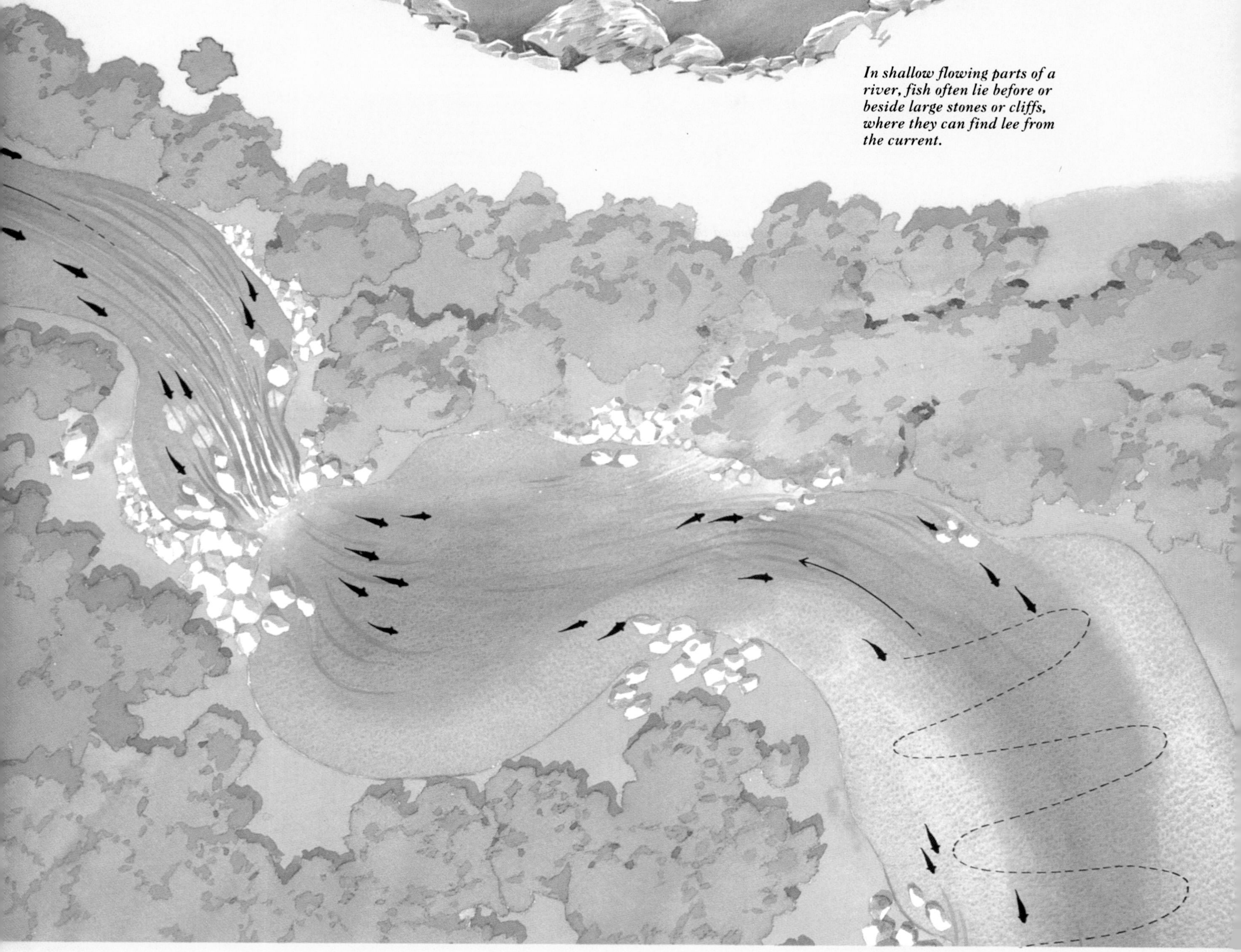

A stretch of river is illustrated here in top view and cross-section. As can be seen, the fish prefer to lie at the inlets of pools – gathering their strength for the next stage of migration – and to rest at the outlets after having overcome previous obstacles. In long wide pools, though, the fish try to lie in the outer edges of the current.

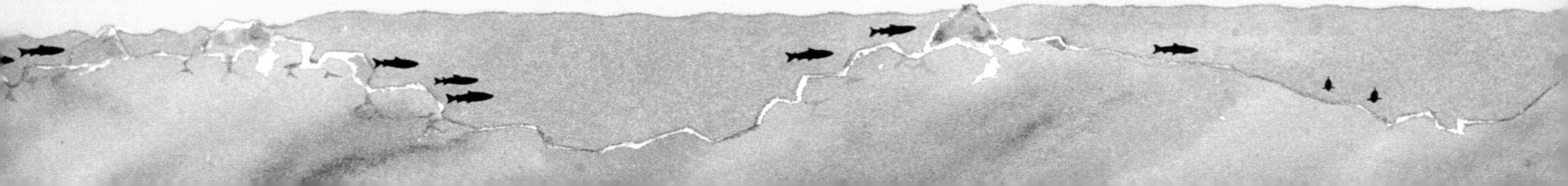

The salmon has taken the fly, yet many long and dramatic minutes remain before it can be landed.

The taking times

At least one British salmon writer has observed that it is impossible to overfish a salmon river. What he meant was that it is not easy to put fish permanently into a non-taking mood, and that they may always – at some time of their own choosing, for some unknown reason – suddenly "come on the take" and grab the first lure they see. In any case, we must evaluate the condition of the fish. A fresh fish entering a new lie for the first time, and taking a brief rest, may be quite likely to snatch at the first thing to antagonize it. Until we know why salmon take our flies, we are naturally only speculating – but experience shows that fresh-run salmon are very vulnerable in this respect, and that many are caught when running without staying long in a lie. Here I

feel that it is almost impossible to overfish the lie or the river. But where the fish have run into holding pools and stayed for some time in a lowering water, it does seem possible to over-intimidate them into a non-taking mood.

There are undoubtedly many instances, in salmon and sea trout fishing, where "familiarity can breed contempt". Moreover, what can we gain by continually flogging a stretch of water when there is a total lack of response? It may make better sense to rest, as well as giving the fish some respite.

The idea of resting a stretch of water, of course, poses hard questions. On many rivers, it is impossible to tell exactly what is happening under the surface. Only by having a fish-counting device at the inlet and outlet of every pool could we determine just what stock it contains from one minute to the next. But since the stock is often a matter of pure speculation, it may be that resting a pool will reduce the chance of familiarity breeding contempt. Indeed, the next time your fly is shown to the fish, some new stock may have moved in, or one of the old residents may have changed its mood.

It is not strictly true that one can never predict the taking times of the fish. Those that settle into lies for several weeks are known to be residents. You may even recognize some of them by the positions in which they show, by their leaping style, and by their size or colouring. However, it is important not to overfish for them – and to fish at times when "all of nature is in tune", as suggested by a knowledge of the behaviour and feeding times of other animals.

Although salmon and sea trout are known to be non-feeders in fresh water, some memory of their heavy marine feeding may trigger a reflex and make them respond at some times of the day better than at others. One of the most predictable taking times, throughout the season and in any kind of weather, is the last hour of daylight.

The weather in Scotland may vary greatly during April and May. One day might have air and water temperatures around 5-8° C (41-46° F), while another may have the air at 15° C (59° F) and the water at a magical 10° C (50° F). In any event, when fishing with a fully floating line, it is very important that the air be warmer than the water. Choose a day when the opposite is true, and you may well draw a blank.

As emphasized above, the angler who does best with salmon and sea trout is usually one who lives on, or near, the river he is to fish. He gets to know all its moods and whims, ignoring the temptation to try a new river every year. For this reason, I am now reluctant to try new waters. Age does not leave me enough time to learn them as intimately as I know, for instance, the Castle Grant beat of the Spey, or the Upper Floors beat of the Tweed.

A salmon often rises calmly and slowly towards a fly in the sub-surface. If it decides to take, which is far from certain, it usually does so heavily and decisively rather than violently.

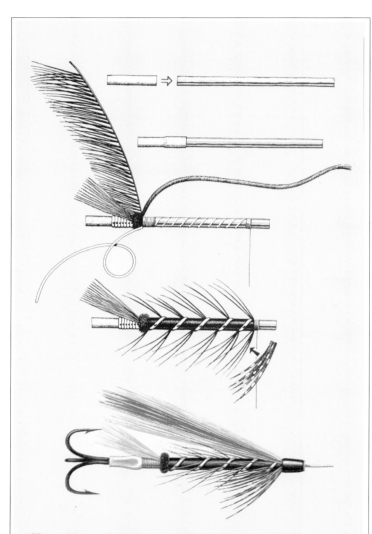

How to tie a tube fly is shown here. The example is Garry, an all-round pattern that has proved to catch salmon throughout the year, but is perhaps most effective in the early season when the river water is at a high level and low temperature.

GARRY SPECIAL
Tag: oval silver tinsel
Butt: black ostrich herl
Tail: golden pheasant crest feather
Body: black floss
Ribbing: oval silver tinsel
Body hackle: sparsely tied black
 cock hackle
Front hackle: blue guinea hen
Wing: red and yellow bucktail
Head: black

Practical flyfishing

Suppose that you are fishing early in the season, and the river is at nearly perfect height, with a water temperature of around 4° C (39° F) or perhaps a bit warmer as in Scandinavia. You are using a 15-ft (4.6-m) rod, a sinking line, and a garishly coloured 2.5-in (6.3-cm) tube fly. Taking up a position that enables you to cover the lies, you make your first cast.

Initially a few short casts should be made toward the opposite bank, pulling a yard or two of line from the reel at each cast, until you have enough line out. But it should be remembered that a longer cast will allow the fly to get farther down in the water – and that by holding up the rod tip, immediately after the cast, you will keep more line off the water as the fly begins to swing, so that it will sink farther.

Do not be in too much of a hurry to strip back line for the next cast. Let the fly dangle for a few seconds, then casually pull in the first two or three loops of backing. Sometimes during the cold weather of the early or late season, fish will slowly follow the fly and take it only as it is being withdrawn upstream. On occasion, especially in the autumn, my fly has been snatched while hand-lining back at full speed.

These slow tactics offer the best chances in cold weather, but it may be useful to speed them up a little as the water warms. However, salmon – notably the Atlantic salmon – react much less quickly than do sea trout, which can grab a fly and take you down to the backing in a single rapid movement. Besides, Atlantic salmon differ in behaviour from the same species in North America, which often display real pyrotechnics. All Pacific salmonoids, particularly when fresh-run, are fairly savage on the take, whereas the more ponderous Atlantic salmon of the early spring are rarely willing to snatch and flee like summer sea trout.

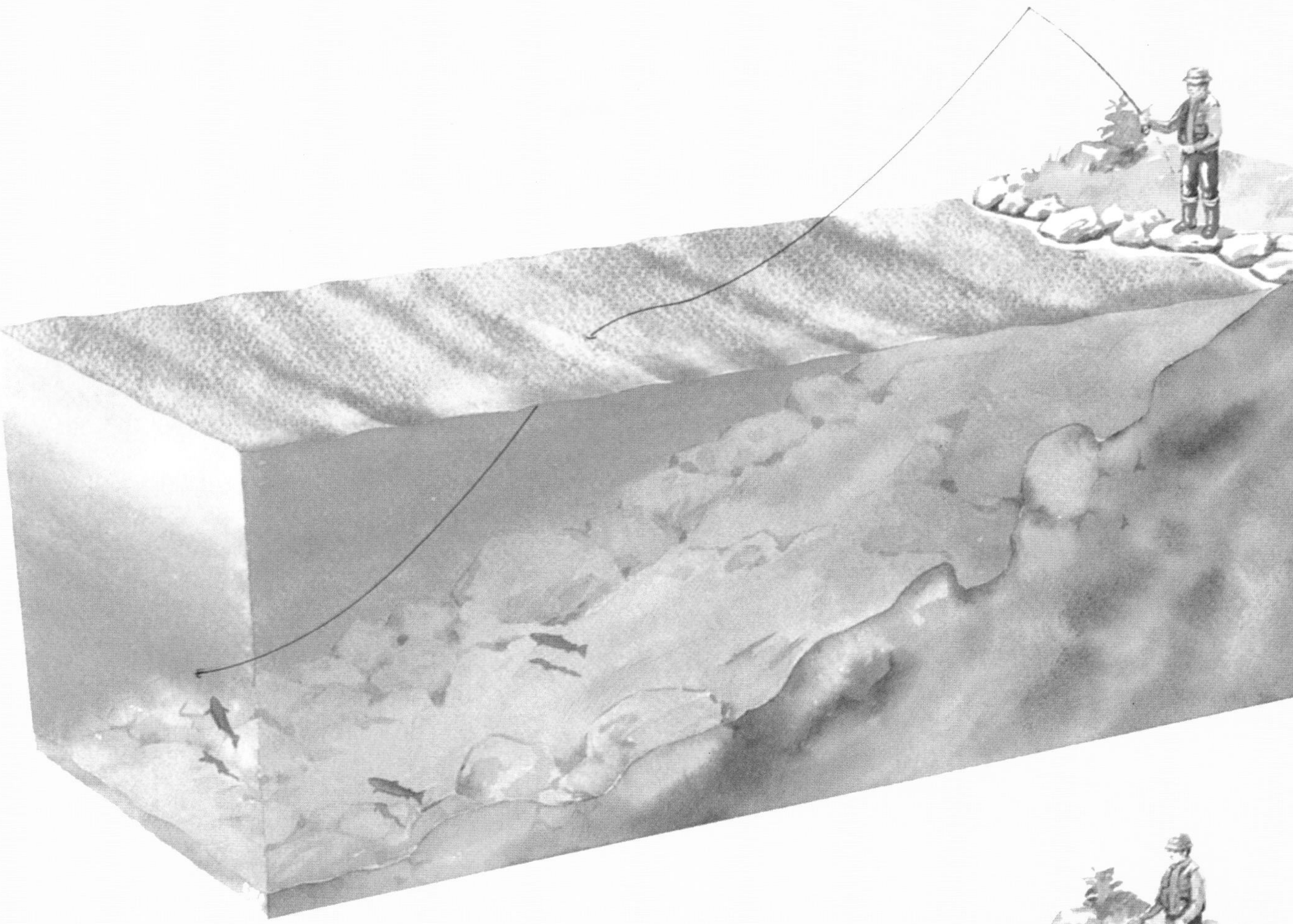

In sink-line fishing, you should always try to hold the rod high. As seen in the upper illustration, the fly then has a chance to sink properly toward the bottom. If the rod is held too low, as in the picture below, too much of the line will float on the surface due to friction, keeping the fly "hanging" a little under the surface.

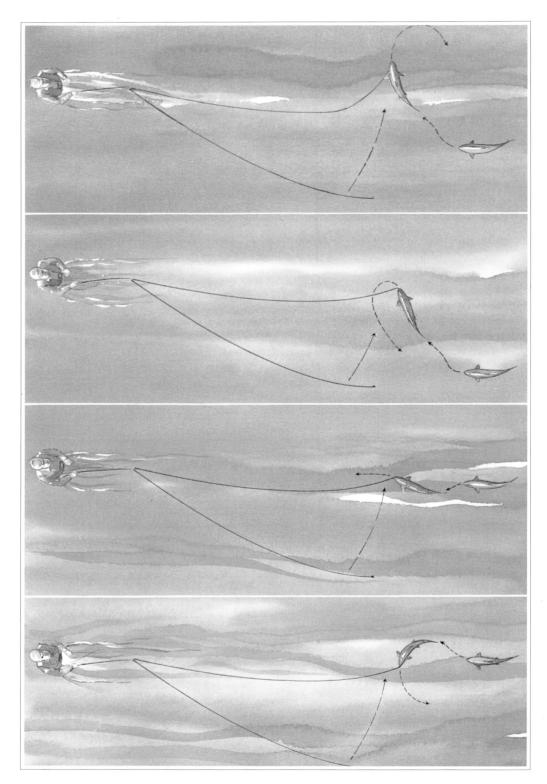

Salmon can take a fly in various ways, and opinions on what to do after the take are almost as numerous as salmon fishermen. Shown here are four common ways for salmon to take. The fish nearly always rises upstream to inspect the fly and possibly take it. Then the fish usually falls back with the current in some direction. Only in the third example does the fish continue upstream after taking the fly.

Though the fish often hooks itself, you should always make a clear strike as soon as you feel it on the rod. No matter how it takes the fly and how you hook it, you should let it work against the rod during the whole fight. Give it as little chance as possible to rest, ideally by playing it in the faster part of the current.

Will the salmon take the fly – and if so, how?

Hooking and landing

There are several opinions about what to do when a salmon takes the fly. Some anglers, especially those who have read a great deal on the subject, seem to be obsessed with feeding line to the fish at the moment of the take. Others, who may have caught a lot of fish, apparently believe that you should hold hard when you feel the fish and let it hook itself. The present writer prefers the latter view. Possibly a fish in very cold water will get hooked on any slack line fed to it, but I see no reason to do this at any other time. I agree with the idea of holding hard, or even striking, at the instant when the fish is felt pulling on the rod tip.

Exactly what you do after hooking the fish depends to some extent on its mood. It may soon take the initiative and do unexpected things, such as rushing away downstream and threatening to break the line. But usually it stays in the pool where it was hooked, so you need only give line when it pulls strongly, and win back some line when you feel it trying to rest. The fish should be kept active, and preferably in the faster current. Do not let it get so far downstream that it can lean on your tackle to resist the current.

But neither should you stay opposite the fish simply in order to keep a side-strain on it. This might lead you far downstream from your starting point. Normally I like to play and land a fish from the place where I was standing when I hooked it. Naturally there are times when you have to move, but a good rule is to stand fast.

Before long, in fishing for salmon or sea trout, you will realize that certain conditions must be met if you are to catch fish by design rather than by accident. The angler who has got to know the water in all its moods – and who has learned to cast far – will, in the long run, score heavily over the inexperienced novice. Yet perhaps the main requirement is a "command" of the water. What counts is not merely casting out to the fish, but being able to make your fly move over the fish in such a way that it is more likely to be taken than refused. Achieving effective water command is possible only with expert advice from your gillie, guide or boatsman, unless you have long personal experience of the water you are fishing.

(Above) Mending in a river with low water and moderate current, where the main aim is to lessen the stronger midcurrent's effect on the line – and thus vary the speed of the fly. Slighter mending is sufficient here.

Mending the line

One of the first lessons a salmon flyfisherman should learn, particularly if he is to fish mainly with a floating line, is the technique of mending the line. This refers to the movement which you give the line after it is cast and has fallen on the water. Normally a sinking line cannot be mended significantly, so it is important to make a good straight cast that will minimize the central current's influence on the line.

Of course, when fishing a river with a floating line, you are always casting across flowing water where the current's strength varies from one side to the other. Often the central current forms a "belly" in the line, and – as shown by the

illustrations – this gives the fly an unnatural movement. A very strong central current may cause so much belly that the fly is whipped round in a fast-moving arc, which is frequently quite unattractive to the fish.

But by switching the line upstream, mending its belly formation shortly after it has fallen on the water, you can slow down the fly and enable it to swing round more gradually. Sometimes the current speed varies widely – and the angler who can continually read the situation, mending or modifying the curves in his line, will have greater success than one who merely casts the fly across the flow and leaves it to fend for itself!

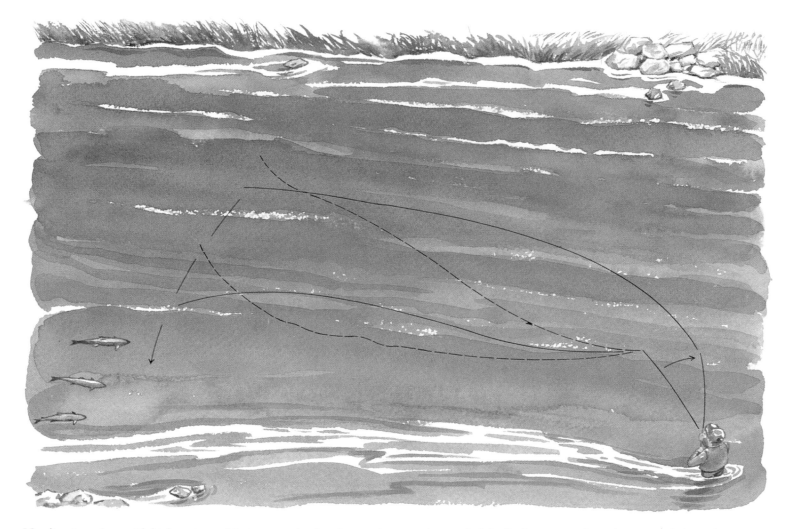

Mending in a river with high water and fast current is often done to decrease the speed of the fly. In waters where the current is irregular and varies in speed, you should keep adjusting the line's curve with bold and slight mendings.

In general, a longer rod improves your chances of creating effective mends. Especially on fast water, an upstream mend is often needed to slow down the fly. But sometimes, in very sluggish water, a downstream mend may be best. This increases the belly in the line, giving the fly more movement and speed to make it attractive.

When fishing with a sinking line, however, there is very little time in which to mend the line. If a sinking line is to be mended at all, this should be done just after the cast, before the fly and line can sink down in the water.

An understanding of the degree of movement which your fly must have in relation to the current, and thus the speed and angle at which it should be fished, will come only with experience. As already noted, a fly that passes too quickly over a lie may not incite the fish to take, while a fly that passes too slowly may be recognized as a trick or may fail to trigger the fish's attack mechanism.

Besides, what triggers a suitable response at one time may not do so at another. There are also variables of air and water temperature and clarity, climate, barometric pressure, oxygen content, and the general mood of the fish at a specific time of day or night. All of these add to the possibilities, and it is still true that no perfect formula can ensure the downfall of fish.

Methods

There are various distinctions between methods of salmonoid fishing. The most common methods on the British, Scandinavian and North American rivers are fishing with a sink-line and with a floating line. The former is most effective when the river is high and cold, whereas the latter is best for a low warm river.

In addition, numerous other approaches are used according to the conditions at hand. For example, on North American rivers it is normal to fish for salmon with a dry fly and a technique called "riffling hitch". In parts of the Scottish highlands, local methods such as "dibbling" are very popular. Large rivers like the Tweed in Scotland, and the Alta in Norway, tend to be fished best from a boat, as when harling.

Fresh-run fish

During the early season, the prime time for salmon fishermen, you can expect to catch some of the freshest fish of the entire season. Some of these may be bearing sea lice – the hallmark of fresh-run fish. It is assumed that sea lice can survive in fresh water for only 48 hours, but they have been known to do so for up to seven days under laboratory conditions. Even then, a fish with sea lice must be regarded as excellent, both for sport and on the table. However, you may get a poor fight from a fresh-run fish, especially when the water has warmed a little and when the fish may have run a long way in a short time. Such fish might be already partially exhausted from their swim, needing several days to get back into prize-fighting trim.

Another fish that may be encountered during the early months is called a kelt. This is an Atlantic salmon which entered the river during the previous year and spawned already during that autumn. Not all such fish return quickly to the sea. Many die, as do all the Pacific salmon species – and other kelts linger in fresh water, not returning to the estuary until March or April, particularly after a hard winter. Kelts are recognizable by their lean and lanky appearance, ragged fins, and distended vent. One should also look for maggots in gills, and not be fooled by an overall silver appearance – somewhat like that of fresh fish. Such kelts are merely in the process of donning their seagoing coat.

When hooked, a kelt does not normally fight as hard as a fresh salmon. But well-rested kelts may prove to be more stubborn fighters than is generally appreciated. The law in several countries is that all kelts must be returned to the water, although there are instances in North America where it is permitted to keep them. In any event, they are fairly useless as food.

Late spring salmon

Some Scottish rivers are famous for their early runs of salmon in January, February and March – a period often curiously called "spring" by anglers. Others become better for the sporting angler when spring turns into summer, from April to June. This is the heyday of the flyfisherman who enjoys fishing with a floating line, and when wading is more comfortable, with a general sense of spring in the air. There may still be lots of snow on the mountains, and a strong flow of water in the rivers – but for many of us, this is the peak of the season.

During the past few years, I have almost given up the early season so that I can concentrate on the latter period of better weather. This is a wonderful time to be alive on many of Scotland's classic rivers. Although the spring run on several of them is no longer as prolific as it was thirty years ago, the stocks build up gradually as summer arrives, and the big migrations of fish often do not come until late summer or early autumn.

However, in many other countries with stocks of Atlantic salmon, the season tends to be much shorter. In Norway it is confined to June, July and August, while in Iceland and North America it is more or less the same. There the angler is limited to the fine-weather season, and the styles of fishing are dictated only by the condition of the water. North American anglers often fish from canoes, making it easy to use a single-handed rod and small flies. Nevertheless, there must be situations where the American angler decreases his chances by adhering almost ritually to the single-handed rod.

The choice between treble, double or single hooks for flies is a popular subject in angling magazines. I like to have

The salmon could not resist the fly, fished with a single-handed rod and a floating line.

195

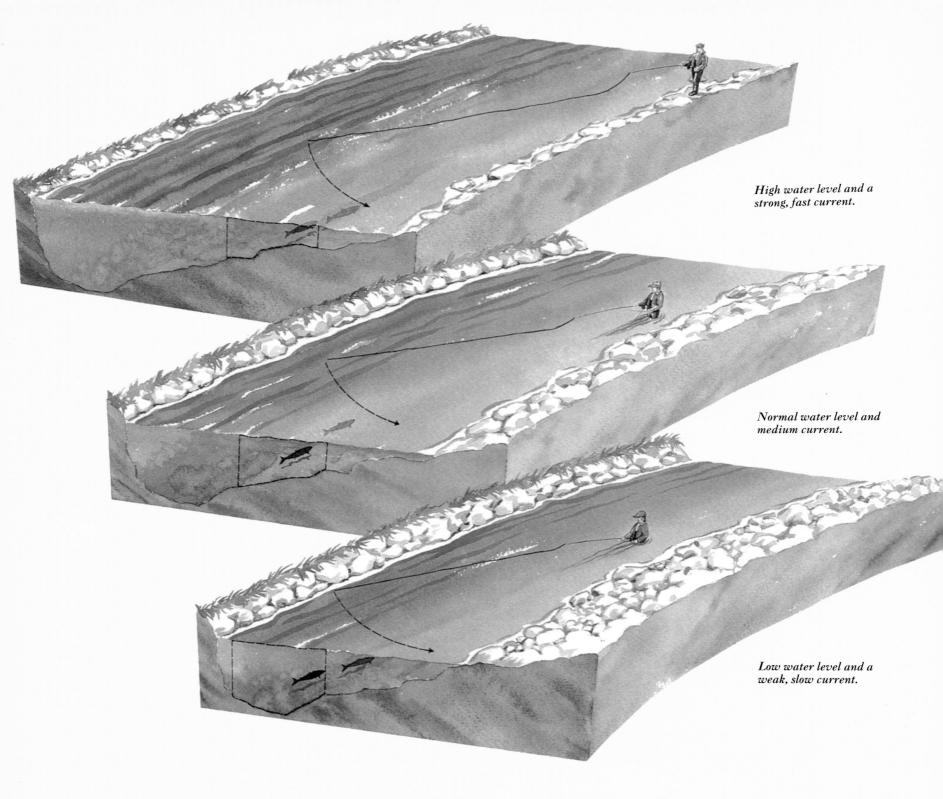

High water level and a
strong, fast current.

Normal water level and
medium current.

Low water level and a
weak, slow current.

A knowledge of bottom conditions and holding pools is
essential for successful salmon fishing. Above is shown an
area with high water level and strong current. Fish then
lie rather close to the shore, so the fisherman can – and
perhaps should – stand on land. At centre we see the same
stretch of river with normal water level. Wading may be
necessary to reach the fish. At bottom the river appears
with a low water level. Waders are now frequently a prerequisite for going in deep enough to fish the current, even
if it runs at the opposite bank as in this example.

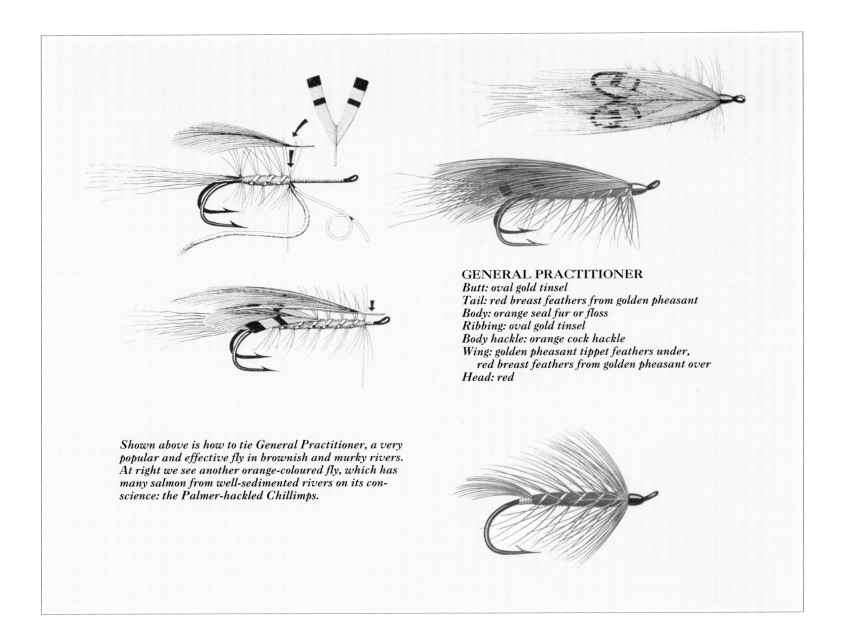

GENERAL PRACTITIONER
Butt: oval gold tinsel
Tail: red breast feathers from golden pheasant
Body: orange seal fur or floss
Ribbing: oval gold tinsel
Body hackle: orange cock hackle
Wing: golden pheasant tippet feathers under,
*   red breast feathers from golden pheasant over*
Head: red

Shown above is how to tie General Practitioner, a very popular and effective fly in brownish and murky rivers. At right we see another orange-coloured fly, which has many salmon from well-sedimented rivers on its conscience: the Palmer-hackled Chillimps.

all three types on hand, and their relative merits should now be considered. Advocates of the treble hook rightly claim that it offers wonderful hooking potential. That a fish can take a treble hook, and then pull against the rod and line without becoming hooked, seems impossible. Of course, we all know that fish can and do fail to become hooked – but it may be reasonable to assume that they do so less frequently with treble hooks.

The problem with a treble hook – and this may be news to you – is that, for a given size, it experiences relatively great drag, or water resistance, when dangling in a current. The smaller treble-hooked flies tend to rise well up in the water in a strong current, and may lose effectiveness by skating on the surface or too near it. Interestingly, many North American anglers make use of this as a technique. They even put a half-hitch (sometimes called a riffling or

A simple trick can pull out a fly that has snagged on, say, a stone during sink-line fishing. By releasing line in the water, a downstream belly is formed. Then the line is tightened up with a subsequent strike, and the fly will frequently be released from its snag.

Newfoundland hitch) on the fly, so that it hangs at right angles from the leader. But in most North American salmon rivers, they are often limited to the use of a single-hooked fly, which may also have to be barbless.

The fewer hooks involved in a salmon fly sometimes cause it to swim a bit deeper. This can sometimes be an advantage, and the angler should be aware of the varying tactics made possible by using different hook styles, in order to use them when conditions dictate.

For much of the fishing in April and May, it is advisable to have already changed from a sinking line to a full floater. There may be occasional advantages in using a sinking line or a floating line with sinking tip, but these are not easy to cast, and I consider them virtually needless on most of the rivers I fish. In this chapter I will therefore concentrate on fishing with a floating line.

The months of April and May in Scotland correspond very closely, as regards weather, with the months from June to August in North America, Scandinavia and Iceland. On the other hand, it is true that August may be a disappointing month anywhere. Consequently, if I had to restrict my salmon season to a specific period, I would choose the period from April to July.

At left is shown how to tie a hairwinged salmon fly, Blue Rat. The fly above is a hairwinged Cosseboom. Hairwinged salmon flies, which come originally from North America, are much easier to tie than the classic English salmon flies. It has thus become ever more common to tie even classic patterns with hair wings. These hardly fish worse, and are far cheaper.

BLUE RAT
Tag: oval gold tinsel
Tail: a bunch of peacock herls
Body: rear part of light-blue floss,
*   front part of peacock herl*
Ribbing: oval gold tinsel
Wing: blue and gray hair
Sides: jungle cock
Cheeks: blue kingfisher
Hackle: grey cock hackle
Head: red

Low-water flies, as the name indicates, are used for low water levels, especially in summer. Since hairwing flies became accepted on European salmon rivers, however, low-water flies have declined in importance, since a sparsely tied hairwing fly fulfils the same function. Shown above are Blue Charm (left) and Silver Blue (right), tied as low-water flies. Both of these classic "killers" can, of course, also be tied as fully dressed and as hairwinged variants.

Summer fishing

One basic difference between Scotland and Scandinavia, as regards fishing, is the size of fly to be used. In Scotland during June, most of the snow has already melted and the rivers are fining down to summer level. A similar river in Norway or Iceland, however, still has a large run-off of melt-water; although the sun is high and air temperatures may be above 20° C (68° F), the water may be little more than 5-8° C (41-46° F). Often, therefore, the Scottish angler who is fishing water around 15° C (59° F) uses flies of smaller sizes (8-12) while the Scandinavian fisherman is still using big tubes and trebles up to 3 in (7.5 cm) long – the type used in Scotland during February and March.

Tactics in Scotland at this time may involve fishing mainly in the early morning and late evening. Certainly little can be achieved by fishing over low water on a hot sunny day when the air temperature soars over 20° C (68° F). Even in Norway, where the fresh fish are then entering the rivers, it might pay to delay your main effort until the sun has sunk behind the lofty mountains – or even, in the region which enjoys the midnight sun, to defer all fishing until evening and continue through the night. Some of the northernmost rivers, such as the famous Alta, are fished only between 6 PM and 6 AM.

Fishing for sea trout

Although salmon and sea trout have been treated above as similar species, they differ subtly in behaviour, and some-times so much that entirely different tactics are needed when fishing for a specific species. Certain writers even suggest that the two types of fish cannot be related when discussing tactics. However, in reality you will often catch sea trout when fishing for salmon, and vice versa.

Handtailing is perhaps the most gentle and sports-manlike way of landing a salmon. The fish is held by the tail so that your little finger points toward the tail fin. A woolen finger-glove improves the grip greatly and is especially helpful if the salmon is large.

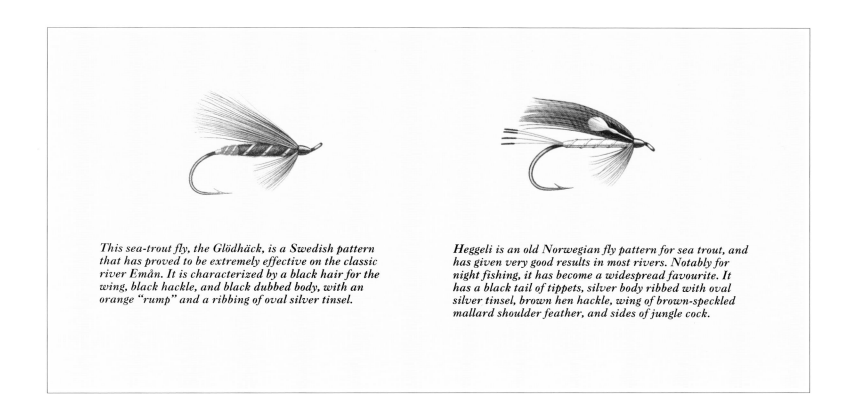

This sea-trout fly, the Glödhäck, is a Swedish pattern that has proved to be extremely effective on the classic river Emån. It is characterized by a black hair for the wing, black hackle, and black dubbed body, with an orange "rump" and a ribbing of oval silver tinsel.

Heggeli is an old Norwegian fly pattern for sea trout, and has given very good results in most rivers. Notably for night fishing, it has become a widespread favourite. It has a black tail of tippets, silver body ribbed with oval silver tinsel, brown hen hackle, wing of brown-speckled mallard shoulder feather, and sides of jungle cock.

(Below) A sea trout usually takes the fly near or in the surface. The fly should be fairly small, size 6-10. Unlike salmon, sea trout actually feed also after starting their spawning migration, so they tend to take decisively and can seem quick, even violent.

A single-handed rod is the commonest choice for sea-trout fishing, just as for salmon fishing in North America.

On most British rivers, sea trout begin to run only in late spring. They are often regarded as a summer fish, and in many places they are not encountered until July. At this time northern Europe has long periods of daylight, and fishing with a fly can offer greater rewards at night than at any other time.

Sea trout, particularly those that have been in a river for some time, are very shy. On their first run into fresh water, they may be quite easy to catch – but after only a short interval, it may turn out that they can only be caught at night. In midsummer, on the rivers of northern Europe, this may mean starting as late as 10 PM or so.

On normal waters, you should usually begin with a single-handed rod and a floating line, using flies of sizes 6-10, and fishing in the traditional style – casting across the current and letting the fly swing round. The water's sporting potential will tend to be indicated by the amount of surface activity among the sea trout. Takes are often savage, and the fish present some huge thrills as they charge about, trying to throw your hook.

Such sport may last until midnight and complete darkness. But sometimes a dead silence falls, leading you to conclude that the fish have gone down and ended the game for the night. However, this may be only a "half-time" pause by the fish, so that you can take a brief rest and resume fishing – with a sinking line and a big lure as long as 3 in (7.5 cm). This "second half" may be just the time to catch the larger sea trout, and you may be able to continue fishing until dawn.

Nights with a cold wind, or air colder than the water, should be avoided. Moonlight is not advantageous. The best nights are those with balmy breezes from the southwest, a little moisture in the air, and a myriad of insects dancing in the shadows of late evening. Sometimes, later in the season, the darkest nights offer the best sport of all.

Yet at other times, it is frequently possible to catch sea trout along with salmon. Despite notable differences in tactics, sea trout may respond in much the same manner as do salmon. Indeed, although salmon rarely take after dark, it happens on rivers like the Spey that a fish is caught in late

Dry flies are often used for salmon fishing in North America, and when fishing for sea trout in a few Norwegian rivers. Among the best-known dry flies is the Wulff series, created by Lee Wulff. Here we see Grey Wulff, which floats very well due to its tail and wings of hair, and to its bushy hackle of cock feathers.

GREY WULFF
Tying thread: black
Tail: bucktail
Body: dubbed grey wool
Wings: bucktail
Hackle: grey cock hackle

evening and you do not know what it is until you have netted it. Usually I do not care whether it is a salmon or a sea trout, for both are equally welcome on the table!

Salmon are commonly caught with dry flies in North America, but rarely in Europe. At times a dry fly is very effective for Scandinavian sea trout, even in the middle of the day – yet salmon can seldom be induced to succumb. Only a few times have I caught salmon on a dry fly which was intended for trout, and there have been a few more occasions when I caught sea trout.

Pacific salmon

Of the five principal species of Pacific salmon known in western North America, the most important for sportsmen are the chinook, or king salmon (also called the tyee in parts of Canada), the coho or silver salmon, and the sockeye or red salmon. The others, the pink and the chum salmon, are plentiful but not very interesting for sport, and make only low-grade canned salmon.

My experience of fishing for these species has been confined to Alaska. There I have found that the coho, sockeye, and chinook can provide exceptional flyfishing when they are fresh-run. It is rare to see anyone using a double-handed rod, and only occasionally might one be needed. A light single-handed rod of 9-10 ft (2.7-3.0 m) is usually sufficient. Balance this with a floating line of size 7, sometimes with a sink-tip, and a test leader of 8-10 lbs. Then you can have some super sport, particularly with the coho and sockeye. The chinook does not respond very well to small flies, so it is advisable to use a sinking line and large lures, on extra-strong leaders of 20-25 lbs, in case you tangle with a monster weighing over 50 lbs (23 kg).

Much the same techniques as with Atlantic salmon are used for fishing with a floating line. But it pays to go very deep for the chinook, and to fish as slowly as possible. The fight from a chinook is about the same as from big Norwegian salmon, although it lacks the same lustre and cannot be compared on the table. Perhaps the highest gourmet marks are earned by the fresh-run sockeye. Indeed it is this species, when caught at sea, which goes into expensive cans of "prime red salmon". None of the other Pacific species get beyond the "pink salmon" label.

The most popular sea trout on the west coast of the United States is the sea-run rainbow trout called the steelhead. Among the most highly favoured by American flyfishermen, it is reckoned to be the "fightingest" fish on that continent. Many of the biggest specimens are taken with bait-fishing techniques, but a flyfisherman can get good results with large flies on sinking lines.

Most of the Pacific salmon species, however, are not seriously fished after they have been in fresh water for some time. Sockeye, for example, undergo a great physiological change soon after entering fresh water, acquiring the colour of goldfish with a green head. They are then pretty useless for food and sport, although they can be very eager fighters when fresh from the sea.

Perhaps the greatest sport is provided by the coho, or sil-

The king salmon is a first-class fighter, and is readily coaxed with a large fly fished deep and slow.

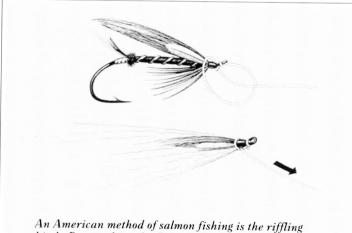

An American method of salmon fishing is the riffling hitch. By attaching the fly to the leader with the knot shown above, the fly can be made to imitate an animal that swims on the surface across the current.

ver salmon. It resembles Atlantic salmon more closely, and fights like a tiger when it is fresh from the sea. While it responds well to smaller flies and lures fished on a single-handed rod, it may sometimes react better to a sink-tip floating line than to a full floater.

Many Alaskan rivers have favoured fly patterns. But the fish are ready takers to most lures, and a "Happy Hooker" or "Street Walker" is not always needed for success. To be sure, these patterns are highly decorative, as are many patterns for Pacific salmon in Alaska.

The Bristol Bay area of Alaska abounds with salmon rivers, and a visit by European anglers may prove less expensive than they expect. In fact, comparing the rent of a

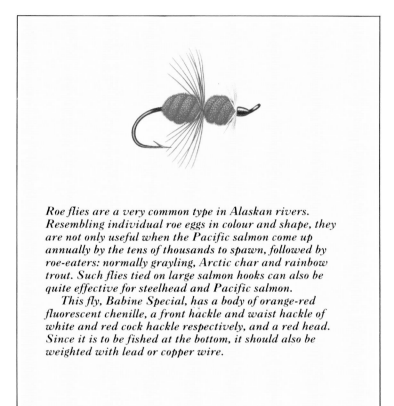

Roe flies are a very common type in Alaskan rivers. Resembling individual roe eggs in colour and shape, they are not only useful when the Pacific salmon come up annually by the tens of thousands to spawn, followed by roe-eaters: normally grayling, Arctic char and rainbow trout. Such flies tied on large salmon hooks can also be quite effective for steelhead and Pacific salmon.

This fly, Babine Special, has a body of orange-red fluorescent chenille, a front hackle and waist hackle of white and red cock hackle respectively, and a red head. Since it is to be fished at the bottom, it should also be weighted with lead or copper wire.

Still-water salmon and sea trout fishing

Catching migratory fish in still waters is not possible at many places in the world, but it can be done effectively on a number of Scottish lochs and small Norwegian fjords. Of course, the water must not be too deep and you have to know that it contains fish. Usually a boat offers much better chances than fishing from a bank. On the whole, still-water fishing calls for a special skill, and may be less simple than it seems at first.

Quite often, a short line on a single-handed rod will catch salmon, while a long line will get the sea trout. Flies tend to be very small in comparison to river flies. The best results with salmon are frequently obtained just as the fly is approaching the boat and is suspended on the crest of a wave, as you prepare for the next cast. But sea trout may respond best to a long cast on a very long leader. Sometimes it pays to use a light fly line (AFTM class 5-6) and a leader with up to 20 m (65 ft) of fine monofilament of about 6 lbs test. The best response is often made to a fly near the surface, and a light line enables you to bring the fly up to the surface soon after a cast.

It is important that the water has a good wave on the surface. A windless day may well produce no results. If you have a boatman, he will doubtless row slightly upwind, so that the track would take you in a crosswind direction. If you cast with the wind, the boat's movement will slowly swing the flies round in a neat arc.

I prefer to fish still waters with two flies, but there is no reason not to use three, or even just one. Sometimes in mid-summer, I also use two flies when fishing in a river – yet there can be problems in playing a fish if it has taken the dropper. Then the tail fly is dragging about, and may get caught in weeds or another obstacle. Usually I put the salmon fly on the tail, and a sea-trout fly on the dropper, although the fish are certainly less concerned about this than we are. When fishing at dusk on a late June evening, you will indeed frequently get salmon on the sea-trout fly, and sea trout on the salmon fly.

private beat in Scotland, Iceland and Norway, then adding travel and hotel costs, it is quite likely that Alaska offers better value for the European fisherman. All fishing in Alaska is free, and you need only a state visitor's licence (about 20 US dollars), besides transport to a suitable location. Accommodations range from a simple tent to highly equipped lodges with all modern conveniences, which are situated on some of the best rivers. These, and a daily fly-out facility to remote rivers, are where the expenses begin to climb.

Alaska is definitely the place to go for that once-in-a-life-time fishing trip. However, this must be carefully planned according to the type of fish you want. The chinook come in first, usually around mid-June to mid-July. They are quickly followed by the sockeye and chum salmon, in July and early August. The coho tend to arrive last, providing best sport in August and September. Throughout this time, of course, there is superb fishing for wild rainbow trout and Arctic char. It all adds up to an unforgettable experience.

Saltwater flyfishing

*Flyfishing in salt water
has grown from an infant to a giant
in the past few years. Where only a few
anglers practised the art, principally in the
Florida Keys three decades
ago, there are now fishermen who
are journeying to all parts of the world to
fish new and untested waters. The
unexplored frontier
for the sport is undoubtedly
in the Pacific. Australia, New Guinea,
Fiji and many other islands in this region
are already being sampled. The results
have been outstanding!*

*T*ackle has improved dramatically. Rods for graphite are available that are light enough even for women to easily cast, making it comfortable to fish with larger and stronger tackle, which is often needed to subdue these powerful fish. Reels developed just for salt water are now so over-designed that they will handle far more than will ever be demanded of them. Fly lines have improved, with special ones developed just for saltwater use. In the world of fly patterns there are now several hundred, where a few years ago anglers only used several dozen basic flies. Even the materials that today's saltwater patterns are made from have changed. Vast improvements have occurred.

For many Europeans shut off from fishing private waters in their countries, and for other fishermen around the world who see their fresh waters deteriorating or disappearing, flyfishermen are looking to other areas where they can enjoy their sport. Salt water offers unlimited opportunities for this. Flyfishermen can effectively catch fish in waters to about 60 ft (20 m) deep with new tackle and flies. In waters less than 10 ft (3 m) deep, fly tackle is often more effective than other types of artificial lures. In very shallow waters (2 feet or less) realistic flies can be presented so quietly that often the flyfisherman can catch fish better than someone using any other tackle, or even bait! This is especially true with wary species such as bonefish which, when feeding, will frequent waters so shallow that their dorsal fins often protrude above the surface. Under these conditions many fish are extremely wary and will flee at the slightest splash of a lure or bait. The silent entry of a fly is often the best way to present to such fish.

Great fighters

Salt water also offers other bonuses. Most fish sought by fly rodders in fresh water do not have many predators. The fish they seek are at the top of the food chain and it is they who are doing the chasing. But in the sea, nearly every fish is being eaten by another that is larger and more fierce. While some bottom-living species, when attacked, can retreat into a cave or under a rock, most saltwater species can only escape by going away. And they must swim faster and farther than the predator or they will be eaten. Such an environment produces fish that are much superior to freshwater fish, as far as speed and endurance are concerned.

All of this is a plus to the flyfisherman. When the hook is set in most saltwater species (other than some bottom-living types), the fish give a far better fight and run off more line than almost any freshwater species. The first time an angler hooks a 5-lb (2.3-kg) bonefish and watches the line melt from his reel as this relatively tiny fish pulls off more 100 yards (30 m) of backing in that first burst of speed, he cannot believe that it is the same fish that took his fly. To battle a tuna, trevally, large mackerel, or any swift open-sea fish is a delight and surprise to the angler who first hooks one of these speedsters. And because of their strength and speed, special tackle is often required to subdue these fish.

There are two basic kinds of flyfishing in the sea: inshore and offshore. Inshore waters are those within about a half mile (1 km) or so of the coast, and usually not more than 12-15 ft (4-5 m) deep. Waters deeper than that are generally regarded as offshore, and usually require different tackle and different fishing techniques.

In colder seas, such as off the coasts of Europe and the northeastern and northwestern United States, flyfishing is not productive for much of the year. Even when it is, generally the numbers of species and times that you can catch them on flies are limited. There are some bottom species in all of these estuaries that will take a fly; mackerel, bluefish and some other species may appear during warmer months. But the most exciting world of saltwater flyfishing is confined to waters where temperatures in the sea rarely drop below 60 degrees and often are 80 degrees or warmer. The closer one gets to the equator, the more opportunities exist for year-round flyfishing. In these warmer seas, food is abundant all through the year and there are many predators that take flies. Many of the species that inhabit these warmer oceans in cold weather will migrate briefly north and then return as the water temperatures drop.

Sharks belong to the true big game of the seas, and can be caught with flies in many parts of the world. Offering a long hard battle, they are superb to play on a fly rod.

Flyfishing inshore

When fishing the shallows, two basic approaches are taken. In very shallow, clear waters, such as the flats along the coasts of Africa, Florida, the Bahamas, Yucatan and islands in the south Pacific, many species of fish live in slightly deeper waters, but move into the shallows to feed. Such species include the famous bonefish, permit, tarpon, snook, trevally, threadfin salmon, barramundi, snappers, groupers and channel bass. Much of this is sight fishing, among the most interesting of all kinds of fishing. The angler either wades or else is propelled in a boat (usually with someone poling it) across the flats (shallow saltwater areas are often called flats); it is a combination of hunting and fishing. Both the angler in the bow of the boat, armed with a fly rod, and the person poling the boat are looking for fish. Once the fish is seen, the poler attempts to position the boat so that the angler can make a productive cast. This hunting/fishing offers great appeal to many fishermen, and is a major reason why tarpon, bonefish and permit are among the most publicized and popular of all species sought with a fly rod in salt water.

Noticing the fish

Sight fishing, and knowing how to look for and see fish in the shallows, require some skills. Fortunately, most of them are easy to master. First, the angler needs the proper equipment, so that he can see. A hat is essential, preferably one with a dark under-brim. This cuts down glare reflected from the water and allows the angler to see much better; hats with bright under-brims reflect the glare from the water into the eyes. The other piece of equipment that helps the angler's vision penetrate the surface is a good pair of polarizing glasses. These help to remove most of the glare from the surface. While it is a personal choice, most experienced "flats fishermen" prefer brown or amber-tinted glasses, rather than gray or green-tinted ones. The brown or amber builds contrast and makes it easier to see these fish. It should be remembered that tarpon, bonefish, permit and many other species have silvery sides, which act much like a mirror. When a tarpon, whose back is dark green, swims over light sand it is very easy to see: the back stands out against the light sand. But when the same fish cruises over

dark-green turtle grass, it becomes very difficult to see. This is true of all flats fish that are silvery in colour.

Fortunately, there are some skills you can learn that help you to see fish with mirror-like sides. You look for any fish swimming in very shallow water differently than when they are moving in deeper water. A fish swimming in water less than 1 ft (30 cm) deep will create wakes, ripples and small swirls on the surface. Indeed, some fish stand on their heads to root out a bit of food. This means the tail may protrude above the surface, so the angler should look intently at the surface. Anything that moves will instantly be noticeable.

When the fish are in water deeper than that, the angler

Like many other species on the "flats", permit have silvery sides that can make them almost undetectable to us. Being very shy, they are also considered difficult to attract to take.

cattle, the walker would interrupt his vision and be seen. By looking at the bottom, any movement of fish between the bottom and the viewer is instantly noticed.

The angle of the sun is also important when looking for fish in the shallows. The best angle is to have the sun at your back, or at the back and a little to one side. That is when the least glare occurs on the water. Sometimes it pays to plan your approach according to existing conditions. If there are white clouds in the sky, it is a good idea to move across the flats so that these clouds are not in the direction of movement. By approaching the clouds, the angler will be looking at the glare on the water, and even polarizing glasses will not penetrate the white reflection. Near islands or tall growth, the fish will be much easier to see if the angler looks in the direction where their dark green is reflected on the surface. This type of background allows the viewer to look clearly at the bottom.

Any unusual disturbance of the surface is also an indicator. If waves are moving in the opposite direction from the wind, something is pushing them. Often bonefish, especially, can be discovered by observing that some waves are moving in a different direction. And nervous waters (any small ripples) are a tip-off that something is creating the disturbance. Many kinds of fish, such as bonefish and sea trout, muddy the water as they root on the bottom. Try fishing where the mud is most dense or bright in colour. That is where the fish are active. By fishing a sinking fly through mud, you can often get terrific fishing. Once in Belize, we found a large mud, and caught bonefish for more than two hours on nearly every cast, using weighted bonefish flies. Casting into the muddiest area of the water, we allowed the fly to fall to the bottom. Then it was moved along in little hopping motions. Rarely did the fly travel more than a few yards before a bonefish found it.

Many fish can be caught near rays, such as sting rays and mana rays. Rays often get their food by descending to the bottom, where they pound their heavy wings against it. This frightens shrimp, crabs and other food morsels from the grass and mud, which attempt to flee. The ray then grabs what it can. Rays are slow-moving, but predator species are much swifter and will often hover over the ray. If a shrimp or crab slips out from under the pounding wings, the predator often grabs it before the ray can. This means that the hovering predator is in a feeding mood. The ray creates a long streak of mud that is swept away by the current. By locating the muddiest water, and casting a fly a foot or so uptide from it, the fly can be retrieved over the ray, and into

should look at the bottom. If you look at the surface, you will often miss seeing fish that are cruising below. To understand this, visualize someone looking at a person walking along a road. The viewer does not see the cattle in the field behind the walker. But if the viewer were looking at the cattle and the person walked between him and the

the mouth of a predator. Fish also have a tendency to follow rays – even in deeper waters. Anytime a flyfisherman notices a swimming ray, it should be checked to see if a predator species is following it. Mutton snappers are extremely wary fish (more so than permit, which are famous for being difficult to fool) but can be caught with flies rather easily, since they have a habit of cruising over a ray and can then be deceived.

Planning your catch

Perhaps the main factor in successfully hooking a saltwater fish, especially in the shallows, is how you approach and make your presentation. A noisy approach or a loud splash of the fly or line near the fish will frighten it. Because these predators are in the shallows and they know they can be seen easily, they are wary and will flee to the depths at the slightest indication of alarm. So the approach to such fish must be silent and carefully planned, and the presentation of the fly must be very correct.

When feeding, most predators working a flat approach it from the downtide side. Therefore, if the tide is flowing from the north to the south, the fish will enter the flat usually from the south, working into the current. The reason is that the tide carries the scent of their prey to them. It is amazing how far fish can smell shrimp, crabs and other food. In fact, some experienced anglers will anchor uptide on a white sand spot. They deposit chum (cut shrimp, conch crab or other fish food) in a sealed pipe drilled with holes to carry the scent to the fish but not allowing them to eat it, or scatter the bait on a white spot on the bottom. Smelling the bait more than 100 yards (30 m) downcurrent, fish will come into the white sand. This makes them easier for the angler to see, so an accurate cast can be made.

It is good to understand that fish feed in the shallows much as a bird-dog hunts. The dog goes into a field downwind, lifts its nose and catches the scent of the birds as it manoeuvres through the field. Fish do the same thing. Entering a flat from the downtide side, a fish moves into the current, picking up the scent of shrimp crabs and other food. It wends itself back and forth into the current. Armed with this knowledge, an angler has an advantage. By wading or moving in a boat from the uptide side, the angler is in a good position to cast to approaching fish.

Presenting the fly correctly

Of paramount importance in both fresh and salt water is the awareness that, when a fly is offered to a fish, it expects to pursue this baitfish, crab, shrimp or other food source. It does not expect to be attacked by a prey species. Yet we often wrongly give that impression when we present a fly to a fish.

Any fly which is retrieved so that it approaches the fish from the rear, or is brought back directly at the fish, is an unnatural occurrence and the fish will usually not strike. The very best method of retrieving to a fish is in the natural way. If the fish is swimming or facing into the tide, the angler should either wade or move the boat to one side and in front of the fish. Then a cast can be made upcurrent and a few feet to the far side ot the fish. As the fly is retrieved, the current draws it down to the fish. A few feet (1 m) in front of the fish, the fly makes a turn and begins to move upcurrent, back toward the angler. A fish is used to seeing prey species drift toward it on the current and then suddenly, realizing the danger, turn and move away. Such a retrieve is the best of all. Another good method: if a fish approaches you, throw the fly several feet (2-3 m) to one side and in front of the fish – not in a direct line with it. As the fly is brought back, the fish notices it appearing to escape.

Three incorrect or bad retrieves are often made. The angler casts well to the other side of the fish and begins to bring the fly back, but the current sweeps the fly downstream of the fish, and it comes from the side appearing to attack the fish. If a fish is swimming away from you, never throw over its back and retrieve it straight toward the fish. And perhaps the worst retrieve is to throw a fly to a fish lying directly below you, so that the fly lands behind the fish and approaches it from the rear – this almost always results in the fish fleeing.

A typical scene from the tropical and subtropical shallow flats, where flyfishermen challenge permit and bonefish – among other species. The inset picture shows a tailing bonefish that stands on its nose digging out morsels of food with its tail protruding above the surface.

Flyfishing offshore

Flyfishing in water deeper than 10 feet (3 m), and on the open sea, requires different techniques than fishing in the shallows. In most cases something is used to lure the fish to the angler. Then a fly is presented. One common method is trolling a lure until a fish is hooked and brought near the boat. Many species tend to swim in schools, and others follow the hooked fish to the boat where the angler can make his presentation. Chuggers, sometimes called bloopers, are another way of luring fish within range of the fly caster. A large, floating casting plug devoid of hooks, with a scooped face, is thrown out on the surface. By giving hard jerks on the rod, the lure makes a loud gurgling sound, which many fish find attractive. As they rise to attack the plug, the fly is dropped nearby, usually resulting in a strike. Another method of luring fish is to chum. Ground or chopped pieces of fish, or sometimes even small whole fish, are sent overboard on the tide. Fish are lured to the food source, where the angler can make his cast. This is perhaps the most commonly used method of luring fish within casting range on open water.

Another method is used by billfishermen seeking marlin and sailfish. A hookless bait or artificial lure (called a teaser) is trolled on the ocean to attract a billfish. The angler has a partner who manipulates the teaser. The fish attacks the bait and mauls it, while the teaser is pulled closer. When the enraged fish is lured within a few feet of the boat, the teaser is jerked out of the water and the fly is placed in front of the billfish – which usually attacks it.

The use of lead-core shooting heads, and extremely fast-sinking fly lines that are loaded with lead dust, also allows anglers to fish to depths of 60 feet (20 m) if the tide is not running too strongly. This is often slow fishing, but anglers who are willing to cast the fast-sinking lines and allow them to descend into the depths are catching some very large reef species.

In flyfishing at sea, the quarry is often teased close to a boat by suspending small live fish in the surface layer. Then they are removed and a fly is substituted.

Poppers are used mainly in the USA when fishing for cobia, shark and sailfish. These bugs, having a flat or bowl-shaped front part, are often made of plastic, cork or balsa wood. But foam rubber material has become ever more common, since even big bugs are then easy and simple to cast. Popping bugs emit their sound when they scuttle across the surface as you take in the line fast. This sound may be fairly loud and probably makes the fish think some large prey is fleeing. It certainly seems attractive to many saltwater species and often triggers strikes.

Divers are bugs tied with deer hair. For fishing in shallow water, this Dahlberg Diver is superb, although bugs are usually heavy and hard to cast. Most typically, they have a deer-hair head that is trimmed to slope backward in a conical shape. Like many other bugs, this one has a hook shield of monofilament nylon line, so as not to snag on underwater plants. It can be fished floating – by taking it in with jerks at the surface, to make a popping sound – and as a streamer, whose slithering movements seem very attractive to fish.

Sliders are a variant of popping bugs, with a conical front body. Due to its streamlined, rocket-like tip, the fly is easy to cast even in windy weather. It also moves more quietly and calmly in the water, which is most useful if you are after shy fish in the shallows. This type of fly is meant to imitate small, wounded prey fish at the surface – that is, rather easily caught ones. The colour of a slider has little importance, whereas its size and the way it is fished at the surface often determine whether or not the fish will attack it.

Saltwater flies

Size, colour, shape, and sink rate are all important factors when considering flies to catch saltwater fish. Size is perhaps the most important. Some fish, such as bonefish, have a small mouth; others, such as cobia, snappers and groupers all have large mouths. Offering a 5-in (13-cm) fly to a bonefish is almost certain to result in a refusal. And presenting a very small fly to a big fish with a large mouth will rarely convince the fish to strike. Bonito, for example, roam the world's seas, and they seem to prefer feeding on small 2-3 in (5-8 cm) slim minnows. A streamer fly that imitates these baits will do well. Cobia, sharks, and many other species all want larger flies. Cobia are a good example of where size is often vital to drawing a strike. Even a big 10-in (25-cm) bulky sailfish fly will often be refused by this fish. But a large popping bug that makes considerable noise will often result in a powerful strike. I believe that the popper, though smaller than a streamer, creates so much disturbance that it persuades cobia and other species that here is a much larger prey – and so they strike. Barracudas often scorn streamer flies, but a 0.5-1.0 (2-3 cm) popping bug that is manipulated quickly across the surface will often cause them to hit. Apparently such a disturbance creates the impression that here is something large and edible that is rapidly getting away.

Frequently size is more important in fly patterns than how the fly is dressed. For some species, however, colour often plays a key role in whether the fish will strike. Striped bass and European bass often like a certain colour better than others. This can vary during the same day, so it pays to experiment with these fish. Sea trout and weakfish will often prefer a chartreuse or bright yellow colour. Fish that live on reefs, where the fly is fished at least 10-30 ft (3-9 m) down, can often be caught sooner on flies that have the dressing made from fluorescent colours, which can be seen in their true tints at greater depths. Snook seem to go for bright yellow combinations. Many offshore species are best caught on streamer flies that have a blue or green back and white belly. Almost all streamer flies fished in open waters are better if their belly is white, the colour of every prey species that predators feed upon.

Coastal flyfishing along the shallow coasts of northern Europe is sometimes extraordinarily rewarding. Common catches are garfish (see inset), sea trout, mackerel, cod and coalfish.

Surface flies

The most popular surface flies are popping bugs. They were made originally of cork, then of balsa wood, but lately the use of closed-cell foam plastics has increased. These are much lighter and easier to cast, and fairly large bugs can be made that weigh far less than those of the same size in cork or balsa wood. The buoys used by commercial fishermen to mark their traps and pots are an excellent material to fashion popping bugs from. Tough, very light and easy to work with, they make superb popping bugs.

Poppers come in two different designs. The standard bug is one with a flat or cup-forward face. On the retrieve, the line is stripped quickly and the bug moves forward, pushing water and making a popping sound. This is very attractive to many species of saltwater fish. The other type of popping

bug is called a slider, shaped more like the cone on a rocket or the front end of a bullet. This pointed bug makes little disturbance on the surface. In situations where fish are wary, or easily alarmed when in shallow water, the slider can be manipulated without a great deal of disturbance, which may frighten the fish. The slider is usually tied to resemble a minnow or baitfish. It represents an injured minnow, struggling on the surface – appearing to be an easy meal for a predator. Many experienced anglers, myself included, feel that the colour of a popping bug is not important. What is important is the size of the bug and how it is manipulated on the surface.

Deer-hair popping bugs are rarely used in salt water, but are a favourite of many freshwater fishermen. The deer-hair bug is bulky, difficult to cast against the ever-present sea breeze; and after being fished for a while, the deer hair soaks up water. This makes it heavier and more difficult to

This streamer, of the synthetic material organza, is very common for coastal flyfishing in southern Scandinavia. An organza streamer nicely imitates a little silvery prey fish, and is thus extremely effective in catching, for example, sea trout. Like most streamers, this one is usually tied on straight-eyed hooks 3-5 cm (1.2-2.0 in) long.

Ullsocken is a Swedish fly that has long been used in the country's southern salmon and sea-trout rivers. But coastal flyfishermen discovered that it can also be fished as an imitation of a ragworm. Not least the sea trout, which seek shallow coves during the spring in order to feast on these hairy worms, find it hard to resist the fly. Its tail is tied with red wool, the body of peacock herl or floss, and the hackle of brown cock or hen hackle feather.

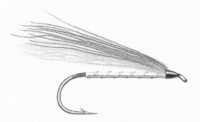

The above streamer has been given a wing of marabou feathers, and represents an effective type for several species. It can naturally also be tied with hair wings, but its movement in the water is then less lively. The fly can be fished either superficially or deep – for sea trout, garfish, mackerel, cod, coalfish and many other species. The wing colours may be varied, yet green, red, yellow, orange and/or blue flies have proved good.

cast, and it doesn't work as well on the surface. However, one deer bug is superb in shallow saltwater situations around the world: the Dahlberg Diver. This has a body and wing of a baitfish, but the head is made from spun deer hair and clipped. The result is a cone-shaped head that slants back to a large collar. When manipulated on the surface, the bug makes a popping sound. Yet if the retrieve is constant, the bug dives under the water and swims in a wobbling motion. Thus, the lure can be worked as a popper, streamer, or sometimes a combination of the two. It can be popped several times, then made to dive and swim a short distance. The retrieve is stopped and the bug slowly rises to the surface, where the retrieve can be repeated over and over. The bug is almost always dressed with a monofilament weed guard, which allows it to be cast into or near brush, without fear of getting it snagged in the trees.

Streamers for deeper water

There are also lures that work in the water column, not on the surface or bottom. These are the most familiar to fly-fishermen. Most are called streamers, and are meant to imitate minnows or other baitfish, shrimps or crabs. Some are dressed lightly and without weight, to travel just under the surface. Others are weighted, usually with lead wire or lead eyes, to drive them deeper. Many are imitations of baitfish, usually with a white belly and a green, gray or blue back. The addition of large eyes to some of these streamer flies seems to increase the number of strikes. Large, weightless eyes can be placed on streamers by painting an eye on a duck feather attached to the forward portion of the fly.

Lead eyes are often useful in getting flies deeper in the water. These are miniature dumb-bells made of lead, in five sizes from 1/100 ounce to 1/10 ounce (0.28-2.8 g). They offer two attributes. By using various weights of lead eyes, you can control how deep you want the fly to dive. And eyes on flies, in my opinion, always help draw strikes. These eyes can be painted in any colours.

One streamer that has become very popular in saltwater flyfishing is the Bend Back. This is a standard streamer, but tied on a hook that is slightly bent. The wing is tied in reverse style. This causes the fly to ride with the hook up – nestled inside the wing, which makes it nearly snag-proof. A Bend Back can be tossed into mangroves or other brush and very carefully retrieved without snagging. It can also be fished close to the bottom with the same benefits.

Another method commonly used in tying flies that will not catch on weeds or obstructions is the use of a monofilament weed guard. This is a loop of stiff nylon monofilament, usually 15-30 pounds in test. It comes from the back of the hook down under the point and is attached at the hook eye. This mono loop also allows flies to be fished where they would snag without it. A further method of making weedless hooks is with stainless-steel trolling wire, tied on the hook just behind the eye, then bent downward to form a metal guard that protects the hook point. When a fish grabs a fly with a nylon or monofilament weed guard, the material is soft enough that it collapses on the strike, allowing the angler to hook the fish. But both materials are strong enough to push the fly away from weeds or snags.

This typical tarpon fly, like all other flies for saltwater fishing, obviously should be tied on a corrosion-resistant hook. The long wings made of hackle feathers must be tied on the hook back, and the shank wound tightly with coloured tying thread or stainless tinsel. The fly can also be given a hackle just in front of the wing.

Black Deceiver is an example of a dark, contrasting all-round streamer for fishing in deep water. Its wing is tied with black hackle feathers and, on the outside, black hair. Some long strips of silver tinsel are also tied into the wing. The head has painted eyes to give the fly a more realistic look, which can often bring a strike.

Joe Brooks' Blonde series of flies are now classic all-rounders for saltwater fishing. They are typical bucktails and have brought good memories to flyfishermen around the world for many years. Their colour variants include being tied entirely of black or white bucktail, or with an orange tail and red wing, or a white tail and green wing.

Tides

One prerequisite to successful saltwater fishing with any tackle is an understanding of the tides. Unlike fresh water, where rivers flow and lakes are static, gravitational pull affects large bodies of salt water, causing movements of current and changes in water height.

What is not generally realized by light-tackle and fly-fishermen is why tides are so important. Baitfish are a major source of food for many predator species that flyfishermen try to catch. Minnows and other small fish in the sea have no home. In a river, when a flood occurs, the minnows that live in a certain pool hide behind rocks or under cut banks, away from the current. They attempt to stay in the pool where they were born. But saltwater baitfish make no such attempt. They were born in open waters and they allow the current to take them wherever it may. It would be foolish for them to burn energy and try to stay where they are, when there is no reason to do so.

Thus the tide moves the baitfish – and predatory fish know this. They prefer places where the tidal flow moves the bait or concentrates it. The fish must understand tidal effects in order to survive, while the angler must learn the effects on the bait and predatory species if he is to consistently catch fish.

While the sun is much larger, the moon is much closer to the earth. The gravitational pull of the moon is the main cause of tidal flows on Earth, but the sun also has an effect. When there is a line-up of the moon, sun and earth, a major gravitational pull occurs. When the sun and moon are at right angles to the earth, a lesser gravitational pull occurs. In most places, the seas rise slightly higher and fall slightly lower than the week before; the following week they will not rise as high or fall as low; then the effects are repeated. In other words, every other week there is an extra high and low "spring" tide, followed by a week of "neap" tides that are not as pronounced.

It is useful to remember that tides repeat themselves every two weeks. If you were at Rum Bottle Bank on Saturday morning, and fishing was great on a high falling tide, you should not return the following Saturday – for the tides would be almost opposite. But if you go back two weeks later, you find almost identical conditions, unless there is a major weather change such as strong wind.

It is easy to tell when there are spring tides and when there are neap tides. On weeks with no moon or a full moon, the spring tides occur, and the rise and fall are much greater. When there is a quarter-moon week, the tides will not rise and fall as much.

How do tides affect flyfishing? Many shallow-water species will not come up on flats until these are flooded with water. In most situations around the world, flats-feeding fish, such as bonefish and permit, will move up on a flat as the tide is rising, and retreat as it begins to fall. However, some flats do have better fishing on falling tides than rising tides. This is a good reason why guides are often useful.

In a small bay that fills on a higher tide and exits through a narrow opening, the flyfisherman has an advantage. As the water pours in, filling the bay, it will carry baitfish. As the bay empties, the tide will flush the bait along with the water. Fish know this, so they feed at the inlet side when the tide is coming into a bay, and on the outside as the water is leaving through its natural funnel mouth. In areas where flooding tide rises and drowns mangrove and other rooted plants along the shoreline, baitfish swarm there to feed. The predators do not try to chase them at this stage of the tide, but locate a depression or ditch that is among the last places to drain from the root system. Here is a natural funnel, and the baitfish will wait until the last moment before coming out of it. Locate these outlets and fish the last half of the falling tide, and you stand a good chance of hooking predatory fish.

The Flyfisherman's dream waters

*Salmonoids are still
ranked highest among our catches,
but several other kinds of fish are becoming
ever more interesting. Except in the very
deepest waters, nearly all
predatory fish can
be caught with a fly and fly rod.
Committed flyfishermen have developed
into the most lively travellers of our time,
and it is not unusual that
summer fishing for salmon in Alaska is
followed by winter trips to the tropical flats
for bonefish. A flyfisherman on the move is
thus always in high season – whatever
the place and species.*

All of us naturally have our own favourite waters, which best suit our individual temperaments for one reason or another. Even so, there are certain fishing waters that pop up again and again in the historical literature and the many current sporting magazines. These are often waters that have meant a lot for the development of flyfishing, or have recently brought modern flyfishing a big step forward, or else simply offer a marvelous opportunity for good fishing.

In the Northern Hemisphere, flyfishermen originally sought only salmonoids in flowing waters. But today, our fly rods are being swung over almost every type of water – and at species which were previously thought to be out of the question. Our equipment, too, has undergone significant improvement during the past few years, and this is the immediate reason why flyfishermen have been able to take command of new, different waters. If we choose, we can now cast farther, and fish deeper, than ever before. Thus we can adapt to conditions everywhere from the smallest streams to the wide stormy oceans.

Sadly, a number of the fishing waters that are most significant in historical terms cannot be included in the following "world tour", since they have fallen victim to man's rough treatment of nature. Yet such former dream waters may belong to the Happy Hunting Grounds where those who once experienced their grandeur still wander along the banks to challenge their denizens with simple flies, twined horsehair line, and split-cane rod in hand. Blessed be their memory!

Scandinavia

Among the colder parts of the world, we find some of the indisputably best fishing waters for salmonoids in the far north of Europe. Here, ideal conditions have been established by nature for large, strong stocks of big salmon,

trout and grayling. Not that we have always understood the value of these resources – and many of the region's finest flyfishing waters have been abused, or even devastated, through the decades.

Denmark

Beginning in southernmost Scandinavia, the flat confines of Denmark hold outstanding trout streams. One of them is Karup Å, which annually yields fish of 10 kg (22 lbs) to its faithful worshippers. Most are caught during the evening and night hours, when good local knowledge is needed to walk safely on the swampy ground along the banks. The fishing is done with a floating line by night – and with a sinking line by day, since the fish then seldom rise to a dry fly.

The former world record for rod-caught sea trout comes from the Karup Å. It was a silvery female of 14.4 kg (31 lbs 12 oz), caught in 1939 – although not on a fly. The biggest fly-caught sea trout in Denmark, from the Gelså farther south, weighed no less than 13.85 kg (30 lbs 8 oz). This

Scandinavia has some of the world's best fishing waters for salmon or sea trout, as well as for large trout: (1) Karup Å, (2) Gelså, (3) Mörrumsån, (4) Emån, (5) Storån, (6) Kaitumälven, (7) Gaula, Orkla and Stjördal, (8) Leardalsälven and Aurlandsälven, (9) Tana, (10) Alta, (11) Kuusinki, Kitkajoki and Oulankajoki, (12) Laxá and Grimsá.

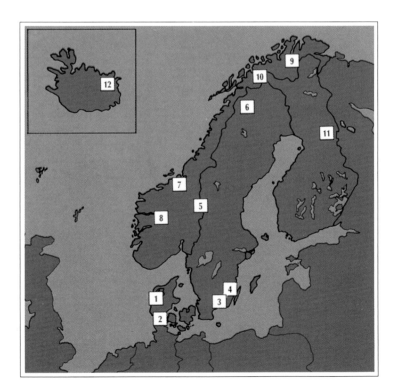

catch is only a few years old, and shows that there are very large sea trout in the nutritious Danish waters.

Also belonging to Denmark, but lying just south of Sweden's southern coast, is the rocky little island of Bornholm. It offers fine winter fishing for sea trout, at times both abundant and sizeable. During the winter, the fish thrive in the cold, brackish Baltic water, which they prefer to the mixture of cold and salty waters of the coasts farther north and west.

Sweden

At least as big are the sea trout in Sweden, for which the rivers Mörrum and Em have long been particularly famous. Quite a few sea trout are landed there at over 15 kg (33 lbs), and fish around 10 kg (22 lbs) are almost daily food. Both of these streams offer, in addition, excellent fishing for Baltic salmon. The big sea trout and the salmon migrate away in the Baltic to hunt the herring schools, which give them a record-breaking growth. Notably during the winter months, many big sea trout swim along the southern Swedish coast, available for anybody who wants to tempt them with a large streamer or bucktail.

In the northern parts of the country, there are naturally a lot of fine trout waters, both still and flowing. The trout and grayling are plentiful, though often not very big. Streams like the Storån – where, by the way, Frank Sawyer fished with great success – and the Kaitum River have earned a firm place in the hearts of many trout fishermen.

Norway

Without a doubt, Norway is the flyfisherman's El Dorado when it comes to big Atlantic salmon. This mountainous country, whose long coast is always in contact with the constantly warm Gulf Stream, has more than 220 salmon-rich rivers. These waters definitely yield the world's largest Atlantic salmon – many of them over 10 kg (22 lbs), some

A record salmon caught in the Mörrumsån, weighing 22.9 kg (50 lbs 8 oz).

over 20 kg and a few over the magic 30-kg mark. The biggest salmon caught on a rod in Norway weighed all of 36 kg (79 lbs 6 oz).

It is difficult to make a small selection of Norway's salmon rivers, but certainly the area around the city of Trondheim offers a range of truly productive waters. Names such as the Gaula, Stjördal, Orkla, Namsen and Surna inevitably arouse strong memories among the flyfishermen who have wet their lines there. And all of these have become still better in the wake of restrictions on professional fishing, which went into effect in Norway during 1989.

Farthest into the Sognefjord, northeast of Bergen, lie two other renowned rivers – the Laerdal and Aurland. Even though at least the Lærdal has very good salmon fishing, they are also well known for yielding sea trout on dry flies.

If we proceed northward in this long-stretched land, we first meet the Alta, legendary for its huge salmon. Then, on the border between Norway and Finland, we reach the Tana – Scandinavia's most productive salmon river. The former is colossally expensive to fish in, and the latter is colossally large.

The northernmost district of Finnmark, too, is obviously worth a visit. Here you have a good chance of catching seagoing Arctic char on both wet and dry flies. But the chief attraction is the grayling, which can be very big in this area. Fish of 1 kg (2.2 lbs) are common in many waters, and those of 2 kg are nothing impossible. Around Råstojaure on the border between Sweden and Norway, the waters are famous for numerous and large grayling. Besides, the fishing for mountain trout is superb.

Iceland

In fishing for salmon and trout, Iceland occupies a special status. This semi-arid volcanic isle is not as unfertile as it might at first seem. The petrified lava is full of minerals which, along with a water temperature that is high by Scandinavian standards, make the rivers and lakes very nutritious. And the main beneficiaries of these conditions are salmonoids.

Salmon are the fish that have brought Iceland world fame. From all over the globe, salmon fishermen come to fight these creatures – which, in spite of their numbers, are rather small in size. A salmon of 10 kg (22 lbs) is considered very big in Iceland, whereas in the great Norwegian salmon rivers it may correspond only to the average weight. Yet

Icelandic rivers such as Grimsá, and Laxá in the district of Adaldal, regularly reveal truly big salmon as well.

If you want to catch a lot of salmon, and to do it on light equipment with a floating line and small flies, Iceland is the right place. Unfortunately the relevant local prices are in dollars, and this has pushed them up to a level which even the natives find it hard to pay. The problem is, ironically, almost self-inflicted. For the excellent salmon fishing is largely due to the fact that Iceland has forbidden net-fishing for salmon and reserved the fish entirely for sport-fishing.

We are lucky that the island also offers bountiful fishing for trout, and at a much lower cost. It is not exactly cheap, but fish of 1-2 kg (2.2-4.4 lbs) are common in many of the waters. One of the best-known trout streams is the Svartá.

Finland

The "land of a thousand lakes" is richly endowed with trout streams. Among the best-known is the Huopana, where there are still plenty of large trout, even though not as many as in the past. Three more streams with big trout exist in the Kuusamo district of eastern Finland – the Kuusinki, Kitkajoki and Oulankajoki. Here the fish migrate up from lakes on the Soviet side of the border to breed, and about a thousand trout weighing 1-9 kg (2-20 lbs) are caught every year. The 1989 World Championship in Flyfishing was held in the same area.

Greenland

In the far north between Iceland and Canada lies the world's largest island. Hundreds of rivers and lakes exist in Greenland, and flies are gladly taken by their steel-hued and red-bellied char, of the seagoing Arctic type. These fish seldom weigh more than 1-2 kg (2.2-4.4 lbs), but are so strong and full of fight that they seem much bigger than they are, when we land them among the turquoise icebergs that drift majestically in the fjords.

In spite of the great numbers of salmon in the nutritious Davis Strait, there is only one salmon-bearing river in Greenland: a little one with a small, variable stock of generally small salmon. The temperature in Greenland's water systems is simply too low, and there is an extreme shortage of suitable spawning sites.

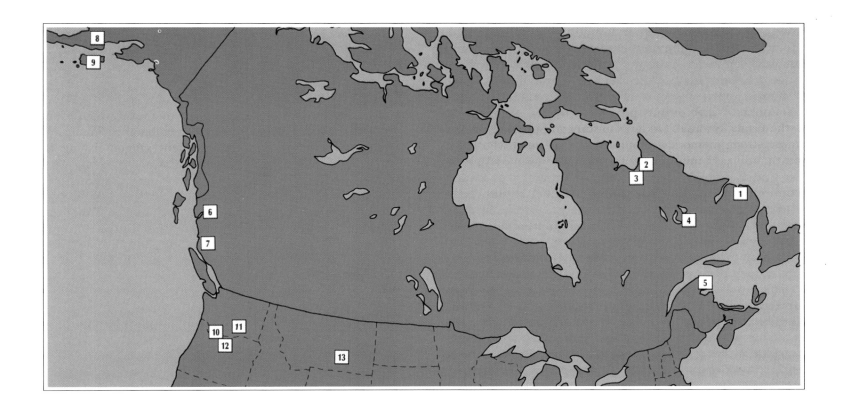

North America

Canada

In North America, the best fishing waters lie mainly in the east and west: (1) Eagle River, (2) George River, (3) Whale River, (4) Minipi, (5) Gaspé Peninsula, (6) Skeena, (7) Dean River, (8) Iliamna Lake, (9) Kodiak Island, (10) Columbia River, (11) Kalama River, (12) Deschutes River, (13) Yellowstone River.

On the other side of the narrow Davis Strait, salmon live under significantly better conditions in Canada. Not least in Labrador, productive salmon rivers abound, the Eagle being probably the most renowned. It is typical of Labrador's salmon rivers, however, that the migration upstream consists mainly of small salmon. In nearby Quebec, whose two best salmon rivers – the George and Whale – empty into Ungava Bay, the salmon are often somewhat bigger.

The northernmost parts of both Labrador and Quebec also provide exciting flyfishing for what must be the world's largest seagoing Arctic char. Fish of 5 kg (11 lbs) are common, and there are opportunities of fighting in the 10-kg class. But doubtless the rare and exotic brook trout is what draws most flyfishermen to this region. The Minipi water system is notably well known for its unusually large brook trout, the biggest weighing over 5 kg. A long series of world records is held by the Minipi, which certainly yields the biggest trout in the world caught on dry flies. During the high season in mid-July, fish of 3 kg (6.6 lbs) are landed on dry flies almost daily. Virtually nowhere else in the world can one experience such stable dry-fly fishing for really big fish, in spite of the variable weather.

Newfoundland, Nova Scotia and New Brunswick, too, feature good and well-organized salmon fishing. Especially the Gaspé peninsula, in the Gulf of St. Lawrence, teems with big salmon. Among the classic salmon rivers in this part of Canada are the Matapedia, Miramichi and Restigouche.

The inner regions of Canada contain many locations with fine fishing for grayling, besides innumerable large lakes with sizeable lake trout. These, however, live in such deep water that they are mostly inaccessible with flyfishing equipment.

We must therefore move to British Columbia, the country's beautiful Pacific province, in order to resume top-class flyfishing. Our interest is concentrated around the powerful Skeena water system, which originates high up in the Rocky Mountains and empties into the ocean near Prince Rupert. The Skeena is one of North America's leading producers of Pacific salmon – but in spite of that, the main target of flyfishermen is the seagoing rainbow trout, or steelhead. The sizes of steelhead caught here are unique in the entire world.

The Skeena's strong central channel is murky and milk-coloured. Only on occasion does the water become clear enough for effective flyfishing. We thus find much better conditions in the smaller, clearer tributaries. Names like the Babine, Bulkley, Kispiox and Sustut can make any self-respecting flyfisherman jump with joy. It is in these rivers that the record fish are landed: steelhead weighing 10-15 kg (22-33 lbs). Most are taken with a sinking line and large flies, in September and October when the water is relatively cold. But actually, if the circumstances are right, August can provide dramatic flyfishing with a floating line and small flies.

British Columbia has, of course, several other excellent fishing waters. One is the Deen River, lying south of the Skeena. Its fish migrate upstream-early, so the summer fishing is its chief attraction.

Proceeding northwest, we reach Alaska – bought by America from Russia for a song towards the end of the last century. Alaska reveals an incredible wealth of salmonoids. The five Pacific salmon species range from the great king salmon to the leap-happy coho, and there are two species of mountain trout, in addition to Arctic char, lake and rainbow trout. All these can be flyfished during a short summer of four months, from June through September.

The fishing is nevertheless far from being equally good everywhere. If you want a wide range of alternatives, the area around the extensive Lake Iliamna is definitely the best choice. All species are represented here, as well as some of the world's biggest and wildest rainbow trout.

These, like the steelhead, migrate out into the lake and feast during the summer. As egg-eaters, they follow the myriad Pacific salmon which migrate up from Bristol Bay to spawn and die.

On the other hand, if you are looking for a fight with really big silver salmon, or coho, it is better to go out on the islands of varying size in the Gulf of Alaska. Silver salmon are Alaska's toughest fighters, and they often weigh 5-10 kg (11-22 lbs) in that area. Reputable places are Kodiak and Afognak Islands in the south, and Montague Island in the north of Prince William Sound. However, it is a sad fact that this very area was the victim of the "Exxon Valdez" oil-pollution catastrophe in 1989.

United States

Turning instead southwards along the Pacific coast, we reach the states of Washington and Oregon. Despite the construction of many large hydroelectric dams on the Columbia River, fishing is still good there for steelhead – though often implanted. It is hard to single out any of these waters, but some that should be named are the lovely little Kalama River in Washington and the classic Deschutes River in the deep wilds of Oregon. The latter is as perfect for flyfishing as can be imagined.

Farther into the United States lie Montana and Wyoming, and the "Mecca" of American trout fishing – Yellowstone National Park. Several of the classic waterways, such as the Yellowstone, Madison, Firehole and Bighorn, flow in this highland. Every year, thousands of American and foreign flyfishermen make their pilgrimage here to catch rainbow, cutthroat and brook trout in the clear, cold, pure waters. The fishing often becomes ever better and calmer as September approaches, when the crowds of tourists have tapered off.

In the northern part of the Rocky Mountains flow several classic trout streams, in majestic natural surroundings.

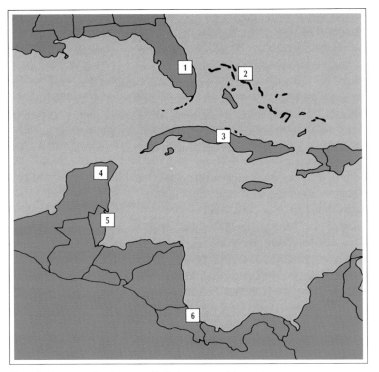

For the bass and saltwater flyfisherman, this region offers many good opportunities. Among the best-known places are: (1) Florida, Lake Okeechobee (for bass) and the "Flats", (2) Bahamas, (3) Cuba, (4) Yucatan Peninsula and (5) Belize.

Central America

Just west of Florida lie the Bahamas, which are also attractive for tarpon and bonefish. Only about 120 miles (200 km) south, on the other side of the narrow Straits of Florida, is Cuba. With the Bay of Mexico to its north and the Caribbean Sea to its south, Cuba is endowed with plenty of exciting fish species. There are tarpon as well as bass in the dense mangrove swamps, and bonefish along the chalk-white coral shores. The flat southern coast offers very good opportunities for flyfishing.

A shorter distance west of Cuba brings us to Mexico and the Yucatan Peninsula, which divides the Bay of Mexico from the Caribbean. Here you can fish with the old Maya ruins at your back, and a fly is gladly taken by the bonefish, tarpon and several other saltwater species. Along the Pacific coast, too, Mexico has excellent places for flyfishing. The golden mackerel and sailfish can give advanced flyfishermen a lifetime memory.

Moving down into the Central American countries, one soon reaches the small land of Belize. Its group of Turneffe Islands is best known to flyfishermen, once again with tarpon and bonefish as the main actors. Farther south in Costa Rica, the Atlantic shore features the world's best tarpon fishing in its estuaries and lagoons. The Pacific coast is also successful with flyfishing for sailfish, although primarily to be done by experienced saltwater flyfishermen.

South America

On our way towards the equator, we first arrive in Venezuela, which is a new area in terms of sportfishing. Here you can find admirable possibilities of fishing for smaller tarpon in the estuaries, and for bonefish on the little atolls in the Caribbean. Deep inside the country – near the Amazon River, where the heat is almost intolerable – there are peacock bass. They eagerly take bass bugs on the surface or large streamers under the surface, and fish of 5 kg (12 lbs) are by no means unattainable.

In the southeasternmost part of the USA, Florida's warm lakes harbour the country's biggest large-mouthed bass. This is a fine sporting fish that has been seriously discovered by American flyfishermen in recent years. Notably huge bass exist in the enormous Lake Okeechobee, on the edge of the Everglades swamp.

Florida is most significant for its role in the development of modern saltwater flyfishing. Its broad "flats" were the scene of the first attempts with a fly rod to make contact with the sprinters of the sea – those shy, fast bonefish and gigantic tarpons. From there, saltwater flyfishing spread like rings on water to the rest of the Caribbean. But Florida still yields the world's biggest tarpons, weighing nearly 100 kg (220 lbs).

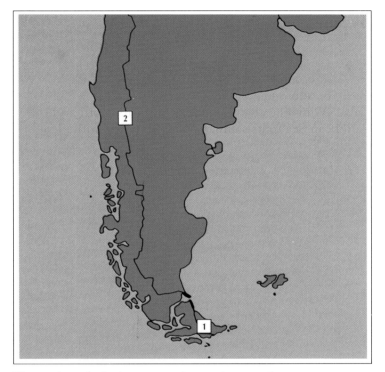

The southern Andes have several trout rivers, such as (1) the Alumine. Farthest south is a fantastic sea-trout river, (2) the Rio Grande.

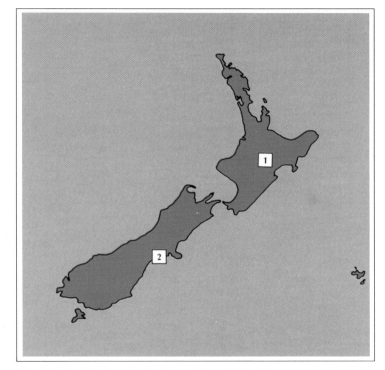

New Zealand is famous for its excellent fishing for brown trout, rainbow trout and king salmon, as in (1) Lake Taupo and (2) Rakaia.

Chile and Argentina

It is a biological fact that no natural stocks of salmonoid fish have ever existed in the Southern Hemisphere. The ability of countries like Chile and Argentina to offer first-class trout fishing is due, instead, to implantation of rainbow and brook trout at the beginning of our century.

In the southern part of the Andes, we find superb trout fishing. However, Chile is probably best known for the sizeable rainbow trout in its large lakes at high altitudes. By contrast, Argentina lies on the other side of this mountain chain and has several rivers that are perfect for flyfishing. Among them are the Alumine, Chimehuin and Malleo.

Farthest to the south, Tierra del Fuego – the "land of fire" – is attractive for the big sea trout in the powerful river Rio Grande. Fish of 5 kg (12 lbs) are common here, and much larger ones are quite obtainable.

Summer in the Southern Hemisphere is at its peak when winter is worst in the north of the world. So the fishing season is opposite – it begins in November and ends in April.

New Zealand

Even in the trout paradise of New Zealand, the fishing season generally occurs at a time just the opposite of what we are used to. But we have to distinguish between this country's northern and southern islands in regard to fishing, as well as between the conditions for rainbow and for other trout.

The two islands are very different in both climate and geology. It is warmer and more hospitable in the north, colder and much more mountainous in the south. This explains why rainbow trout are said to predominate on the northern island, and brook trout on the southern island. It is obviously a truth with exceptions, but still a good rule of thumb.

On the northern island, by far the best fishing is on Lake Taupo, a large body of water 30 miles (50 km) long. Here one can fish both in the numerous river inlets – preferably at night with phosphorescent flies, for rainbow trout that hunt smaller fish – and in the lake's tributaries for fish that are migrating to spawn. Most famous among the latter is the

A big rainbow trout is netted in one of Lake Taupo's many tributaries.

Tongariro, which annually yields more than 100,000 rainbow trout caught on fly rods, the majority with weighted nymphs and roe flies. Farther up this river, there are also very big brook trout, shy fighters of over 5 kg (12 lbs).

The primary trout fishing in Lake Taupo has been created entirely by man. Just as in South America, no natural stocks of salmonoids occur in New Zealand: the trout were imported from Great Britain and North America around the turn of the century. They multiplied so rapidly that the lake's own stock of small fish disappeared. Then the fishing declined a lot, but it was saved by setting out food fish. Today both rainbow trout and small fish, both implanted, dominate Lake Taupo.

On the southern island we find a rough landscape with deep fjords and high mountains, known as the "Southern Alps". The landscape is strongly reminiscent of Norway –

and indeed there are salmon, though unfortunately not the Atlantic species. Instead, king salmon have been implanted in some places and, notably in the river Rakaia, flyfishing for them is purposeful and quite successful. However, interest is focused on the many large brook trout, which thrive in the local lakes and waterways.

Much of this sport is sight fishing, by observing the fish first and then fishing for it. The fish weigh 1-3 kg (2-7 lbs) and are extremely shy in the crystal-clear water. Thus, the southern island's lakes and streams are not suitable for inexperienced flyfishermen, who probably have more success on the northern island. The same applies to the little island of Tasmania, which lies west of New Zealand and just south of Australia. There, the main fishing occurs in several very nutritious lakes, whose sizeable trout are shy and selective.

Europe

England

As we know, the cradle of flyfishing lay in Europe – more exactly in southern England with its clear, food-rich chalk streams full of large and timid trout, where Halford and Skues developed dry-fly and nymph fishing. Their haunts were the streams Test and Itchen, which thus became world-famous. Even today, flyfishermen come from all over the world to this area and wander in the great masters' footsteps, savouring some of the atmosphere from the early days of the sport.

The fishing is, of course, not what it used to be. While the Test and Itchen still flow southward to the Channel coast, they are now but a shadow of their former grandeur. Man has left deep marks in the chalky earth, and modern agriculture has taken a toll as in so many other regions. Rain-soaked grounds have been drained, making it necessary to irrigate them during dry periods. In addition, the intensive fish farming is both a pollutant and a consumer of large amounts of water.

The chalk streams, originally characterized by their stability, have become unstable. Their water level and temperature were once constant all year round, yet are now out of balance. But it is not only agriculture and fish farming that have produced disorder in the natural environment: flyfishermen, too, have made a contribution. We are responsible for the fact that there are more "tame" rainbow trout than wild brook trout in these streams. The Test teems with small rainbow trout that have escaped from fish farms, and with big implanted trout from the fishing clubs. In several places, outright put-and-take fishing has arisen for rainbow trout weighing around 2 kg (5 lbs).

Scotland

Fortunately, the trends are not so sad everywhere in Great Britain. In Scotland, the centre of salmon fishing, it was a couple of centuries ago that the first salmon were caught on flies. This fishing is still done with the longest two-hand rods and the greatest possible enthusiasm.

Scotland is in the enviable position of providing a chance to fish for fresh-run salmon nearly throughout the year.

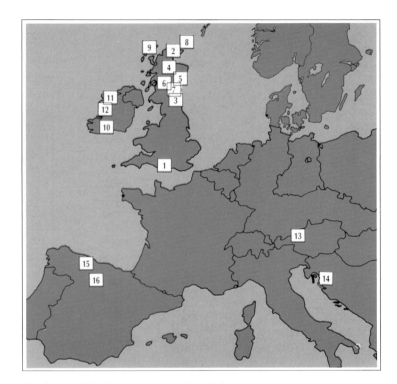

Much as in North America, the best fishing waters in Europe – apart from Scandinavia – occur mainly in certain areas. The classic "dream waters" certainly include (1) the Test and Itchen, (2) Thurso and Helmsdale, (3) Tweed, (4) Spey, (5) Dee, (6) Tay, (7) Loch Leven, (8) Orkney Islands, (9) Hebrides, (10) Blackwater, (11) Moy, (12) Lough Corrib, (13) Traun, (14) Gacka and Unec, (15) Narcea and Sella, (16) Orbigo.

From January until November, the salmon migrate up the rivers. The season usually begins in the north on rivers such as the Thurso, Helmsdale and Oykel, to finish on the classic Tweed at the border of England. Other renowned rivers are the Tay, Dee and Spey, where thousands of salmon have taken their last fly.

The Scots live with salmon, but this region has still more to offer. A good example is Loch Leven, which has long been a favourite destination of flyfishermen from the whole of Great Britain. It is well known for abundant, pugnacious trout, and its traditional drift fishing has been polished to perfection. This method of flyfishing from a drifting boat is also extremely widespread in Ireland. Moreover, it was from Loch Leven that some of the first specimens of *Salmo trutta* were sent across the Atlantic to North America at the turn of the century.

The two small groups of islands west and north of Scotland, the Hebrides and Orkneys, offer superb flyfishing as well. In particular they have sea trout and lake trout, but there are also scattered salmon. The same is true of the Shetlands, and of the Danish Faeroes up in the North Atlantic. But there you must be prepared for rain, mist and high wind as you fish for trout.

Ireland

Across the Irish Sea to the west, there are wild salmon and trout to be caught in rivers and lakes that are still in good condition. Ireland has many salmon-bearing waterways, although most of them are spate rivers – small ones that rise rapidly after sudden hard rain, then fall equally fast, and may even run dry when there is little rain.

Despite this variation, you can experience rich salmon fishing (and at a cheap price) in these small rivers, however uncertain the results are made by the unstable water supply. When the rivers rise, the salmon come up too. And when the water gets lower and clearer, the fish take madly – for a time. After that, the fishing declines and the salmon are again virtually impossible to make contact with. There are, nonetheless, a few large salmon rivers in Ireland with a more constant water supply, and thus more stable fishing. Examples are the Moy in the west, and the Blackwater in the far south.

But Ireland is best known for the trout fishing in its large lakes. Places like Lough Mask and Lough Corrib are world-famous for their fishing opportunities, primarily with mayflies during May and June. This sport brings flyfishermen from far across Europe, and often yields the year's biggest trout – caught either with dry flies, or by "dapping" with a blowline and natural insects.

Austria

A better and more inviting climate is found on the European mainland. Industrialization has ruined most of its sal-

Flyfishing for spring salmon at Castle Grant on the legendary river Spey.

mon and trout waters, but there remain individual ones of high quality. For instance, the Austrian river Traun has long boasted the same importance for German-speaking flyfishermen that the Test has had for the English. The Traun is difficult to fish and contains large, shy, selective trout and grayling, which can give the cleverest flyfisherman a lot of trouble. Nor has the tooth of time passed lightly over this waterway, and today it is hardly comparable to what it was in the days of Charles Ritz.

Yugoslavia

Conditions worthy of paradise can be found by flyfishermen in Yugoslavia, whose chalk streams are attracting ever more attention. Prominent examples are the Soca and Unec, but especially the legendary Gacka near a beautiful national park named Plitvice. Here, some of Europe's largest rainbow and brown trout swim in almost unbelievably nutritious water, at a temperature around 10° C (50° F) that gives the fish a record growth rate.

In Yugoslavia's clean waters, you can also find an amazingly exotic salmonoid: the soft-mouthed trout, which exists nowhere else in the world. This fish has a grayling-like head and a trout-like body. It is an ideal hybrid that developed in the isolated currents of the Adriatic Sea after the last ice age. What can be more fascinating than a *Salmothymus* for the flyfisherman who has seen everything?

Spain

In the southwestern corner of Europe, and notably along the Atlantic coast, Spain provides plenty of thrills in flyfishing. There are still a few rivers with good resources of salmon and sea trout, even though the fishing has become worse in recent years. Among the best known are definitely the Narcea and Sella.

For trout fishing too, it can be worth a visit to this part of the world. The rugged but beautiful Pyrenees contain several waterways thar are rewarding in this respect – as are some of the fine streams that descend on the southern side of the Cantabrian Mountains in Asturia. Another Spanish river that has given lifetime memories to many southern European flyfishermen is the Orbigo.

Index